I May Frustrate You, But

I'm a Keeper!

(Parenting the Temperaments With Love and Confidence)

Ray W. Lincoln

I May Frustrate You, But I'm a Keeper!

Unattributed quotations are by Ray W. Lincoln.
Scripture references are from the New International Version.

International Standard Book Numbers
Softcover 978-0-9842633-9-4
EBook 978-0-9842633-8-7

Library of Congress Control Number: 2009912437

Printed in the United States of America

Apex Publications
Littleton, CO

Dedication

To the one who has enriched my earthly existence with her love;
Filled my closest relationship with its warmth;
Walked with me through dark valleys and sacrificed;
Comforted me with love's fire.
To my dearest treasure and a wonderful mother – my wife, Mary Jo.

Everybody today seems to be in such a terrible rush, anxious for greater developments and greater riches and so on, so that children have very little time for their parents. Parents have very little time for each other, and in the home begins the disruption of peace of the world.

~ Mother Theresa

Table of Contents

Understanding Your Child

Parenting Styles

Strengths and Weaknesses

Beliefs, Dreams, Skills, and More

Appendices

Preface

In the counseling room help is offered and insights are gained. No, not as you might be thinking. Help and insights are often, unknowingly, offered by the client. The counselor is the learner, filing away new thoughts and testing new approaches as the common enigmas of life are unraveled in a fruitful exchange. There is no end to the learning of the real student. When the teacher stops learning, the students freeze in fixed principles that become lifeless. Hope in parenting lies in more understanding and loving, insightful application.

What I have learned from books, professors, and (not least) my clients has led to this book. In excess of fifty volumes on temperament, philosophy, personology and neuroscience have been devoured to prepare parents for a better understanding of their children. Hearing over and again "Our home has been healed," or "This really works! I understand my child now, and the knowledge has brought confidence and hope to me as a parent," have caused me to take my work from the coaching room and put it into the form of a parenting manual, with the humble hope that it will help many more parents and children than I can reach one-on-one or in my seminars and keynote speeches.

I'm a Keeper is intended to equip you with the knowledge of how you and your children are made on the inside, how you can relate to your children with pleasant results and how to build their self-worth to fashion them for their dreams. It hopefully will also reduce the stress of your parenting and return to you the joy that is often stripped away in those heated times of damaging encounters.

Thanks to all who have influenced my life for the better, and particularly to my wife, Mary Jo, who has labored with love and untiring devotion to produce this book. Of special mention are Vandi Deines and Debbie Schutt, who proofed parts of the manuscript and offered their wisdom to make this a better book, along with Jennifer Peters whose expertise and consultation as contributing editor has been very helpful. Thanks also go to Burt Deines, Adrienne Adams, Millie Rogers and many others who have given generously of their time, resources, skills, encouragement and moral support throughout this labor of love. Your efforts and your skills are deeply appreciated. I am indebted beyond my ability to express.

Introduction

The best interest is paid on an investment in understanding!

Most parents are the experts on their children's behavior. We know if little Megan is acting normally or acting up. But what we don't know is how she feels when she obeys or disobeys. Why did she throw that tantrum and kick her mommy? Why did she, only one hour later, show such tenderness and say, "I'm sorry, Mommy. I'm really sorry. Honest I am?" We can guess, and most of us do just that. Sometimes we even oscillate on their "keeper" status.

Guessing causes much disharmony and frustration. However, this book will teach you about the drives that caused the tantrum and what caused the tender attempt at making up. We can understand our children on the inside with an accuracy that will astound us and comfort them. Furthermore, knowing how our children are created on the inside (the part of them we can't see) – where their decisions are made, their drives live, and their preferences are formed – will give us the chance to parent them to be the best they can be. It will also decrease the stress of parenting. Wouldn't that be wonderful?

Actually, what we can learn is so detailed and helpful that no parent should be without this knowledge. Do you long to be the parent who really understands how your children feel and think, or the parent that guides your children to the rich development of their strengths and their potential? Wouldn't you love to know how to lead your children to be all that they can be?

On the other hand, have you given up on understanding your child? Does he or she frustrate and puzzle you at times? Have you been wondering whether perhaps Mars was the origin of birth? Are you turning gray, losing hair, or tearing it out? Age is not the only cause.

Children can be infuriating at times, and a large part of the irritant is a lack of understanding — a very large part!

Is your child going to be like you, think and feel like you, simply because he or she has some of your genes? No! That's another reason to learn how they are made on the inside. Strange as it may seem, they can be the opposite of you, and be made in the mold of a temperament whose actions you find hard to accept. Oh, and in this book you will learn why trying to make them like you is really harmful to them and frustrating to the point of despair for you.

Never fear! The advances in scientific tools and the wisdom of two and one half millenniums will guide us to parenting our children with the understanding of how and why they feel the way they do, act the way they do, and display opposite drives that are, at times, different from those of their parents. Your child's blueprint is all written in something we call temperament. Understanding your temperament and theirs, and how each reacts on the other, is what I want you to know. If you parent by understanding, rather than by trial and error, you will see results quickly.

Perhaps most important, a new relationship with your children will develop. When they realize that you understand how they feel on the inside and have learned to respect who they are, they feel more at home and comfortable around you. And here's the wonderful thing, they will bond with you, and you with them, on a new level. You will be designing your parenting to the individual makeup and needs of each child. They will love the change. Parenting is not all about the parent, but all about the child.

Parenting with understanding and skill actually makes parenting easier and more rewarding. Stresses born of the feeling "I just don't know my child" fall away. As you look forward to the teen years when the bond between parents and children is crucial, you will need more intimate and trusting connections and communications so you won't lose them to their peers. In these pages you will find out how to bond, how to develop your child's potentials and dreams, and how to create a better parenting style. Wouldn't that be great!

There are many methods used in raising children. Most of them are helpful and work under certain circumstances, but they work for only some of the children and some of the parents. Some of them are only disciplinary methods. Methods have always existed because people who have had success in raising their children tell their friends, "This is what you should do, too." Even though it works for them and their children, it may actually be harmful for you and your child. All children should not be parented in the same way.

This book will teach you how to parent your children according to how they have been made, and to respect their inbuilt purpose and design. It is hard to describe in a few words how this is all going to play out, but read on and it will all make sense. We constantly receive feedback at our seminars and in our coaching sessions that parenting according to temperament makes real sense, and it works. Lives and homes have been dramatically changed by parenting with understanding and skill.

The information contained in this book is not just another method for parenting. *I'm a Keeper* asks, "Who is your child? And who are you?" Then it fashions all of its guidance to the individual parent and child, and not to parents and children in general. The emphasis on individualized understanding is its uniqueness and its secret.

Parenting is one of life's major challenges. You are also making a meaningful contribution to life, and shaping the lives of ones you love for their best good. Indirectly, through them, you are affecting the lives of others and playing your part in creating a better future of hope and love in our world. It's called being the "salt of the earth." It is my prayer that this book will help you greatly; and I honor you as you parent with understanding and skill.

A Fast Track!

Yes, there is a fast track for those who need to see some immediate results, and cannot read the whole book first. Turn to the appendix, "Parenting by Understanding and Skill – The Fast Track," and start immediately. You will be referred to the sections where you can get more detail and understanding as you proceed. Preferably, read the book first, if you can.

Some things are repeated in the book, but in a different context and in different words so that those using the Fast Track do not have to read the whole book first. To require that they do would nullify the Fast Track. This repetition will also serve as a needed teaching tool in most cases.

♦

My introduction to temperament and the use of it in my counseling and coaching over the past decades may be of interest.

It was decades ago when, as a college freshman, I was required to study the four temperaments as outlined by Hippocrates, Plato, Aristotle and Galen. I was fascinated! Here I was, understanding myself like I never had before. I wish I had continued my study of temperament at that early stage, but other demands by my professors took my time and attention.

It was a little over two decades later, while attending a personal growth conference that I was introduced to the idea of temperament again. The reference was, in passing, to the four temperaments espoused by the philosophers I had studied in my freshman class. With interest spiked again, I began to see the value of knowing how I had been created on the inside. The idea that we all have similarities and differences, and that they somehow give us an identity that can be called *temperament*, began to intrigue me. A simple scientific way of diagnosing and categorizing these helped me understand their usefulness and make a meaningful application. To be able to know myself, and predict my likely actions and reactions, stimulated my curiosity even more. I could also see why I was making many of my choices in the way I did, and why I felt the way I did about others and their actions. I still had no concept that the four temperaments had been with us for two and a half millenniums (from early biblical literature) and that the observation of the Greeks had so dramatically affected human understanding up to this day.

I also had a new insight and an engrossing game. It was fun to guess the temperament of the people I worked with, especially those who served on my board. My family? That was a constant source of intrigue.

It occurred to me that the knowledge I was acquiring, together with the use of a scientific assessment, could be of help in counseling. Wouldn't it be wonderful to know how your spouse was made on the inside before you married him or her? Not all prospective partners initially shared my excitement, until they realized that the experience was not negative, but very helpful and confirming. Understanding their own and their spouse's preferences in life gave a glimpse of what life together would be like, and how to smooth over the possible rough spots in their relationship.

I was amazed at the accuracy of the assessment and the detail it provided. My consistent use of it in coaching and counseling began with this encouraging experience. But there was much more that would develop as the years went by, and you are about to read of the unsurpassed benefits of knowing how both you and your child are made on the inside. Your child will feel the comfort of being understood. Aberrant behavior will decrease since most of it is a result of relationships that chafe and cause insecurity and distance. You will find that knowing your child will open up a world of help, and you will learn what, I believe, are transforming parenting skills that you can put to the test.

Years of study of human nature with the aid of temperament led, finally, to this book.

The Path the Book Will Follow

Start reading with chapter one, and skip chapter two if you are not interested in the compelling story of the development of temperament psychology, also known as *personology* (David Keirsey's term). However, if you are wondering what temperament is all about, read this chapter.

In the second section you will find the "Temperament Keys." Answer the questions before you read further and the rest of the book will make real sense in terms of you and your child. You will now be reading it with personal interest and profit.

The section, "Understanding Your Child," will give you the basic understanding of your child and yourself, and the picture will begin to come together. Parenting styles that arise out of your temperament's preferences should make many of your interactions with your child understandable and outline for you some changes you may need to make. This is the meat of "Parenting Styles."

"Strengths and Weaknesses" will introduce to you a way of looking at strengths and weaknesses that has transformed the study of temperament for me and many others. You will learn how to effectively get rid of your weaknesses and, also, how to help your children get rid of theirs! "Beliefs, Dreams Skills and More" is about developing some helpful skills. More issues and interpretations are reserved for another book, because if all that we deal with in our seminars were included in this book its size would scare most people from reading it. This book is your basic manual for parenting with understanding and skill, and if you follow its suggestions you will become a **Super Parent** which means...

- Parenting so that each of your children with their different temperaments will reach their full potential and live a fulfilling, rewarding life.
- Parenting with the understanding of our own temperaments, and the interactions they create with our children.
- Parenting to become super-parents who see parenting as a precious trust and an unsurpassed challenge — the greatest opportunity of our lives.
- Facing the difficult times with the knowledge of how to parent your children without damaging them and frustrating you.
- Parenting successfully when you find yourself lost in unknown territory, confused, and crying out for help because nothing

seems to work, and knowing how to find your way and what to focus on.

- Parenting for those who want to bond with their children and maximize trust, mutual love and respect.
- Parenting without undue stress and with control when you feel that your child is damaging you!

Grandparents, remember, you play a vital part in influencing your grandchildren, and (dare I suggest) most of us are not the experts we claim to be. They may frustrate you, but you too, need help in understanding more and in learning new skills.

Don't forget, a *Fast Track* is in the appendices to help those who want a speedy application and immediate results.

Indebtedness

I am deeply indebted to the research of many scholars in the field of Temperament, but particularly to David Keirsey and his excellent contribution in *Please Understand Me II*, also to the superbly readable volume by Stephen Montgomery and others listed in the Bibliography. You will find our ideas run parallel in many instances and digress somewhat in others.

Gender

One more point of clarification is needed. The use of "he" or "she" in text or comment is meant to be inclusive of both genders and neither should be understood to exclude the other.

Happy parenting! And may you have an enjoyable ride to real understanding and personalized skills for parenting each of your children.

REAL HELP FOR PARENTS

Though it costs all you have get understanding.
~Proverbs 4:7

Chapter One ♦

Your Child and Your Parenting

If your child could write you a letter it might read like this:

Please understand me! I'm different from you, and I need to be understood and appreciated for who I am. I don't feel the same as you do much of the time. Sometimes, I wonder if you are for me or against me. When I am hurt and react or shout, you think of nothing but grounding me or punishing me, and I don't understand. Why don't you know the difference between hurt and bad? You seem to be trying to change me to be like you. Don't you think that I am a wonderful person just as I am, or do I have to be like you to be wonderful? I think God did a good job in creating me just as I am? If you can agree we can get along better, and you can help me more."

Sincerely,
Your hopeful child. (Am I a keeper?)

A letter like that might be a wakeup call. This book is intended to be one!

As a parent, I look in the mirror each morning and I see how I am made on the outside. Mirrors are early morning shock treatments! I also observe how I have taken care of, or neglected to care for, my body. But I cannot see how I am made on the inside. I need another kind of mirror. Some people are just plain scared of looking in a mirror that reveals the hidden territory of their inner selves. I had that problem, too, but let me assure you it is not all that scary, and once you get past your fear you will love what you have found. Is there a mirror that helps me see how I am made on the inside? Yes, there is! And that mirror will be explained in the third section, "The Temperament Keys," for both you and your child. You will see yourself and your child in a new way.

You will be able to verify if what the "mirror" says about your inner life is true or not since you are the one who knows what is inside you. If the "mirror" is correct about you, trust it to reveal your children as well so that you can understand how they feel on the inside, and so much more.

Our ignorance of our inner selves is our great loss. Seeing how we are made on the inside helps us understand many things about ourselves. A good assessment can tell us not only the obvious things about ourselves and our child, but also the things we often want to have confirmed and explained. When we have this understanding, we parent with the solid knowledge (based on two and one half millenniums of careful observation and research) of who we are.

I can hear an objection coming, "Surely there are not just four different types of people out there as the Temperament Keys in chapters four and six might suggest. (You may have glanced ahead.) We are all different, unique and precious. How can you reduce humanity to four temperaments?" If you are thinking this way, let me answer this now – before you refuse to complete the Temperament Keys.

We don't reduce humanity to four temperaments and sixteen types. We are all unique and different. You are right about that. However, you may have noticed that we are also, in many ways, similar to each other, and similarly different from each other. Temperament identifies our similar strengths, which we share with others in various degrees of intensity and skill. "Four temperaments" means four groupings of similarities and strengths which are found together in humans. It's a kind of shorthand to be able to understand each other quickly and reliably. Those four groupings are also broken down into four variations of each grouping, which total sixteen types (or variations) of temperament. We are all unique yet, at the same time, recognizably similar.

Hopefully, you will find the best tool for parenting is learning to identify the temperaments and their strengths, and understanding the power of preferences/drives in shaping a person's thinking, feeling and behavior. I cannot overstate the benefit of understanding the drives that govern our children's feelings and behavior.

The accuracy of this simple tool is what I ask you to experience for yourself. You are the judge of all this book intends to teach. The great benefits (of understanding by temperament) that will bless your parenting are sketched below. Read them for a summary of some of the ports our cruise ship will visit and to prime your excitement for an understanding that may change forever what your child thinks of you, and what you think of your child.

Discover How to Parent Each Temperament Successfully

We naturally know how we feel when faced with a choice, and how we felt when we were children. Why shouldn't our children feel the same way as we do? They are <u>our</u> children after all – born with a transmission of genes from the parents. But is it that simple? No, it is not.

Your children may quickly display, even while infants (for those who know what to look for), an indication that they are very different from their parents in how they are made on the inside. Their drives and preferences (which lead to feelings, thoughts, and actions) will increasingly become evident as they grow older, and may even be strikingly different from yours. Obviously, a simple gene transfer doesn't explain all this. My son is wonderful, but not like me. I was puzzled by him and, no doubt, he with me. With the knowledge I am about to give you, parenting will be personalized for each temperament.

Not only does each temperament feel, think and act differently, but each also has different compass directions and goals in life. This means that each temperament needs to be parented differently if their potential is to be encouraged.

Once you learn how that can be done and have the knowledge to do it, you will find, as so many of my clients have found, that a home of discord is suddenly peaceful and happy. Children know when their parents respect their differences. They know when they are understood in comparison to feeling like aliens in a foreign land. The great benefit of parenting with understanding is the bond that develops between child and parent. This bond with the parent, built upon mutual respect, caring and knowing they are understood, makes the task of correcting undesirable behavior much easier and leads to respectful feelings.

Discover How to Avoid Pygmalion Efforts

Avoidance of Pygmalion efforts makes life better for both parent and child, and honors the way both have been made. It is natural to want our children to be like us and is hard for us to conceive that if they are different it will be for the better. "If they are like us we will know them and know how to help them. If they are different, both they and we will have to chart a course in unfamiliar waters," we reason. How can we avoid trying to change them when, for example, we feel they should be more responsible, but in contrast, they feel they must find their freedom to be different? These two ways of living appear to be opposite, and represent a common tug of war between two of the temperaments (SP and SJ). Temperaments don't see eye to eye on many things. In fact, they often repel each other.

We will examine the ways we can understand their seemingly opposite drives and how we can lead those drives to express both their individuality and a sense of responsibility. No, I'm not talking of simple compromise. That would be easy to attempt and, in most cases, impossible to achieve. Understanding how they are feeling gives the parent the advantage of leading them to express their strengths and preferences in a helpful way for all concerned and in line with their drives. A Pygmalion project is then avoided.

We will also examine the ways to calm the spirit and temper the heat of emotion that is the cause of a lot of hurtful engagements when misunderstanding our children.

How Does Your Child See You and How Do You Naturally Tend to Parent?

Have you ever stopped to think about how your child interprets you and your actions? We know what we think about our children. We may be annoyed at what seems to be a lack of responsibility or day dreaming, or we may be in awe of their imagination or ability to be easy going. Our children also interpret us. In fact, they often see right through us. Intuition is seldom as clear as it is in a child. Children cannot tell you how they know what they know, but they often understand more about us than we give them credit for. It is possible for them to see us with a greater clarity than we see ourselves. Frightening, isn't it? Therefore, children sense when we are not real or not honest, and they know if we see things differently than they do. They look at us through their glasses (their temperaments' urges) and interpret us accordingly. Their minds are a colored slate, not a blank slate. If we are all about responsibility (SJ), and they are all about free expression (SP), for example, they see us as aliens in their world. Wow! What will we do about that?

We also parent with our own style, but there are great differences in parenting styles that will unfold for you in the section on "Parenting Styles." Seeing our parenting through the eyes of others should be one of our goals if we are going to increase our parenting and people skills.

So, wouldn't you like to know how your child sees you and your parenting? Wouldn't it make a difference to your parenting? With this knowledge, our parenting style can be examined and altered to meet the needs of different temperaments, thus giving our children the best that an understanding parent can give. When we discuss parenting styles, we will be able to glean the best from all styles, and at least implement the ones that our children respond to.

Not only do the needs and drives built within a child's temperament affect their view of us, and vice versa, but our expectations and experiences (all of which arise out of our temperaments) also create a haze in our relationships, and we often misread each other in critical exchanges. Moreover, in our blindness, we become entrenched in our perceived positions, and create untold damage out of which we have to extricate ourselves. Ever had to apologize for totally misunderstanding your child, or, worse, not even knowing that you needed to understand? This port is where different worlds meet.

Often the lack of understanding can create a situation similar to this.

Jane, an embarrassed but conscientious mother, explained to me that her attempts at disciplining her little boy of eight, who was most of the time loving and considerate, resulted in him laughing at her! "Worse still was the fact that he must have noticed my confusion and loss of control when he laughed at me. I felt totally exposed and stupid," she confessed. "I don't know what to do," she pleaded.

This is an example of a child who knows the parent better than the parent knows the child, and the child, therefore, has the advantage. Jane must understand her child, because if she doesn't, her son will quickly take the lead and dominate her. A child quickly snatches an advantage like this.

So far, we've been discussing the issue in which the temperament between the child and parent is opposite. However, don't make the mistake of assuming you automatically understand your child if you are both of the same temperament. What if you don't understand yourself? Then you also don't understand your child. Jane needs both understanding of herself and her child, along with some reliable tools to put her firmly in the parent's seat.

Discover How and Why Your Children Feel, Think, and Act the Way They Do

Many people, when they answer a temperament key, express their relief at finding out why it is they feel the way they do. The ancient Greek philosopher was right on target when he said, "Know yourself." Our preferences arise out of our urges, which drive our decisions. Knowing our actions is not good enough. We must know the what and why that drive our actions.

For example, you may wonder, "Why do I always seek to please others, and opt for harmony and peace in relationships?" *Answer:* Your temperament drives you to empathy and caring. That's why. You will always (unless angered) find feelings of empathy driving you. These feelings are temperamental drives that fuel your actions. If you are built this way, it is a relief to find that it is not because you are not objective enough, or don't seem to be as tough as others, or even lack a pragmatic, objective view. Really, if someone were to point it out as a weakness, you would probably feel offended and feel the person was a heartless, harsh judge. You will always feel more comfortable empathizing with others than analyzing them, and it is always best to be who you are – always!

My empathizing strength in this case is a gift to wounded humanity, and I need to be what I am made to be. The world needs me the way I am. Your children need for you to lead them in their self-understanding to be who they were made to be — for their happiness.

Our feelings, thoughts and actions are all colored with our temperament's strengths, or the converse (we'll explain strengths and weaknesses later). Our type (and that of our child) is our personality blueprint. In that blueprint are the reasons for most of our behavior, and the information that can even predict our behavior in most circumstances. We all largely run true to form: the form our temperament dictates. Of course we can choose to act in violation of our preferences, but only at a cost to our self-esteem, comfort, and happiness.

Shawn, one of my clients, was secretly disturbed by his volatile temper. Why did he flare over seemingly little things? He had carried the guilt of this behavior with him for years, and had tried without any marked success to eliminate it. He felt he was a failure, and he longed to be different, but his anger would flare before he could turn it off. His witness for his faith had suffered many times. (He was religious and believed he was letting his God down. He thought he was more of a liability than a blessing to his faith.) He was at the point of not revealing his beliefs for fear that he would again stain his cherished cause. This devastated him.

There is a temperament that is vulnerable to the slightest upset and, within it, emotions flare more quickly than others. Shawn's personality assessment revealed this type, and gave him an explanation. He had a super sensitive nature, and it blessed others because he was extraordinarily sensitive to their needs and conditions. Pleasing, caring, and loving others were dominant strengths in him, and his feelings were appropriately located for immediate access. However, unlike the other people around him, he had no shield to defend against the hurts of others. Every time someone would say something derogatory, or not do something that he expected they would do, he would feel a surge of hurt that he had learned to direct internally and hide most of the time.

When Shawn didn't internalize his anger, he delivered a verbal broadside in defense of his defenseless feelings. Of course, to burst out in anger was not constructive, nor what he wanted to do, but to be angry when he was hurt was also an unavoidable reaction. It was what he did once he felt the surge of anger that showed him the way to his answer. Paul (the philosopher/theologian who was familiar to him) was the same temperament, and gave him a path to understanding and finding his answer. Writers often reveal the lessons and the wisdom that an understanding of their temperaments has taught them. ("Be angry [Let's paraphrase: 'It's alright to be angry when you are hurt.']; but don't sin [meaning: don't do the wrong thing]," were Paul's words). Learning that it is not a failure to burst out in the anger of hurt, but to simply make sure to follow up and do the right thing, was a revelation for Shawn! He had always felt guilty for his anger. Now he did not need to.

There's more to this story (and others like it) that we will return to later. For now, know that much of your behavior and feelings may be explained by the strength that you have been given and in its right or wrong use – not in some supposed weakness over which you seemingly have no control. What a benefit for our children to know who they really are when they are troubled like Shawn. They, and we, can feel a deep sense of relief that only knowledge and understanding can bring.

Discover Your Purpose and Your Satisfaction in Life (Child and Parent)

Our strengths are the foundation of our temperament. We love to use them because it feels natural to us and indeed can be our natural high. We also feel fulfilled when we operate in our strengths, and that feeling is a great reward. Now, think with me. If our strengths lead to our fulfillment, is it not also likely that written into our strengths is the purpose for our lives – a plan that shows us what will be most rewarding for us to be and do?

The discovery of our strengths makes our purpose in life discernible. All people must find their true purpose, or they break down and malfunction. If we know our children's makeup we will also know where their fulfillment and long term pleasure lie. We can lead them to it. Most of the time we pray, worry, and sweat over what we should be and do, but right there in the pattern of how we are made our answer is waiting. Unfortunately, instead of finding it we often keep searching in all the wrong places.

When I was formed, a purpose for me was declared. It is as though my Designer said to himself, "I want Ray to be a speaker and life coach and help people." So, he gave me the strengths (strengths, gifts, drives, and temperament are used synonymously here) to be what he purposed for me to be. Bingo! I feel fulfilled and useful whenever I use my strengths. I have a map for my life written into who I am on the inside, and I feel a deep satisfaction when I am who I am and live that purpose. When we know our purpose, we know one of the most important things we need to know about ourselves. Learn your strengths and those of your child, and you can both move in the direction of lifelong satisfaction. Your child needs this guidance. You can't go wrong, because your children know if something is their strength or not and will resist being led in the wrong direction.

Many of our children are growing up disturbed (and disturbing others) simply because they have not found their purpose in life and are not using their strengths. They wander aimlessly, unsatisfied and forever looking for satisfaction in all the wrong places. For them (and for all who don't know where they should be going), anything, anywhere, will do. It won't!

Purpose and satisfaction are inseparable. Created things operate with satisfying purpose and contentment when they run according to their maker's purpose. A car operates best when it is used for its created purpose. It fails miserably as a battle-tank. Live in your strengths, and you will live with a sense of deep fulfillment. I have seen it hundreds of times, when people see how they are made on the inside and learn their strengths they discover a new happiness. Life without happiness is life without the fuel that powers our systems and motivates us to be the best we can be.

Without a sense of fulfillment and purpose our children can also suffer from depression and low self-esteem. Finding our strengths and our purpose in those strengths will also lift our self-esteem. I have said to so many, "Be what you are created to be; it's the only way to real happiness." When they take that advice, the happiness is very evident.

Jon was such a case. Designing buildings would seem, to some, a perfect way to express creativity, but he hated going to work and was becoming more depressed by the day. He had spent four years obtaining his architectural degree – four laborious years wondering what was wrong with him since he couldn't summon up the excitement that his classmates exuded. But he kept at it because he was told this was the perfect outlet for his creative juices and that he would discover it to be true once he graduated and found a job.

Distressed and depressed, Jon attended a conference I was conducting, and he had the opportunity to take a personality assessment. He discovered that his strengths were all in the field of creative people skills, which suited him for helping, encouraging, and developing people — not buildings. Jon was a people person, designed to be an inspiration to others. Developing people, not buildings, was his calling. He quit his job and started his training all over again in the field of helping people to personal growth and health. Happy? At last, he was glad to go to work because each day was a fulfillment of who he was. He is now living his inbuilt dream.

Lead your children to know their strengths, and they will likely not make this mistake. You, at least, will see it coming.

You are about to learn how to guide your children to their purpose, not your (or someone else's) purpose for them. This is crucial if you want them to be fulfilled.

Discover How to Be Your Best (Child and Parent)

To know our strengths is to know where our potential lies; strengths lead to potential. We all have great potential, but most of us do not reach it. We often fail because of low self-esteem, but when we use our strengths our self-esteem rises, and the ceiling of possibility lifts. We are wonderfully designed to succeed in all areas of our lives, including spiritual, physical, mental, and the field of relationships.

As your children grow, they need to develop and sharpen their strengths in order to reach their highest potential. In order to reach full potential, they must feel they are capable, which will be assisted by a healthy self-esteem. At the same time, the reaching of one's potential feeds the self-esteem. Encouragement of goals and building the self-esteem are crucial to develop together.

A teenager, Susan, felt the urge that most of us feel, to be the best she could be. "I knew I had strengths," she said, "but I didn't know all of them, nor did I know for sure what any of them were. I knew I was good at many things, but I hadn't found what made me feel whole and complete." (Like so many, she could have wasted some of her life trying to find them.) "When I took a reliable personality assessment and found my strengths I knew instantly that I had discovered them. I knew I had to develop them with training and experience, of course, but now I just know that I'm on the right course to being the best I can be."

Discover How to Get Rid of Your Weaknesses (Child and Parent)

Weaknesses always seem to attract more attention than strengths. We can become obsessed with our weaknesses very quickly, which leads to personal defeat. Children become obsessed with their weaknesses, and we must know how to help them. Perhaps, if we get rid of our weaknesses we will be what we were created to be. Not so! We will only be what we were created to be when we <u>develop our strengths</u>. Yet, developing our strengths usually takes a back seat to getting rid of our weaknesses for most of us. We even settle for the goal of minimizing our weaknesses. Can you believe that?

Persistent weaknesses were called *besetting sins* in the last century. I don't hear the term much these days. The phrase is out of vogue. When people focus on getting rid of their persistent weaknesses, they inevitably fail to dig them out by the roots. I think it is the urge to rid ourselves of the negative – the weeds of our weaknesses – that gets our wholehearted attention. Negatives drain us and make us feel empty. We want to be rid of them because it is painful to be controlled by negatives. But if we focus on the negative we pay no attention to the positive. Wherever our attention is directed, our energy is expended. Therefore, we do not grow by focusing on the removal of our weaknesses. Focus on your strengths and your child's strengths, and you will both develop fast. Hopefully, among other things, this book will change your focus and your results.

In addition to learning to change focus, part of getting rid of our weaknesses is a matter of first learning how we formed them. Knowing how we form our weaknesses will be one of the most important things we will learn and be able to teach our children. Consider the case of Charlie:

He was a pleasant individual who always tried to please, and (when he wasn't angry and overtaxed) he was a loving, kind husband and father. That was Charlie most of the time. However, his wife and friends described him as unpredictable. One of his strengths was his passion that seemed to be very near the surface. Whatever he was passionate about drove him to extremes and to obsessively focused behavior. Distract him when he was passionate about something, and his irritability would flare. He would snap angrily at you. Charlie was all too aware of his impatience with people under these circumstances and hated himself for it. It had gotten his attention in a big way, and he tried to control his reactions. He had been trying for years. Even though he was successful in many things, he regarded himself as a failure because of his inability to control his emotions.

Charlie was unaware that his weakness was related to his strength of passion. It was the last place he thought of looking for the cause of his impatience. When he finally understood that an overuse of his strength (which he was focused on with an <u>obsessive</u> passion) caused his impatient reactions to others, he directed his energy to using his passion intensely, but not obsessively. This misdirection of our energy's focus upon weakness instead of strengths can be due to a misunderstanding of how our weaknesses are related to our strengths.

When he changed focus, his weakness did not show itself because he had focused on using his strength constructively and properly, thus dismissing his weakness. Control and the right use of his strength banished his weakness.

This misdirection of our energy is probably also due to the false idea that both strengths and weaknesses make up our temperament. They don't. You will learn more about this in "Strengths and Weaknesses."

Discover What Motivates You Most (Child and Parent)

This is what a parent really wants to know. How can I get my child off the couch? What is it that makes them misbehave? How can I get them to do their homework?

Motivation comes from a myriad of sources like love, sensual things (that plush couch), hope, money, belonging, rewards, and on and on. Unfortunately, parents (in their frustration) often use material things to motivate — like gifts, rewards, or the removal of a material reward — but that won't substitute for activating the real motivations that lie deep within us. When we discover how we are made on the inside, and focus on our strengths, we feel empowered. Nothing motivates like discovering and unleashing your powers. Children's journeys are more often being hammered with reminders of what they can't do and shouldn't do. They are told to stop dreaming, and that great motivation of the spirit is squelched. Some temperaments live mainly within themselves, and others live mostly in the external world. They find their motivation in their world and its adventures. For the child blessed with intuition and imagination, the world that motivates is the world of dreaming. Understand your children, and you will understand their world.

Our future is written within ourselves and our children, and will also thrill us like no other material thing or experience on this earth, since it is centered on the use of our strengths. Motivations live in the hope, vision, and understanding that we can encourage in each other.

Some are motivated by learning that they will lose the pleasure of their parents; some, by a little more freedom; others, by bringing personal meaning into relationships; and still others by study and learning. Let's just say the ability to motivate a child lives in the knowledge of that child, not so much in methods and enticements. Temperament is a kind of shorthand that guides our decisions and perceptions. This promises to be a wonderful port of call.

Discover How to Create Positive Behavior and Beliefs

Help! What do I do when undesirable behavior shows up? I'm in the line at a grocery store, and my little darling throws a temper tantrum that rates on the Richter scale! We will look into this problem and offer some help and some methods to handle these "earthquakes." There are positive steps we can take to lessen the occurrence of "earthquakes," as well as ways for immediate treatment. This book's full title, *I May Frustrate You, But I'm a Keeper,* is not only meant to show you how your children are "keepers", but also to help relieve frustration.

You have, no doubt, noticed repeated undesirable behavior, and wonder where it is coming from. From beliefs! Learn how to change damaging beliefs and replace them with positive, helpful beliefs. It is far more beneficial to both parent and child to learn how to infuse positive beliefs, because it lessens the chance of aberrant behavior. Is this a necessary task of parenting? Consider the consequences for your children if they are left untouched, unchallenged, and (most importantly) unchanged. Challenging destructive beliefs and behavior is all some parents know to do. They don't know how to effect change. Herein is help far beyond your desperate efforts to silence destructive behavior. You will become, in your child's eyes, their most needed help.

What a journey! This book promises a new beginning and changed results in the challenging world of parenting. Each port of call will hopefully enrich your knowledge and give you understanding of the different cultures of temperament.

THE COMPELLING STORY

A compelling story is evidence not to be lightly dismissed.

Chapter Two ♦

Two and One Half Millenniums Effectively Understanding Human Makeup

This chapter is more technical in content, but it helps us put the observation of temperament into historical relief. And it will answer some of your questions about how we came to the detailed, scientific assessments we have today. Knowing the roots of the knowledge we have about any given subject always puts that knowledge into perspective, and we can better appreciate its contribution to our lives – in this case, the life of two and a half millenniums on this planet. For those of you who are interested in the religious roots of temperament, refer to Appendix II. The source of any idea paints it in its original colors.

Walk through its sources and you will gain valuable insights as you jump-start your understanding of the temperaments. If the history of temperament studies does not intrigue you, come back to this chapter later as your interest dictates, and skip over to chapter three.

The Secular Science of Temperament

(Some Main Contributors)

The following is meant to provide a brief sketch of some major contributions to the understanding of Temperament and their places in history.

Geographical Spread of Temperament Observations in Ancient Literature

These geographical notes show the widespread influence of temperament observations in the ancient world. First, Ezekiel (a Jew) received his vision of the four faces of humanity in Babylon, an ancient city located in modern-day Iraq. John saw his vision while he was on the Island of Patmos, which is located off the coast of modern-day Turkey in the Aegean Sea, not far from Cos. Hippocrates was born on the Greek island of Cos. Plato (circa 428 – 347 BC) and Aristotle (384 – 322 BC) lived in Greece, and Irenaeus (circa AD 175), who studied and taught in Rome, wrote about the temperament of the four gospel writers while he was Bishop of Lyons in France. The observation of temperament was not localized to one small part of the ancient world.

Hippocrates

The study of human temperament has a long impressive history. It stretches from Hippocrates (circa 460 – 377 BC), who is known as the father of medicine and the source of the Hippocratic oath that has played an important role in medicine, to our present day – almost two and a half millenniums. Hippocrates is no obscure figure. So great was his influence in the medical world of antiquity that he is attributed with writing a collection of 70 works called the *Hippocratic corpus*. We suspect few were actually written by him. These works probably formed a library for medical students, and Hippocrates' influence in the world of his day may have been, in part, due to his training of others and his interest in learning all that could be learned. He saw a connection between the inner world of temperament and the outer physical world of the body – a connection that runs uninterrupted, but not unchallenged, for 2500 years.

Hippocrates is attributed with the observation of the four temperaments: sanguine, melancholic, phlegmatic and choleric. Later, Galen would further flesh out the descriptions.

Plato

Plato (circa 428-347 BC) made use of the four temperaments in *The Republic* where he sketched their contribution to the social order. Hippocrates' Sanguine (SP) [I will use the Myers/Briggs letters — SP, SJ, NT, NF — to denote the four temperaments throughout this book] is the one who plays out his artistic skills in society. The Melancholic (SJ) watches over the material interests of society. The Phlegmatic (NT) is the reasoning person who keeps society on a rational course. The Choleric (NF) is the passionate, intuitive, ethicist who keeps society pointed in the right direction.

Plato, a philosopher of whom it is said "all philosophy since Plato is but a footnote," understandably shows concern for society's values. After the death of Pericles (428 BC), imperial Athens declined. The resultant excess of the conservative political party, the strife that followed, the high-handed actions of the restored democracy (which saw to the death of Plato's mentor, Socrates [399 BC]) – all of which he witnessed – must have left a lasting impression on his mind and a longing to understand it all. He turned to what drives us – our temperament – for a model of society, which he described in *The Republic* as a celebrated Utopia.

Our lesson from Plato is, in part, that how people function and what drives them must be understood in order to contribute according to their strengths in any successful society. All societies, even the family, are no exception.

Aristotle

Aristotle (circa 384-322 BC) used the temperaments to describe four sources of happiness. People get their pleasure in different ways (he maintained.) Some get it from the pleasure of the senses (SP); some from the ownership of property, what they possess (SJ); some from the rational enquiry of the mind about life and its puzzles (NT); and others from being pure and ethically beneficial to themselves and to society (NF). It is most likely that Aristotle was an NF himself, since his ethical concern, his tender, affectionate caring for his wife and family, and his influence and reputation as a speaker (he was known to walk up and down the covered walkway as he spoke, giving him and his followers the nickname "peripatetic lecturers," or "walkabout lecturers"), indicate this type. (My opinion is contrary to some who feel he may have been an NT.)

Aristotle was enormously influential, affecting philosophy well into the Renaissance and even to this day. His recognition of temperament, though not expounded as a theory, could well have been a cause of its revival in, and after, the dark and middle ages.

Galen

Galen (circa AD 130 – 201), a Greek physician and philosopher, was born in Pergamum in the ancient Roman province of Asia Minor (Turkey). He studied in Asia Minor and Greece, and later lived in Rome. Galen was an outstanding source of knowledge in his day. He compiled all the medical knowledge of his day, writing volumes on both medicine and philosophy, and he became the quoted authority, particularly in the medical field, until the 12th century. Like Hippocrates, he made the connection between the inner world of the spirit, and the outer world of the body and expanded the ideas of Hippocrates. The Sanguine temperament, in which the bodily fluid (blood) predominated, was lively and optimistic. The Melancholic temperament was, he believed, due to a predominance of black bile which caused a rather serious, doleful outlook. The Phlegmatic temperament dominated by phlegm, turned out to be slow, or calm. The Choleric temperament ruled by yellow bile, was passionate (emotional) in expression.

This erroneous, but quaint theory of body fluids controlling our temperament is, of course, not based in scientific fact. However, the classifications of Sanguine, Melancholic, Phlegmatic, and Choleric, with some renaming and adjustments, would stand to this day. They were to be referred to for centuries as *the four humours* (or humors), the different spellings being a matter of English variants.

The Dark Ages and the Middle Ages

The Dark Ages produced very little comment on temperament. No doubt this was because Galen's theory was well in place, and on the whole, slavishly followed.

Geoffrey Chaucer (circa AD1343 – 1400), whose body is laid in the part of Westminster Abbey called the *Poet's Corner,* and who was in life a prosperous wine merchant and a royal confidant, is described as having immense powers of human observation. Chaucer, in his writings, describes a psychic doctor as "knowing the cause of every malady, and where from, and of what humour [temperament]." The four humors remained the basis for understanding of how we are made on the inside and were still an influence in paramedical practice at least.

The Renaissance

The interest in the four temperaments continued and was advanced with the awakening of knowledge in the Renaissance.

Paracelsus, whose real name was Theophrastus Bombastus von Hohenheim, believed that healing was a matter of mental health (a concept that has modern day support) and found temperament a useful tool in understanding people and their ailments. He re-described the four temperaments as: (1) Salamanders, impulsive and variable – an apt description of the SP; (2) Gnomes, industrious creatures, full of guardian traits – the SJ; (3) Nymphs, whose passion and skill at inspiration certainly nailed the temperament of the NF; and (4) the Sylphs, supposedly calm and curious – the NT. With these descriptions he formed a curious and mystical interpretation of the temperaments.

Philosophers' and Novelists' Use of the Four Temperaments

Philosophers, such as Hume, Brune, and Kent, to name a few from the sixteenth through the twentieth centuries, accepted the four humors as self-evident.

Novelists, particularly eighteenth to twentieth century writers, such as Thomas Hardy, Jane Austen, Tolstoy, C. S. Forester, D. H. Lawrence, Ernest Hemingway, and Albert Camus, are only a few of the great writers who made use of the four temperaments to accurately portray their characters so that people would recognize themselves in the fictional personalities. When we read their character portrayals, we feel we are in contact with real people, and this is a testimony to how accurately the temperaments describe a basic orientation of human nature.

Stephen Montgomery has written an excellent examination of classical novelists' characters in terms of temperament in his trilogy, *The Pygmalion Project.* I readily recommend these books to those who wish to study temperament.

The Challenge

Pavlov and Freud

It was not until the advent of two scholars, Pavlov and Freud, that the idea of people being formed in four distinguishable temperaments with different drives, urges, behaviors, and desires was seriously questioned. Ivan Petrovich Pavlov (AD1849-1936), a Russian Physiologist, studied conditioning in animals and sought to show that they could be conditioned to be what the conditioner wanted, despite supposed inborn tendencies. Man was effectively, in his belief and in that of those who popularized his beliefs, reduced to a machine that could be altered by environment or other conditioning agents. Since he believed that humans could also be manipulated by others to be whatever the conditioner desired them to be, behaviorism was born. Behaviorism is no longer the dominating belief.

At the same time, Sigmund Freud (AD 1856-1939) was proposing that humans are not different by nature, nor do they have a predetermined temperament. All of us are the same, with one drive (namely, sexual desires) that adequately describes all our actions. Freud's works had the effect of changing the way people thought about personality, and how people are motivated. Humans were this time reduced to animals that were moved by blind instinct, in his thought, rather than automated machines as Pavlov saw them. Many psychologists ditched any adherence they had to temperament and bought into either or both of these new philosophies with abandon. Behaviorism and psychoanalysis almost swept the field. This was a radical redefining of human nature and (with the impetus that any revolutionary idea creates) it gained a strong foothold. Like behaviorism, it is also no longer the dominant understanding of human nature.

However, not everyone bought into the apparent demise of temperament psychology. A few scholars still clung to the theory of four temperaments. Moreover, their struggle with defining the temperaments they still observed in humans eventually added significantly to the knowledge of how we are made. One saw the temperaments as four world views, another as four values that people treasure, and so on. They looked at both the negative and positive sides of temperament. A scientific evaluation was underway.

Knowledge and research has advanced a long way since the time of Freud and Pavlov. I think it fair to say that behaviorism has suffered some fatal blows in the estimation of many scientists, and the ideas of Freud have been abandoned for analysis less predisposed to the idea that we are all the same.

Carl Jung

Even Carl Jung (1875-1961), one of Freud's favored students, parted company with him and his ideas and emphasized the fact that we are not all the same. His influence was to equal Freud in many ways. We have different drives and desires, he maintained, "Different in essential ways!" Jung called the drives or instincts of humans *archetypes*, and saw that what made a big difference in basic psychological functioning was the extraversion or introversion preferences that are inborn in all of us. He further defined four basic functions that operated in our inner worlds – thinking, feeling, sensation, and intuition. He was to be influential in the rise, again, of temperament psychology and would be the focus of two brilliant housewives who studied his works and based their conclusions on their own observations of human nature as well as Jung's theories.

Myers and Briggs

Isabel Myers and Kathryn Briggs would devise the Myers-Briggs type indicator, and temperament would be catapulted to first place again with popular personality tests. In one year alone (in the 1990's) over one million assessments were taken. But these two brilliant ladies were not trained psychologists and, therefore, they were not taken seriously by most of the psychological community (a case of sour grapes, I think). The world of academia has a way of punishing "unqualified" research, meaning research and study conducted by people without psychological degrees or training. However, their influence was destined to surpass most of the psychologists who disregarded them.

David Keirsey

Then came David Keirsey, a psychologist who had been profoundly impacted by the Myers/Briggs type indicator. He has, along with others, devoted at least 30 years to further research and understanding of the four temperaments and the sixteen types (four further distinctions within each of the four temperaments). For a brief history of the four temperaments, and for what I regard as the best understanding of the temperaments from a secular point of view, see his books *Please Understand Me* (which was written with Marilyn Bates) and *Please Understand Me II*. Keirsey is today the leading authority in Personology or Temperament Psychology. His studies have been intense and scholarly. Millions have taken his Temperament Sorter II, and his definitions of the temperaments have added significantly to our knowledge of temperament. Temperament studies that do not take note of Keirsey's contributions lose much credibility, in my opinion.

A Compelling Demonstration

The first suggestions of people being formed in recognizable temperaments came as visions from God (see Appendix.) By observation for over two millenniums, among different nationalities (beginning with the Greeks), in many countries, with many profitable applications, and with millions of people assessed, it has established itself with an authority and track record that is impressive indeed. People do fall into four distinct temperaments. When tested, they concur. This is how we are made on the inside, and the sooner we discover ourselves as seen in our temperament the better we will understand ourselves and be the best that we can be.

A tested theory that has proven true over millenniums should not be easily set aside by some recent idea that is yet to be tested over at least half a millennium. The consistency of temperament observation is striking, and the story is compelling.

Current Interpretations of These Ancient Classifications

Many systems claiming to be able to assess one's personality are available today. They may even use Galen's designations – sanguine, choleric, melancholic, and phlegmatic – or some other new terminology. The question is whether they accurately assess the temperament or type of a person? Mostly, they fall short and are inaccurate. I have relied heavily on Keirsey's work because it follows the detailed research of Myers/Briggs. Keirsey has advanced on their research to show the continuity of temperament with the existing observations of the last two and a half millenniums. I strongly recommend that you use either the temperament keys in this book or similar sorters, and avoid the many substitutes available today. They are not in the tradition of Meyers/Briggs or Keirsey and do not utilize their vast research.

THE TEMPERAMENT KEYS

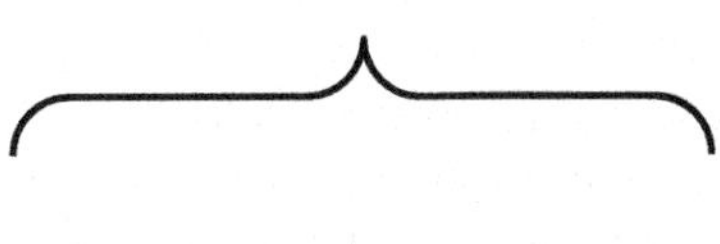

Instruct a wise man [person] and he will be wiser still.
~Proverbs 9:9

Chapter Three ♦

PARENTS

Great Parents Know Themselves! Know Yourself — Stay Ahead of Your Child

Why should we know and understand our temperaments as parents? Isn't it enough to understand our child's temperament? No! Here's why. We should know our own accurately **because our child does!**

This chapter will prepare you for completing the Temperament Keys, so let me remind you of several relative benefits and facts.

The Child's Intuition

The intuition of a child is not clouded with doubts or inability to "see" clearly, and it is often very penetrating. They have a clear view of us parents. Adults have accumulated a lot of "static" on their "intuition lines" and don't seem, in most cases, to see others as well as once they did. The static distorts the reception. The only exception to this is the adult who uses intuition a great deal and has developed it.

Children's learning ability operates at a maximum as it develops and adds to their intuitive insights. They soon learn to piece together the data from people's reactions. Children will often surprise us by turning our statements against us for their own gain – a sign that everything on the intellectual front is progressing with purpose! This learning curve is operating all the time as they pick up all the data they can from their world. A gap in our understanding, particularly about ourselves, is a vulnerable spot for the child to explore.

Parents who want to remain in control must stay ahead of their progeny or give up the game. For the child's sake we can't afford to give up. Know yourself so that you can know how your children see you and what expectations they have of you.

Under the Microscope

Children focus on their parents. A large percentage of the early world of children is their parents. Parents interact with their children at a more intense level of engagement and interest as well. They seek to earn the love and respect of the child. This higher level of interest does not go unnoticed by the child. The truth is that it focuses the child more intensely on the parent. Children's developing brains have little in the way of distractions compared to an adult, so they soak up every little detail and process everything, even though their brain does not make all the expected connections at this early age.

This soaking up of all details accounts for some of those embarrassing moments when a child reports what a parent has done. "Mommy was mean to daddy!" Now mommy has been declared guilty by her own home court! Sometimes the child also tacks on further damaging evidence! "Mommy threw a vase at daddy, and she missed!" The case is heating up by the microsecond.

It's in moments like these that the parent can benefit greatly from self knowledge. How do you typically react? (Do you explode in self-defense, make a joke of it, scold the child, or even lie about the incident to other adults present?) Are you knowledgeable enough about yourself to know what your knee jerk reaction typically is, so you can buy time with a response like "If I was mean to daddy, I will say I'm sorry. That's what we all should do."

Know your temperament because there won't be much time for you to think and learn how to react or defuse those undesirable reactions we all make at times. (In the chapter on strengths and weaknesses we will learn much more about how to handle our moments of challenge.) The child may have meant no harm. She was simply reporting and using her newfound mental abilities to recognize unusual happenings and remember them. Or did the child intend to harm? Do you know your child and how your child sees you? Temperament will tell you. Perhaps your child actually meant to harm you. Maybe it was a tasty moment of revenge. Also, you could benefit by asking, "Why does my child see me as mean?" Has your firm, unbending pursuit of appropriate behavior (SJ temperament) rubbed your child the wrong way? Is your child the SP temperament who typically is lying in wait for just such a moment to assert his or her own tactical skills and deliver a rewarding stab, precisely timed, in the presence of others? In such "warfare" you need to know who you are as well as how they see you. Knowing ourselves is the only path to effective self-management.

How does an SP child see an SJ parent? Not in the way the SJ parent thinks about themselves. The prescriptions for both you and your child's temperament glasses are best known, not guessed. Of course we don't want to see family life as warfare, but the reality often is that opposing temperaments end up engaged in some kind of offensive or defensive action that knowledge of each other can defuse. This is why you are about to engage in self-discovery.

The parent exposes himself, or herself, when these kinds of things happen. We don't like to be exposed, particularly by a child. It also doesn't have to be an embarrassing moment. All concerned can learn valuable lessons. We will seek to equip you with what that might be for each of you. Every temperament will need to return to its strengths in times of challenge, or loose respect. The trillion-dollar question (important questions used to be "million-dollar" questions; no longer so in this economy) is: What are our strengths?

To know our strengths and to be aware of how our weaknesses develop can be the difference between reactions that teach and affirm the child or damage the child and raise the temperature of the home. Know yourself!

Benefits from Knowing How We See Our Children.

Understanding should be a two way street. It is a busy street at that. We understand how they are made, and they increasingly understand the patterns of behavior in our reactions. Learn who you are, and you will also know when your child perceives you correctly or has a very different view of you. Clear knowledge about the child for the parent begins with knowing how the parent is made on the inside, which gives a clear understanding of how you are seeing your child. Simply put: you understand the prescription of your own lenses.

An SP parent may see an SJ child as weak and timid when, truthfully, the child is desperately seeking security. Once the child finds the security needed he is hard to scare and appears determined and brave. Understand that the SP sees the child through a prescription that says "Be bold, take risks, and test the limits." Their prescription causes them to see others in terms of <u>their</u> standard for bravery, through risk taking. Bravery can also contain an element of thoughtful determined planning (SJ). The SJ child sees the SP parent as lacking in this quality and they see the parent as reactionary, impulsive, and possibly as a threat to their safety or the safety of society. None of these things, the SP may think, fairly describes their intention or makeup, but the SJ sees the SP this way. Only with this knowledge can we understand our children's reactions. Know yourself and your child.

Finally, Two Methods

There are two ways to get an understanding of how we are made on the inside. We will use both.

1. Our temperaments (similarities and differences of strengths and drives) can be determined by taking a personality assessment such as "The Temperament Key.". For all who are old enough to have had enough experience to answer questions about their

preferences we use this temperament key or some other reliable assessment.

2. For the child, temperament can be known by observing a person's actions and reactions and, from this data, estimating the preferences under which that person operates. Once you know how someone prefers to act, you can then either consciously or intuitively (a child processes this knowledge intuitively) assess the drives that make them prefer to act in a particular way. As a result, we can get an estimate of their temperament. We will ask you, the parents, to report your children's behavior under differing circumstances so that their temperaments can be determined sufficiently for your parenting decisions and, in most cases, accurately.

Our children are constantly reading us, perhaps with more intense purpose than we read them. So, let's pay real attention to how they see us, and we see them, and to the differences temperament glasses make in this ongoing journey of discovery.

Chapter Four ♦

🗝 The Temperament Key for Adults

Let me introduce you to the Temperament Key for Adults. Both the Adult Temperament Key and the Child Temperament Key used in this book have been developed using the principles of research into temperament that Myers/Briggs, Keirsey and Harkey/Jourgensen, among others, have used for the development of their assessments. These principles, when used in assessments, have proved very reliable and can be depended upon. Any of the above named assessments of temperament are excellent guides to the discovery of how you are made on the inside.

As long as you carefully follow the instructions for both of the Temperament Keys presented here, you should get excellent results.

This is a very positive assessment. We are looking for your strengths, not your weaknesses. There are no wrong answers since it is a self-evaluation. However, be as accurate as possible. Read these instructions carefully since a knowledgeable guide is not looking over your shoulder, and you can't ask for help. <u>It is imperative that you answer according to these instructions.</u>

- Answer these questions according to your preferences (what you prefer), not according to what you think others would have you become.
- Answer each question individually. Don't try to be consistent.
- Aim to get through the key in about 20 minutes or less.
- Think carefully about each answer, but avoid over-thinking, which can lead to confusion. If you are over-thinking, ask yourself, "What am I the most?"
- Again, let me put it this way, if you see yourself as both (a) and (b) in some of the questions, your answer should be what you see yourself to be the most, or what you prefer the most.
- Your preferences are often different at home than at work. This can be due to the fact that, at work, certain things are required of you, and therefore they have become your work preferences. You prefer to do it that way at work, since that's what is good for you. If your work preferences differ from your home preferences, answer according to your home preferences.
- We want to know what really beats in your breast, what really satisfies, fulfills, or pleases you the most.

The results should be accurate, but if you attend one of my seminars ask to be checked again. It's a service we provide. When you read the descriptions of the temperaments in chapters 8, 10 and 13, you can determine whether they match your results in the temperament key. If they do not match the descriptions, then you answered with something else in mind, and you will need to switch to the temperament most like you.

This verification of your answers is very helpful. The ones who are most likely to be confused about themselves are the NFs. They are the complicated temperament and have the greatest difficulty in understanding themselves for that reason. Now, proceed with careful thought.

ADULT TEMPERAMENT KEY

Check (A) or (B) for each question. Please answer ALL questions.

1. At social gatherings do you prefer to
_____ A. Socialize with everyone
_____ B. Stick to your friends

2. Are you more in touch with
_____ A. The real world
_____ B. The world inside your mind; the world of possibilities

3. Do you rely more on, or take more notice of
_____ A. Your experiences
_____ B. Your hunches/gut feelings

4. Are you (most of the time)
_____ A. Cool, calm and collected
_____ B. Friendly and warm

5. When evaluating people do you tend to be
_____ A. Impersonal and frank
_____ B. Personal and considerate

6. Do you mostly feel a sense of
_____ A. Urgency/upset if you are not on time
_____ B. Relaxed about time

7. When you see a mess do you
_____ A. Have an urge to tidy it up
_____ B. Feel reasonably comfortable living with it

8. Would you describe yourself as
_____ A. Outgoing/demonstrative/easy to approach
_____ B. Somewhat reserved/private

9. Which are you best at
_____ A. Focusing on details
_____ B. Catching the big picture, the connections, the patterns

10. Children should be
_____ A. Made to be more responsible
_____ B. Encouraged to exercise their imagination and make-believe more

11. When making decisions, are you more influenced by
_____ A. The facts/impersonal data
_____ B. Personal feelings

12. Do you feel more yourself when giving
_____ A. Honest criticism
_____ B. Support, approval, and encouragement

13. Do you work best
_____ A. Scheduled; to deadlines
_____ B. Unscheduled; no deadlines

14. For a vacation do you prefer to
_____ A. Plan ahead of time
_____ B. Choose as you go

15. When you are with others do you usually
_____ A. Initiate the conversation
_____ B. Listen and tend to be slow to speak

16. Most of the time, facts
_____ A. Should be taken at face value
_____ B. Suggest ideas, possibilities, or principles

17. Do you mostly feel
_____ A. In touch with the real world
_____ B. Somewhat removed/lost in thought

18. When in an argument/discussion do you care more about
_____ A. Defending your position and being right
_____ B. Finding harmony and agreement

19. With others do you tend to be
_____ A. Firm
_____ B. Gentle

20. Do you see yourself as
_____ A. Predictable
_____ B. Unpredictable

21. Do you mostly prefer to
_____ A. Get things done; come to closure
_____ B. Explore alternatives; keep options open

22. After two hours at a party are you
_____ A. More energized than when you arrived
_____ B. Losing your energy

23. Which best describes you
_____ A. Down to earth, practical
_____ B. Imaginative, an idea person

24. Which do you finally rely on more
_____ A. Common sense
_____ B. Your intuition/insights or your own analysis

25. In other people, which appeals to you most
_____ A. A strong will
_____ B. Warm emotions

26. Are you more controlled by
_____ A. Your head/thought
_____ B. Your heart/emotions

27. Are you typically
_____ A. Eager to get decisions made
_____ B. Not keen on making decisions

28. On the whole, do you spend your money
_____ A. Cautiously
_____ B. Impulsively

29. When you have lost energy, do you find yourself mostly
_____ A. Seeking out people
_____ B. Seeking out solitude/a quiet corner

30. Do dreamers
_____ A. Annoy you somewhat
_____ B. Fascinate and interest you

31. Do you rely more
_____ A. On your five senses
_____ B. On your sixth sense/intuition

32. Are you more
_____ A. Tough-minded
_____ B. Tender-hearted

33. Would you more likely choose to be
_____ A. Truthful
_____ B. Tactful

34. Do you see yourself as more
_____ A. Serious and determined
_____ B. Relaxed and easygoing

35. Do you feel more comfortable when
_____ A. Things are decided
_____ B. Your options are still open

36. Would you say you mostly
_____ A. Show your feelings readily
_____ B. Are private about your feelings and keep them inside

37. Would you prefer
_____ A. To be in touch with reality
_____ B. To exercise a creative imagination

38. Is your way of thinking more
_____ A. Conventional
_____ B. Original and creative

39. What motivates you more
_____ A. Solid evidence
_____ B. An emotional appeal

40. Would you rather be known for
_____ A. Being a consistent thinker
_____ B. Having harmonious relationships

41. Do you tend to
_____ A. Value routines
_____ B. Dislike routines

42. Do you live more with
_____ A. A little sense of urgency
_____ B. A leisurely pace

43. Do you have
_____ A. Many friends and count them all your close friends
_____ B. Few friends, and only one or two that are deep friends

44. Do you place more emphasis on what you see
_____ A. With your physical eyes
_____ B. With your mind's eye

45. Are you
_____ A. Thick skinned; not hurt easily
_____ B. Thin skinned; hurt easily

46. When you are asked to create a "To Do" list, does it
_____ A. Seem like the right thing to do and do you feel it will be helpful
_____ B. Bug you and seem more like an unnecessary chore

47. Which word attracts you most or describes you best?
_____ A. Talkative
_____ B. Quiet

48. Which words attract you most or describe you best?
_____ A. Present realities
_____ B. Future hopes

49. Which word(s) attracts you most or describe(s) you best?
_____ A. Logic
_____ B. Loving heart

50. Which word attracts you most or describes you best?
_____ A. Plan
_____ B. Impulse

51. Which word attracts you most or describes you best?
_____ A. Party
_____ B. Home

52. Which word(s) attracts you most or describe(s) you best?
_____ A. Common sense
_____ B. Vision

53. Which word attracts you most or describes you best?
_____ A. Justice
_____ B. Mercy

54. Which word attracts you most or describes you best?
_____ A. Concerned
_____ B. Carefree

SCORE SHEET

Instructions for the score sheet (located on page 57):

1. Place a ✓ in the appropriate column (A or B) to indicate the answer you chose for each numbered question. [*Please note that the numbers run from left to right across the chart.*]
2. Count the number of "As" in column #1 and write that number at the bottom of the chart above the "E". Count the number of "Bs" in column #1 and write that number above the "I" at the bottom of the chart.
3. Count the number of "As" in column #2 and write that number in the left-hand, shaded box at the tip of the arrow beneath column #3. Count the number of "Bs" in column #2 and write that number in the right-hand, shaded box at the tip of the arrow beneath column #3.
4. Count the number of "As" in column #3 and write that number in the left-hand box beneath the dark gray box at the bottom of column #3. Count the number of "Bs" in column #3 and write that number in the right-hand box beneath the dark gray box at the bottom of column #3.
5. Add the number of "As" for columns 2 and 3 together and write the total above the "S" at the bottom of column #3. Add the number of "Bs" for columns 2 and 3 and write that number above the "N" at the bottom of column 3.
6. Repeat the steps in instructions 3-5 above for columns 4/5 and 6/7.
7. Which did you have more of, "Es" or "Is"? ___________
   Which did you have more of, "Ss" or "Ns"? ___________
   Which did you have more of, "Ts" or "Fs"? ___________
   Which did you have more of, "Js" or "Ps"? ___________

8. In the four letters you listed in Instruction #7, which two-letter combination below is present? Circle it!
   S and P S and J N and T N and F

	1			*2*			*3*			*4*			*5*			*6*			*7*	
	A	**B**		**A**	**B**		**A**	**B**		**A**	**B**		**A**	**B**		**A**	**B**		**A**	**B**
1			2			3			4			5			6			7		
8			9			10			11			12			13			14		
15			16			17			18			19			20			21		
22			23			24			25			26			27			28		
29			30			31			32			33			34			35		
36			37			38			39			40			41			42		
43			44						45						46					
47			48						49						50					
51			52						53						54					
	E	I					S	N					T	F					J	P

> *Everything I understand, I understand only because I love.*
> *~Nikki Giovanni*

Chapter Five ♦

CHILDREN

At What Age Can I Assess the Temperament of My Child?

I get asked this question often, so let's answer it before we complete the Child's Temperament Key. You can begin this fascinating task at infancy and observe the elements of your children's temperaments as they emerge and become obvious. Understanding the **emerging temperament** can lead to a more meaningful, early bonding with your child.

Around two years of age, you should be able to put most of the pieces together and know your child's temperament with enough certainty to make a **big difference in parenting**. Until then, focus on bonding with your infant, meeting their needs, and understanding the temperament you see developing. Your children are discovering this strange world they have suddenly been thrust into and will face inevitable struggles with their world and with their own needs. Struggles are necessary for development. You can't protect your child from all struggles, and you don't have to. In those struggles you will more likely observe your child's temperament.

From two years until around eleven years of age, your knowledge of your children's temperaments will make a major difference in your parenting and the way your children feel about you, their early authority figure. Even by two years of age, they are forming their assessment of you. Also around this age, your children will be trying to understand why and in what way you appear to be different from them.

During this stage of your child's life temperament is asserting and reasserting itself, giving you many opportunities to confirm your observations. Your observations of your children's behavior from two to eleven years of age will also be more accurate, and you will better understand why they act the way they do and how they feel when they act or don't act. Most of you will be able to accurately determine your child's temperament, since it will be frequently confirmed. Remember, the only way we can assess a child's temperament is via his or her actions. We can't see inside to know the child's thoughts, feelings, drives, and preferences. We can only observe these in the behavior that results. So, be sharp observers of behavior and don't try to play a guessing game with the reasons for their behavior. Sometimes, you will be right and sometimes, you will be wrong. Depend on your understanding of their temperament to lead you to the right conclusions about how they feel on the inside.

As we have noted, knowing temperament gives us the insight we need and helps us take advantage of its long history of observing and understanding how people are made on the inside. This is the way we can know how they are feeling; and I, along with countless others, have found this to be surprisingly accurate. Accurate observation of behavior never fails to reveal what is on the inside, because it was inspired and formed by what is on the inside.

From eleven years of age (these days eleven seems to begin the teenage struggle for identity and purpose) through the teenage years, I believe, the knowledge of your child's temperament is <u>crucial</u> to excellent parenting. Teenagers are struggling to know who they are in the deepest and most important way. We wonder why they behave the way they do and why they fail so often to meet the expectations of others. Introverts sense they are different from the majority and withdraw if they don't understand why they act the way they do. Struggles ensue that often lead them to unnecessary and harmful experiments with life — all so often with the goal of being understood and accepted. Both emotionally and socially, the teenage years are a traumatic adventure because our emotions are the most difficult part of our makeup to understand and manage. Therefore, teenage trauma and unpredictability is understandable.

If your children are teens, this knowledge of temperament is not too late. They are still in the formation stage, and even though you may not have developed a close tie or bond that is meaningful to them, you still can get through to them with understanding. They see everyone in a new light every day, and you can be one of those who undergo a major change in their minds. Take advantage of these years of change and, if necessary, change your image and your relationship with them through the tough times (when you also gradually release them to their own responsible management of everything in their lives). Most teenage struggles with parents are over misunderstanding or mismanagement of the teen's feelings. Other major issues, such as the teen's beliefs, will be addressed later in this book.

Wouldn't it be wonderful to help your teenager or child understand how they are made and teach them how to be the best they can be? It all starts with understanding their temperament. The journey continues with helping them understand themselves and helping them become comfortable with who they are. Without this knowledge as your tool, you will be at a disadvantage and you will face many a trial you could have wisely averted had you "discovered" your child's true temperament and the purpose for their lives that is built into their fundamental makeup.

Hopefully, you have already completed the Temperament Key to assess your temperament. We will now address the question of how your child is made on the inside. Once you have the knowledge of who you and your child are, this book will then help you understand how to apply this knowledge.

Chapter Six ♦

Identifying My Child's Inner Preferences

The Child Temperament Key

Because we can't ask your children the questions in the Adult Temperament Key and have them understand, we will ask you, the parent, questions about their behavior. These questions will give us knowledge of the same four areas of temperament that the Adult Temperament Key examined and will result in four letters that reveal their type just as we did for you. There is more explanation in this key due to the need to help the parent really understand what we are driving at with the question. Behavior is one step further removed from our preferences and, therefore, we must advance with all appropriate care.

A score sheet is provided at the end of each section to help you record your responses to the questions for all of your children/grandchildren. Please write the name of each child at the top of each grid, and then answer each question appropriately for each individual child. If you have more than two children make copies of the score sheets as needed.

Again, let me point out that I have included lengthy explanations of the questions, at times, to help you understand what the question is asking and to aid the accuracy of your answers.

CHILD TEMPERAMENT KEY

Is Your Child an "E" or an "I"? (Extrovert versus Introvert)

Please check the appropriate choice. **If you have more than one child please check the appropriate choice under the "A" or "B" column for each child on the score sheet that follows this section.**

1. Is your child normally

_____A. Outgoing and engaging
_____B. Reserved and quiet

2. Does your child

_____A. Approach people and things seemingly without hesitation, head erect and confident
_____B. Hesitate and hold back when faced with unfamiliar people and things, dropping their head and acting a little shy

3. Does your child

_____A. Tend to gain energy in the company of other children
_____B. Tend to become drained after a period and lose energy, stand on the side and take breaks from the energy center, or seek adult company

4. Did your child

_____A. Develop good social skills quickly
_____B. Develop good social skills slowly or not yet

5. Does your child

_____A. Love to be on the phone with strangers and seem animated when on the phone
_____B. Show shyness and reserve when on the phone to a stranger

6. Does your child
_____A. Chat naturally with other people, particularly other children, when in line at a grocery store
_____B. Keep close to you and try not to be seen or spoken to

7. Is your child
_____A. Rather talkative in the company of others
_____B. One who tends to listen and talk only after gathering confidence

8. Is your child
_____A. Easy to approach
_____B. Difficult to draw out

9. Does your child
_____A. Respond quickly when asked to do something or when asked a question
_____B. Respond slowly, as though he or she is musing over the request and as though he or she is trying to figure it out; or as though he or she is stubborn and doesn't want to respond

10. Does your child seem to
_____A. Have no secrets
_____B. Hold part of themselves in reserve, hidden from public view

11. Does your child tend to
_____A. Seek and need the company of others
_____B. Enjoy solitude and play alone happily

12. Does your child attempt to make friends
_____A. Easily and openly
_____B. Cautiously and selectively

13. Would your child prefer

_____A. A noisy environment
_____B. A quiet, more subdued environment

14. Does a new environment with new people
_____A. Seem to excite your child
_____B. Seem to stress your child

15. Does a house full of people
_____A. Bring your child out of hiding
_____B. Cause your child to retreat to his or her room

16. For your child, is becoming the focus of attention
_____A. Exciting
_____B. Embarrassing

17. Which pair of words describes your child best?
_____A. Outgoing, approachable
_____B. Reserved, shy

Please transfer your "A" or "B" answers to the score sheet on the next page if you haven't already done so.

Q#	Name		Q#	Name	
	A	B		A	B
1			1		
2			2		
3			3		
4			4		
5			5		
6			6		
7			7		
8			8		
9			9		
10			10		
11			11		
12			12		
13			13		
14			14		
15			15		
16			16		
17			17		
Total			Total		

Count the As and Bs. The higher score indicates your child's type. More As indicates that your child is an E; more Bs indicates an I.

IS YOUR CHILD AN "S" OR AN "N"? (Sensing versus Intuition)

This is the hardest of the four categories to determine in someone else due to the difficulty of relying on observation alone when we are determining internal perceptions.

At an early age, only the extreme N's can be spotted. If you are doubtful in your responses to the following questions, you may have to wait until age three or four before you can identify with accuracy.

Again, if you have more than one child, please write one child's name above each grid on the score sheet and record your answers on the next score sheet that follows this section.

1. Does your child prefer

_____A. Action to stories

_____B. Stories to action

2. Does your child prefer

_____A. Down-to-earth, real life stories about things that are familiar

_____B. Imaginative tales full of fanciful characters and larger than life heroes (Fairy tales like: *Jack in the Beanstalk*, *Cinderella*, *Star Wars*, *and songs like Puff the Magic Dragon*)

3. Does your child

_____A. Bounce up ready to go to play when the story is over, or even before

_____B. Plead for you to read it again or read more stories

4. In picture books, does your child

_____A. Prefer the simple, bold, graphic illustration

_____B. Prefer the detailed, rich and colorful pictures

5. Does your child

_____A. Seem always to be focused on the real world in their play (their toys, things, and people around them)

_____B. Daydream often, make up imaginative characters, or weave fanciful stories into their play (making their toys whatever the story wants them to be, and seem hungry for fantasy)

6. Does your child

_____A. Seem to be an average child, getting upset and then getting over their upset like you would expect

_____B. Remain hurt for long periods and/or hate passionately and seem to be able to hurt skillfully and put his finger on your vulnerable spot (push your buttons)

7. If the toy he is playing with is a truck

_____A. Is it always a truck

_____B. Is it sometimes a submarine, an airplane, or a monster (but seldom a truck

8. When you break a promise to your child (i.e. "Sorry, we can't go to the zoo as promised,") does he (or she)

_____A. Get upset and get over it reasonably quickly

_____B. Get deeply hurt and take a long time to get over it

9. Would you say that your child is

_____A. Comparatively easy to handle

_____B. Difficult to handle

10. Does your child seem

_____A. Normal

_____B. Strangely different from other children

11. There are two ways to answer this question. Answer the question that is based on YOUR temperament.

If you are a very practical, down to earth person (SP or SJ) answer this: Does your child

_____A. Seem like you

_____B. Bewilder you, and do you find yourself often getting angry with your child out of frustration

If you are an NT or an NF, answer this: Does your child

_____A. Seem NOT to be like you

_____B. Seem like you

12. Has your child had any strange premonitions or the like?

_____A. No

_____B. Yes

13. Would your child be likely to have an imaginary friend?
_____A. No
_____B. Yes

14. What does your child focus on most?
_____A. Today and its excitements
_____B. Tomorrow and its possibilities

15. Does your child's mind
_____A. Function as a database
_____B. Bubble with ideas

16. Do you see your child growing up to be comfortable in
_____A. The world of facts and figures, the real world
_____B. The world of imagination, ideas and books

17. Which pair of words describes your child best?
_____A. Organized, realistic
_____B. Insightful, imaginative

Please transfer your answers to the score sheet on the next page if you have not already done so.

Q#	Name		Q#	Name	
	A	B		A	B
1			1		
2			2		
3			3		
4			4		
5			5		
6			6		
7			7		
8			8		
9			9		
10			10		
11			11		
12			12		
13			13		
14			14		
15			15		
16			16		
17			17		
Total			Total		

Count the As and Bs. The higher score indicates your child's type. More As indicates your child is an S; more Bs identifies your child as an N.

IS YOUR CHILD A "T" OR AN "F"? (Thinking versus Feeling)

Please follow the same routine you did for the last two sections.

1. Does your child

______A. Always want a reason, always ask "why," and never seem happy with "because I said so" (obviously an <u>extra</u> curious type)

______B. Express normal curiosity, not ask why continuously, accept most things at face value

2. Does your child seem

_____A. Impervious to getting his feelings hurt

_____B. To get his feelings hurt very easily

3. Does your child

_____A. Give the impression that he or she doesn't favor being touched and appreciates it less than you expect

_____B. Love being touched

4. Is your child

_____A. Reserved about sitting close to you and touching you, or does your child seem as though he or she doesn't need closeness and touching

_____B. One who cuddles easily and always wants to touch you

5. Would you say your child

_____A. Has difficulty with showing affection to others

_____B. Is the real affectionate type

6. Does your child normally

_____A. Show little expressiveness and feeling

_____B. Show frequent expressiveness with emotions

7. Would you say your child

_____A. Seems to live just for himself

_____B. Wants to please adults and shows a strong concern to please them

8. Has it been

_____A. A long time since your child performed a little service for you and showed that he was looking for your approval and appreciation

_____B. Only a short while since your child performed one of these little services, frequently touching your heart

9. Is your child
_____A. A cool and even-tempered child (more of a cerebral child)
_____B. An emotionally warm-hearted, friendly child (more about the heart than the head)

10. Is your child
_____A. More firm than gentle
_____B. More gentle than firm

11. Does your child seem
_____A. Unaffected by sad endings to stories
_____B. To obviously prefer happy endings

12. Unless angered, is your child
_____A. Straight forward, even blunt, in representing the truth
_____B. Careful not to hurt the feelings of others

13. Do you think your child would
_____A. Enjoy debate and argument
_____B. Prefer to be a peacemaker

14. Which pair of words best describes your child
_____A. Strong-minded, winning
_____B. Kind, forgiving

15. Which would please your child most
_____A. Being praised for excelling over others
_____B. Being praised for being kind

16. Which might touch your child most
_____A. Reason
_____B. Emotion

17. Would your child be more likely to
_____A. Praise the winner
_____B. Comfort the loser

Q#	Name		Q#	Name	
	A	B		A	B
1			1		
2			2		
3			3		
4			4		
5			5		
6			6		
7			7		
8			8		
9			9		
10			10		
11			11		
12			12		
13			13		
14			14		
15			15		
16			16		
17			17		
Total			Total		

Count the As and Bs. The higher score indicates your child's type. More As indicate a T; more Bs define an F.

IS YOUR CHILD a "J" or a "P"? (Likes things decided or likes to keep things open)

This is the last set of questions to round out your child's personality profile.

1. Does your child
_____A. Tend to be ready for school on time and get worried about being late
_____B. Appear indifferent about being late and mostly show little concern
2. Are your child's closets and drawers

_____A. Comparatively neat and orderly (for a child)
_____B. Better described as a "rat's nest" (Does he show signs of not understanding why mother is upset about it?)

3. Does your child
_____A. Show signs of wanting his life settled and in order, preferring routines, in fact gets disturbed when routines are changed
_____B. Show little concern about changes to routines and seems to let things just happen in any way, chafes at routines, and is rather happy-go-lucky

4. Does your child
_____A. Like decisions made quickly, can't stand to be in limbo
_____B. Prefer to procrastinate and keep all options open, putting decisions off

5. Does your child tend to
_____A. Run the activities of other children
_____B. Accept what everyone is doing, or plays as he or she pleases in a group of children

6. Is your child
_____A. Always making "for sure" statements as though he or she knows everything for sure (exaggerates)
_____B. Seldom a user of an exaggerated degree of certainty in their speech

7. Does your child show
_____A. Respect for rules and regulations
_____B. An indifference to the established rules unless he made them himself

8. Does your child show
_____A. A contentedness to be like other children
_____B. That he wants to be different in some unusual way

9. Does your child

_____A. Wake up and get dressed, usually without being reminded to dress
_____B. Need to be reminded constantly to get up and get dressed

10. Does your child wake up and
_____A. Want to know what is happening that day
_____B. Show little concern and is happy to let things happen as they unfold

11. Would you describe your child's style of living as
_____A. More hurried
_____B. More leisurely

12. Would you describe your child's style of living as
_____A. More deliberate
_____B. More spontaneous

13. Would you say your child is more
_____A. Meticulous and particular about things
_____B. Free-wheeling and casual about things

14. Is your child more
_____A. Directed
_____B. Changeable

15. Does your child
_____A. Want to get things done, want to come to closure
_____B. Want to keep things open-ended; seem not to be in a hurry

16. When your child cleans up his or her own room
_____A. Is your child neat about it (puts things in a specific place)
_____B. Does he or she show little care for organization ("away" means anywhere out of sight)

17. Does your child tend to
_____A. Safely store all treasured items
_____B. Get distracted easily and not complete the task

Q#	Name		Q#	Name	
	A	B		A	B
1			1		
2			2		
3			3		
4			4		
5			5		
6			6		
7			7		
8			8		
9			9		
10			10		
11			11		
12			12		
13			13		
14			14		
15			15		
16			16		
17			17		
Total			Total		

Count the As and Bs. The higher score indicates your child's type. More As indicate a J; more Bs define a P.

Now write the four letters that received the highest score on the four blanks beside each child's name below (Example: Lynda - ESTP). This is that child's personality type (one type of a possible 16).

Name: __________________________________ : ___ ___ ___ ___

Name: __________________________________ : ___ ___ ___ ___

Name: __________________________________ : ___ ___ ___ ___

Name: __________________________________ : ___ ___ ___ ___

NEXT, do you have in your four letters for each child an S and a P, an S and a J, an N and a T, or an N and an F? Write the two letters below that occur in the four-letter combinations for each child. This is the child's temperament. Your child will be one of four temperaments: an SP, an SJ, an NT, or an NF.

Name: __________________________________ : _____ _____

Name: __________________________________ : _____ _____

Name: __________________________________ : _____ _____

Name: __________________________________ : _____ _____

Remember, when assessing a child's type or temperament, we must remain somewhat tentative, not that the child's temperament will change, but because the child can't provide us with feedback to our questions about the internalization of his or her thoughts and feelings. However, you can proceed with confidence since inaccurate assessments are rather rare. You can use the next section's descriptions to help verify the letters if you wish, but make sure to verify the temperament by reading all four descriptions of the temperaments (pages 57 – 138) and identifying the one that fits your child the best. You will, of course, see a little of all four in your child.

In the next two chapters, we will describe the behavior, goals, feelings, and characteristics of the four temperaments and four

letters so you can understand your child. You will soon have the understanding you need to know your children, and your children will experience the comfort of being understood according to how they are made on the inside. Moreover, you will be able to avoid the damage parents can unwittingly inflict on their children when they do not realize their words and actions are hurtful to their child's self-esteem.

Gracefulness is to the body what understanding is to the mind.
~ Francois de La Rochefoucauld

Chapter Seven ♦

Tell Me about My Inner World

Now that you have four letters…

Let's understand what they mean. Who am I? What am I? Wow! I'm an ESTJ! What's that – a monster or an angel? An angel, of course! Now, if you put it after my name it sounds really important: Joe Blow, ESTJ. Actually, in a world of alphabet soup I'm not sure that being part of the soup is good or bad. So let's talk just a little about the ingredients of this "temperament alphabet soup."

My First Letter Is E or I

These Myers/Briggs letters stand for extrovert or introvert. You may have noticed that you answered some of the questions in this category as an extrovert and some as an introvert. The same was probably true of your child. A few people will answer all of them as one or the other, but for the majority of us we are somewhat extroverted and somewhat introverted. However, one dominates. We are either more extroverted or more introverted. Whatever dominates is going to rule. One must rule. Our personality does not like confusion. We will lean the way that rules us, particularly in times of stress. Whatever rules us will also fashion our personality more than the other. When the chips are down, we will act either extroverted or introverted and this can be predicted about us.

An adult introvert may have been forced to act in an extroverted fashion at work, but reveal another side (the real side) of himself or herself at home. A child is likely to be easier to read.

Extrovert

What is an extrovert? Most people think an extroverted person is one who is more outgoing, perhaps more engaging in social situations. Usually, they are. However, the definition is inadequate because this is only one aspect of extroversion and not the core aspect. Using our system of letters to identify our tendencies, we have a possibility of eight extroverts and eight introverts. Two of the introverts are quite outgoing and socially engaging and look like outgoing, socially engaging, extroverts. Therefore, outgoing, social tendencies cannot be the core definition of an extrovert.

Extroverts are more accurately defined by what they do to recharge when they are low on inner energy. Interaction with people recharges them. Therefore, they seek the company of people. If you are an extrovert, and you are in need of replenishing your spirit or inner energy, you will invade the space of other people in an attempt to get the needed fuel for your spirit. "Space invaders" are what they have been called with good reason. They can endure parties almost endlessly because while losing energy in engaging people they also gain energy from the interaction at the same time. And they never seem to run out of energy. An extroverted child is difficult to keep at home or pull away from his playmates because he is feeling the energy, and for him to pull the plug seems the wrong thing to do.

People must be within an extrovert's reach for them to benefit. In our technological age, this means not only in person, but on the cell, texting, emailing, blogging, etc. Your teenage extrovert is sutured to an iPhone. If you choose to take it away he (or she) will be reduced to ancient methods of communication. Horrors! Most obviously, you see them massing together and feeding off of each other's energy in person. When you see someone driving down the road, endlessly talking on the phone, they may be using the time to top up their inner battery! Since 75 percent of the population are extroverts, it is likely they will find more ways in this technological age to stay connected and protect their rights to do so. We will ask (and answer) the question, "How do you parent the extrovert without damaging and angering them?"

Introvert

The introverts, only 25 percent of the population, are clearly more reserved and quiet. However, two of the introverts are not always observably reserved on first encounter, the INFJ and INFP. How they recharge their inner batteries is also what defines introverts. Since (unlike the extrovert) people drain the introverts' batteries, they seek solitude (not people) to recharge their batteries when their inner energy has been depleted or is low. The introvert (unlike the extrovert) is most often contented, and even happy, when alone in his or her own world. They are, therefore, territorial (protective of their space) when drained. If someone invades their privacy (or their space) they often show resentment or irritability if their battery is really low. You have to expect this. They need to recharge, and they will fight for air when they feel their spirit is being suffocated by too many, or too long a contact with people. This comfort with and need of solitude is the core definition of an introvert.

The introvert is the more fragile of the two, and their needs are also more often trampled on since they are not appreciated as much in social settings. An introvert can show signs of being withdrawn when, in truth, they are simply in need of down time to recharge. They, more than the extrovert, will appreciate an understanding parenting.

As we will see, these two preferences, extrovert and introvert, are vital for the parent to understand and identify in their children lest they anger and frustrate them.

My Second Letter Is S or N

The S stands for "sensing" and the N for "intuition." I know that N is not the first letter of the word *intuition*; but we used "I" in the first couplet, so we need to be inventive here. Being highly creative theorists chose the second letter in the word! (You may have noticed that you answered some questions as an S, and some as an N. Most do. It is the same as for the E and the I. One will dominate and that becomes the tendency that rules.)

Sensing

The S stands for sensing, and by that we mean the dominant use of our five physical senses — sight, touch, hearing, smell and taste — to give us the information we need about our environment. It does not mean that the S is more sensitive than the N. In fact, the opposite is usually the case. S means using the sense gates as the main means of gathering information about the world around. Both of these letters are trying to define how we get our information from the world around. You may suppose there is only one way: namely, by using our five physical senses. You would be wrong. It is the way the majority of people depend on getting their information; but there is another way that is not usually appreciated by the S. Your S-child appears in touch with his or her surroundings, and that is all they tend to observe. If you are an S- parent, don't be surprised if you don't understand this next one: the mysterious N.

Intuition

Intuition is the word we use to identify our sixth sense, which is not physical. These "sixth sense people" rely on their intuition a great deal to tell them what they want to know about their world and its happenings. They consult their "gut feeling" or their hunches more than their experiences, and sometimes they seem to the Ss to be a little removed from reality — living in the clouds. They often daydream. All children daydream a little, but these daydream much of the time, even when you think they are just playing happily. They live in their inner worlds more than the outer world of the senses. Some of them bump into things frequently because they don't seem to be paying attention, and the parent wonders what is wrong. People who complain about "space cadets" at times are probably referring to an intuitive.

Intuition is hard to define in practical terms since it is non-physical and shares the vagueness and mystery of the non-physical universe. There are fewer Ns than Ss; and the Ns are usually considered by the Ss to be dreamers who don't have their feet solidly on the ground. Living by such a shadowy guide as feelings or intuition is often sarcastically put down by the Ss as less than real, or even a mental deficiency. Deep wounds result from the criticisms of those who are all about their five senses. Yet the giftedness of these intuitive imaginers makes them indispensable. Monitor your home and protect the more vulnerable N from unfair disrespect. Ns are every bit as good as Ss.

Yes, you have already guessed that there is a big difference between the S and N in the way they live and in their inner makeup. Does your child daydream a lot? Then the explanation may be in their natural tendency to rely on the inner world of thought and feeling more than the outer world of the five senses. Treat both the same in parenting, and one is going to suffer and resort to undesirable behavior out of frustration and pain. Because this is the biggest divide in temperament, it is the one we can't afford to get wrong

Of course, all people use their five senses and all have intuition. It's how they use their six senses and what they depend on to determine their actions and decisions that makes the big difference.

There are some who criticize the woman who "wears her heart on her sleeve" and makes decisions based upon feeling rather than logic, while others criticize those who seem heartless, cold and calculated, making decisions void of feelings. Now, rather than criticizing or holding dismay or disgust toward one, we can realize the pendulum is part of our temperament.

<u>My Third Letter Is a T or F</u>

The T stands for "thinking" and the F for "feeling." Again, everyone does a little of both. It is to be hoped that we all think and all feel! However, the balance of thinking and feeling we resort to is not equal. Some seem to feel a lot and think a little. Some seem to think a lot and to be devoid of feelings. The pendulum usually swings to one or the other. Let's get a better understanding of these alternatives.

This category, thinkers versus feelers, is best investigated by asking how we make our decisions, not just whether we think more than we feel, or vice versa.

Thinkers

When we make decisions, do we scan the facts and, realizing what they are telling us, say to ourselves "I can see what they are telling me; so let me do what they say"? In other words, we act on our knowledge of the facts, and that is the end of the matter. The decision is made. These are the ones with a T in their profile. Decision-making is usually a comparatively easy matter for them. Most Ts view feelings as lesser or even encumbering elements in the decision-making process. When the parent is a T and the child is an F, the child can be unfairly thought of by the parent as not logical, or too emotional, and slow about coming to decisions. This is often not the case. The F can value feelings more, and uses them effectively in the decision-making process.

Feelers

On the other side of the pendulum swing you have feelers. Making decisions is a much more problematical matter for them. They scan the facts like anyone else, and they, too, see what the facts indicate they should do. However, they must consult their feelings before the decision is made since their feelings affect their comfort with the results. This is where difficulty enters. If they feel contrary to what the facts tell them, they must either make their feelings fall in line with the facts or make the facts subservient to their feelings – perhaps even discounting them altogether. Either their feelings must change, or the facts must be ignored, at least for the time being.

It takes time to deal with emotions. So, the Fs are usually slower to make a decision. Force the Fs to go against their still unsatisfied feelings, or force the Ts to ignore what they think makes sense, and you have a battle on your hands.

The Ts can seem heartless and cold, especially to an F. And the Fs can seem soft and, at times, like chameleons, changing their positions frequently. Neither is a fair description. Perhaps we should note that both facts and feelings are important in a decision. For the Ts to insist that the facts are all that matters is to miss half of the factors involved in the decision: the emotions. Don't forget that sometimes the facts are not the elements that will determine the outcome of a decision. If neglected, emotions can ruin the outcome of a logical decision. Emotions are "facts" to be dealt with.

For the Fs to place too much emphasis on emotions is to skew the importance of the facts. Should we then strive for an equal balance? Well, imagine what that would mean when you had to make a decision. The facts would be balanced by the feelings and the feelings by the facts. What decision would you make? A leaning to one side or the other is a welcome tendency when it comes to decision making, even though we need to consult both. Sometimes feelings are more important than the facts; and sometimes the facts are more important than our feelings. Could that be the real issue at stake?

In a home, you will often find some Ts and some Fs. Decision-making can become a real problem as the Ts want immediate action while the Fs are not ready yet. When sitting around making a family decision, the Ts will jump to what is, for them, an obvious conclusion. They will then become impatient, and even make derogatory remarks toward those who are still consulting their feelings. The Fs must be allowed time to come to a decision if their makeup is going to be respected. Fights break out and hurt is everywhere when both temperaments are not respected. As with all the differences of temperament, appreciation of each other is the way to peaceful encounters.

My Fourth Letter Is J or P

I know you are going to ask: "What do the J and P stand for?" If I tell you it is my opinion that it will mislead, and may even confuse you. I will tell you, however (just to satisfy your curiosity), and then ask you to forget it. Okay? The "J" stands for *judgment* and the "P" for *perceiving*. Now, forget what I just said! The problem is that the Js perceive just as well as the Ps, and the Ps are as judging as the Js. So the words (judging and perceiving) get us nowhere in our understanding of these choices. They only bias us toward one or the other.

So what do they really stand for? This fourth category in your profile is asking what lifestyle you prefer and lean toward. Is it a lifestyle that likes to get things done? Do you like to come to closure, to get decisions made; and do you tend to live your life with a little sense of urgency, favoring routines and wanting to get on with it? Then J is your lifestyle.

The P is almost the opposite. If you are a P you like to keep your options open. You don't like coming to closure, and you chafe at routines. You prefer to be spontaneous, and you like the world to come to you instead of you forcing things to happen. You don't "sweat it" if you are late. Why get an ulcer? "Why do people feel so pressured?" you wonder. This is the P lifestyle.

If you are a J parent who has a P child, you have probably lost much hair, pulling it out frantically trying to get the P child to get dressed, or get ready on time. On the other hand, if you are a P parent with a J child, you are constantly urged and prodded by your child into hurrying up! When the Js have made their decision and are ready to move, they can be merciless in their impatient nagging of the Ps who are not in a hurry. The Ps take their time and are usually quite effective at paying the Js back for their nagging. Don't punish different lifestyles because you won't change them. You will simply push them out of your center of influence and instead you will also be the proud creator of many unnecessary wars.

Percentages

Percentages can flag us about the world our child faces. All the choices of the four categories are not evenly distributed in our society. The differences can flag us about our child's place in the world (ours too, for that matter).

Es, or extroverts, make up 75 percent of the population, and Is, or introverts, only 25 percent. (Understand that these figures are approximate since, as of yet, all the people in the world have not been assessed by the use of a temperament key! However, a sufficient number have been assessed to make a projection of the numbers for our society and those in many other parts of the world. The numbers are accurate enough to tell a reliable story.

Of course the above figures let us know why introverts feel different, and even odd. They are not the main focus of education, advertising, and all areas of life that are subject to mass treatment by our society. Therefore, the reserved nature of the introvert is often enhanced by this feeling of being the odd person. We will see this in families and discover what it can cause in terms of damage to the child.

The Ss, or sensors, are about 86 percent of the population. The Ns, therefore, are as low as 14 percent. The difference between the Ss and the Ns is the major divide among the temperaments. Imagine how an introverted N, who is only one percent feels! A family of Ns and Ss are at times like oil and water. Mixing is only a temporary achievement. Life is best described as a "solution in suspension."

Between Ts and the Fs, the thinkers and the feelers, they are each about 50 percent of the population. However, here's another curve ball. About one-third of Ts are females, and one-third of Fs are males. The general expectations of society are that males are all about facts (thinkers), and females are all about feelings (feelers). That's not true, of course, but since it hangs on as a societal expectation it means that a female T and a male F are swimming against the current of society.

Lifestyle, the fourth category, is about evenly divided, approximately 50 percent each for the Js and the Ps. Therefore, the struggle in society between the two is an even battle. We don't need any more complications here anyhow!

The Best Way to Know Your Child

There is much more, of course. That's why the book doesn't end here. You and your child will come alive in the stories you will read and the replays in your mind of those moments that please, or frustrate and drive you crazy.

If you don't continue to learn how your children feel and think, you will not only shortchange them, but encourage frustration and failure for you, the parent. Aside from understanding their temperaments, we have no way of knowing our children, except by trial and error. Of course, trial and error can reveal a lot to us. The trial part of the equation is fine — harmless and promising, but the error part is where the damage is done. The bond between you and your child is disrupted, leaving you, the parent, with unneeded, undesirable behavior to deal with and a loss of respect to contend with as well.

The four letters and their meanings are just a beginning. Two of your letters will reveal which of the four temperaments you are blessed to be. That's right, blessed! All the temperaments are wonderful and a gift to us all. The four temperaments, represented by two letters, are the basic differences you will meet, and understanding them is the learning curve that will aid your parenting the most. A good working knowledge of the temperaments will illumine how and why your children are the way they are – how they think, feel, and live on the inside – giving you, the parent, the best way to understand and parent your children to be the best that they can be.

Temperament Percentages

Your temperament, two letters, is also informative. The SPs are approximately 40 percent of the population., the SJ, 46 percent, the NT 8 percent, and the NF 6 percent.

The Ss make up 86 percent and the Ns make up 14 percent. NTs and NFs will also feel their minority status and S parents must be careful not to add to their feelings of being different and strange.

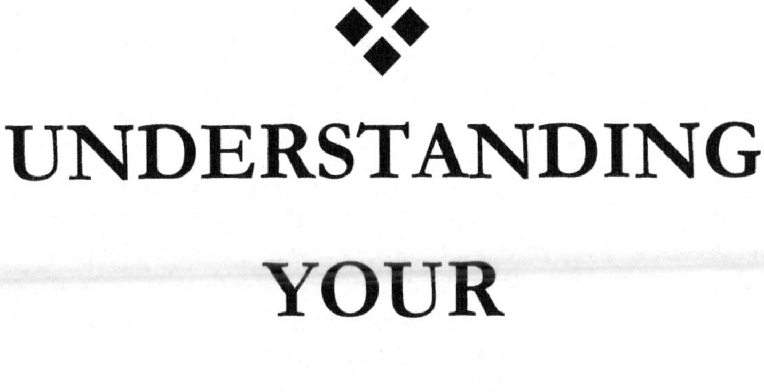

UNDERSTANDING YOUR CHILD

(How We Are Made on the Inside)

> *The human psyche is the most complex instrument in the universe, also, the most rewarding.*

Chapter Eight ♦

How Has Your Child Been Made?

Solving the Puzzle

Now that we've had a better explanation of the four letters, and an introduction to the four temperaments' percentages, we can proceed to the four temperaments

Each temperament has four variations, making 16 variations (types) in all. It would require much knowledge and memory to learn all 16 types, and that might not be user-friendly. Nor is it really necessary for the task of parenting. Knowing the basic temperament of your child is enough for excellent parenting skills to be developed. We will, therefore, focus on the four temperaments. However, I encourage you to read about all four in order to understand where your children stand in the temperament world and how they will relate to other temperaments. Later, we will address some special situations that will arise and that relate to all the four letters.

The two letters you circled on page 46 indicate your temperament. The two letters you wrote on page 66 indicate your child(ren)'s temperament(s). Now you will have the full picture of the world your child lives in: theirs and yours.

I will refer to the four temperaments by the symbols SP, SJ, NT, and NF. Most temperament experts will use a name for each temperament like: sanguine, melancholic, phlegmatic or choleric (or, taking Keirsey's nomenclature: artisan, guardian, rational or idealist). There is a reason I use the symbols rather than names for each of the temperaments. The names immediately color your thinking about the temperaments and suggest they can be known by a one-word description. I don't think they can be reduced to a single word, and I think this tries to reduce a complex description into one thought – however convenient that may be.

Let's take one of the above names (artisan, guardian, rational and idealist) as an example. The very use of the word *rational* for one of the temperaments suggests that somehow the others are less than rational. This is simply not the truth. All would like to be known as rational. The *rationals*, or NTs, are dominated by the use of reason, but this does not mean they are always logical or reasonable simply because they use reason. Each of the other names can be seen to be less than adequate (and even misleading to some people) since our grasp of a word and the emotional meaning we attach to it may not be another person's meaning.

So, let's use symbols and fill each symbol with the full meaning of the temperament, which (if I may say it again) cannot be reduced to one word anyway. At least this will keep us from unintended or unnecessary bias. We will attempt to fill the letters with the meaning (or the temperament) they represent, and that will require describing them adequately.

Remember, the SPs and the SJs are, by far, the most common, comprising approximately 75 percent to 86 percent of the population, with the SJs just outnumbering the SPs. You may have already picked up on the major division. All the four temperaments begin with either an S or an N, and these are the choices for the second letter of the four letter profile. How we gather our information from the world around us is the most decisive factor in temperament, or personality profile.

The Ss are focused on the real world outside of themselves. I don't mean they are not focused on themselves (although that can also be true). In relation to the world of things and people, they appear to be firmly grounded. They focus less on the world inside themselves, turning inward only when they need to. The Ns focus on their inner world primarily, the world of the spirit, and live most of the time in their virtual world, their mind. You could also say they focus on their thoughts, feelings, and imaginings. These Ns make up 14 percent of the population. Of note is that the introverts among the Ns are rarer than any other of the sixteen types.

It may be of interest to you to read the titles for the four temperaments given by various scholars over the last two and one half millenniums. Here are some of the figures we spoke of in Chapter Two and some we didn't mention. Some dates are approximate and some the date of writing. The terms for the temperaments are based on each author's descriptions of the temperaments or the actual terms they used.

Ezekiel c580 B.C.	Lion (brave)	Ox (steady)	Eagle (far-seeing)	Man (humane)
Hippocrates c370	Cheerful	Somber	Calm	Enthusiastic
Plato c340	Artisan *[eikovaike]* (icon or image maker)	Guardian *[pistikos]* (trustworthy, reliable)	Rational *[dianoia]* (thinking-mind)	Idealist *[noetic]* (thinking intuitively)
Aristotle c325	Sensual	Material	Logical	Ethical
John 95 A.D.	Lion	Calf	Eagle	Man
Irenaeus 185	Spontaneous	Historical	Scholarly	Spiritual
Galen c 190	Sanguine	Melancholic	Phlegmatic	Choleric
Paracelsus c1550	Salamander (changeable)	Gnome (industrious)	Sylph (curious)	Nymph (inspiring)
Adickes 1905	Innovative	Traditional	Skeptical	Doctrinaire
Spranger 1914	Aesthetic	Economic	Theoretical	Religious
Kretschmer 1920	Manic	Depressive	Insensitive	Oversensitive
Myers/Briggs 1958	Perceiving SP	Judging SJ	Thinking NT	Feeling NF
Keirsey/Bates 1978	Dionysian (artful)	Epimethean (dutiful)	Promethean (technological)	Apollonian (soulful)
Keirsey 1998	**Artisans**	**Guardians**	**Rationals**	**Idealists**

As parents, you have been waiting to embark on the tour of the temperaments! All aboard!

Action

The SP Temperament in Children

SPs are a delight! They are usually optimistic, pleasant to meet, and appear bright and open. All children are active, but these are seldom still and find down time a real bore. If you have an SP child, you too will be on the move!

While they are still infants, you may be able to spot this excessive activity. They are often called "very active babies." What you observe in the SP baby will only become more exaggerated as they grow older. They will be into everything, searching for excitement and fun. Parents are often concerned about what they observe as "over activity," especially the SJ parents who (remembering their level of activity as children) find little comparison to the level of the SP's activity. "Is my child hyper active?" they wonder. *Hyperactive* is now almost a medical term threatening possible illness. If your child is an SP, he (or she) was born to be this way. There is a compelling drive on the inside that urges them to seek excitement of all kinds and to be on the move – constantly. These are the children who prefer action to stories most of the time. The story must be a good one to hold their attention. To fuel all this activity you may also find they are good eaters. The fun of food, as well as its much needed fuel, is on their early "must" list. Watch out for flying food! It's fun to turn food into missiles!

As you might expect, SPs are often diagnosed with ADHD and given drugs to tame the over-excitable little wonders. I certainly sympathize with the experience of teachers and parents who have to deal with this untamed energy source, but the diagnosis of ADHD is sometimes a misdiagnosis. SPs are dependent on their success in adventure and risk-taking to build their self-image. A child who grows up with a low self-image is not what you want to aim for a parent. The drugs administered to SP children can have the effect of depressing their self-images and damaging their inner development.

His mother was really distressed. Ethan had been such an active child. As she looked back now, she remembered the exhausting days of trying to keep up with where he was, what he was doing, and watching him constantly because he seemed to have no fear. Actually, she recalled occasionally reporting that she swore he loved danger. It was the carrot he chased, the invitation he seemed impelled to accept. And the evidence was there. Ethan was familiar with the emergency room and the doctor's office, which were his repair stops on his constant round of adventure. But those were the good old days.

Ethan was different now. It started with complaints from his teachers that he was disruptive in class, would not sit still, and that his concentration was shorter than "a flea's rest on a hot plate." He was a discipline nightmare for the teachers. His mother felt ashamed and somewhat guilty because he was her child, after all. She consented to having him evaluated for ADHD, and insisted he take his medication once it was diagnosed. This is when the change took place. The medication was effective. Ethan became less active, quieter, more compliant, and everyone breathed in relief. Ethan was at last a normal "good boy." However, something else became noticeable. He became morose, and his personality was changing, too. The sadness deepened, and few, if any, signs of pleasure in Ethan remained. His mother became concerned.

At this stage in the story let me recap what we have learned. Ethan was an SP temperament. SPs have drives inside that impel them to seek excitement and adventure, even to test the boundaries where danger lurks. Their self-image is built on their being brave, impulsive, and on making an impact on others around them. This is what he had been doing. When he was living with action and energy, he was also noticeably pleasant and happy. Back then he was a pleasure to be around – even if exhausting – exuding optimism in his life that was enviable.

Now Ethan looked and acted as though he was seriously depressed. His self-image had been dowsed with ice water. He could no longer be the excitable bundle of energy he once was, and he couldn't think well of himself anymore. Inside he just knew he was not what made him happy.

I'm not against the <u>responsible</u> use of these medications, but I'm opposed to doing damage to a child's self-image and trying to remake a child.

So his mother, after hearing all sides to this argument, eased him off the medication, and soon the Ethan of old returned, together with expressed concerns from his teachers, of course. It was now a matter of dealing with this situation the hard way, walking a fine line between letting Ethan be who he was to fulfill his inbuilt drives, while maintaining respect for others and discovering the value of "cooling it" at the proper times, so that he could add to his pleasant demeanor the less attractive benefits of quiet times.

He had to be taught how to concentrate. He learned, though not without difficulty. He wasn't the best at it, but he tamed the urges when he needed to.

Sometimes, taming urges is what all of us need to learn in order to be prepared for life and succeed in its challenging times. It's hard to learn, and the learning is called self-control. You will find ways in this book to teach this self-control to your child. If you have an Ethan, don't neglect the "natural medications" of self-awareness, self-mastery, understanding, and even a little self-denial — after all, that's what dieting is all about, too! Feed your child's spirit with the much needed nutrition for the human spirit, like patience, joy, love, approval, and encouragement. These will build the muscle of determination and the sinew of perseverance. Sculpting the drives without depressing them is what good parenting is all about. In this case, Ethan's mother will tell you it's not easy, but it's the best thing to do. She is proud of her active, pleasant son who is shaping his inner life, even if slowly.

I'm not on a campaign about ADHD. My campaign is to help you understand your child and take advantage of all that knowledge to teach your child to be what he or she is designed to be. Don't damage a self-image by embarking on a Pygmalion effort, either.

Life is excitement to the little SP, and we cannot deny them this pleasure. To them, time spent in learning is not so attractive, nor is keeping closets tidy, or doing chores. They are just too busy having fun and enjoying the moment to see the sense of tidying their rooms. Teaching them cleanliness will tax you, too. Unless it is fun, like being chased with a garden hose, the very idea of wasting time on such mundane and boring matters is hard for the SP to accept. It's not that they don't love water. They do! But only if water is a medium for more enjoyment.

SPs love to be noticed, and a pool is a good place for attracting attention. They will spend long hours at the pool, provided the attention is available and the fun is fulfilling. This need for making an impact on others is basic to their temperament. Showing off is natural to them. If they cannot make an impression they wonder if they are below average. Depression shows up in SP children whenever they feel they are not succeeding in some physical activity or in making heads turn.

So the agenda for an SP is fun, excitement, movement, activity, adventure, challenges, and anything that spells pressing the limits and taking a risk. As I told you, you will be on the move.

I have mentioned the SPs' gift for turning anything into a contest. They love contests. Let's define the kind of contest they love. It's not so much that they compete against themselves, although they will do that in practice to sharpen their skills. (The NFs are the ones who compete most happily with themselves.) SPs compete against <u>others</u> because they get attention when they do. They also believe they can win, and it puzzles them when they don't. SPs often have a natural athletic ability, and they stand a good chance of winning whenever they step up to compete.

They will initiate a contest over anything. They love to compete with their parents, but please, don't make the mistake of letting them win too often. If they sense you are doing that, they will lose respect for you. "Where is your competitive drive?" they will ask. "Do you have any? Or are you one of those weaklings that are queasy about competing (their point of view)?" A winning parent is admired and followed. Let them win <u>occasionally</u>. When <u>you</u> win, they try all the harder. They must win!

You will notice that SPs move with grace and are naturals at all sports (although they will choose one or two at which they are very good and excel), since competition is the way to fame and attention.

Now, let's turn to play. SPs are artisans with toys. Play dough can bring out the artist in some of them. Artists can be found in all temperaments since creativity is common to us all, but the SPs seem to have an abundance of its gifts. Challenging, creative games are favored, but not games that are too cerebral like chess. (Chess is the loved territory of NTs, since they are the superior strategists and can sit for hours just staring at a board and "living it up" in their minds.) Sitting still while the other player thinks out his move is not an SP's finest hour. SPs are the tacticians, finding the right move at the right time to give them the advantage, and it is best used when the game involves movement, not sitting. Does basketball come to mind?

SPs can play with a toy for hours on end, but when they get bored, that toy is "toast." Once they are through with it, they lose all interest in it. Remember, the secret for the SP is not more toys, but more games!

It may come as no surprise that since the SP loves play, and lives in the present moment, the SP doesn't want to prepare for or save for the future.

Life is enjoyed as spontaneous and impulsive reactions, rather than planned actions. The Js tend to plan life's events and then act with confidence. The Ps tend to favor reacting to life's events as they present themselves, and they seem to have an abundance of confidence in their ability to do so. So why prepare? The SPs are the gifted tacticians and are skilled at living with the greatest effect in the present moment, so this way of life makes sense to them. Preparing for something is wasting the potential excitement of all the moments spent preparing. Why prepare when you know you are good at meeting the moment and its challenges with skill?

If you are not an SP, attempt to get inside this child's restless mind. SPs must be engaged in good things, or they will find activity in destructive things.

Brent, an SP, was restless everyday at school. He found the classroom, and the detailed instructions of the teacher, almost too much to handle. So, when the teacher's back was turned, he would elbow jolt the kid beside him, who would then react with a cry and an accusation. The teacher would turn around to find Brent's friend disturbing the class with his complaints, while Brent (head down and angelic in pose and purpose) went undetected as the cause of the trouble. Brent was delighted, to say the least, and was ecstatic over his success in escaping notice and in causing his classmate to get into trouble. He was tactically brilliant. Seizing the moment like this, and making it into a rewarding display of his success, won him many comments of praise from the other children who were less daring. Brent made an impact on them. Of course, he would soon be detected, but then he would be able to wear his punishment with pride as a badge of his courage and skill.

All the pleading of his parents did nothing to change him because, in his estimation, he was being a brave, daring, risk-taking, tactical, SP. The parents learned to address Brent from his own point of view. The conversation went something like this:

> *"Brent, listen to me," said his father. "You are a brave boy, and I am proud of you for that. Your friends think you take big risks and are very smart. However, what you did at school is more the action of a scared person than a brave person. You disturbed the class, and instead of bravely facing your teacher and admitting it was you, you hid like a coward and let another person get into trouble. I'm proud of you when you are brave, but not when you hide and deceive."*

Brent hadn't thought of it that way. For his father to think he was a coward pierced his heart and made him think.

He did occasionally continue to disturb the class, but owned up to his behavior and took the consequences. It was now the teacher's task to educate her student that it was to his distinct benefit not to disturb others and to find her way of handling him. If the teacher would do this, she would earn Brent's respect and the relationship would improve greatly.

SPs can, as we have already noted, become very bored and disengaged in classes that call for quiet study time or long periods of concentration. When they get bored, they engage in unrelated random activities or, like Brent, in disruptive exploits and are mistakenly classified as hyperactive. Sibling spats are often of the same nature if an SP is involved. If an SP is irritated by a sibling they will usually resort to merciless teasing and picking on the guilty party until they have subdued their opponent and won the contest by persistent wit and determined humiliation.

Trying to change them fundamentally will only lead to maladjustment and damage. They must be reasoned with (starting from their own way of thinking) and shown how they are not really using their strengths in a praiseworthy manner. (Reread how Brent's father addressed him using Brent's way of thinking to start the discussion.) Their desire to perform surpasses their desire for a responsible way of behaving. Therefore, they are hard to parent and they seem to have no fear of consequences. They don't! In their minds, it is the essence of bravery and daring to fear nothing. The very first mention in literature (580 BC) of humanity having four faces, or four temperaments, is in the book of Ezekiel where the SP is seen as a lion: brave and daring, fearing no one and nothing. Your trump card is to realize that although SPs are usually afraid of nothing and no one, they can't stand to be thought of as being cowards or "scaredy cats." Lead them to honest and praiseworthy bravery where their self-image is not lowered, and the reward of using their strength with integrity is felt and enjoyed by them.

The image of a lion suits the SP well. The lion does not prepare for emergencies, but simply reacts to the present moment with a tactical maneuver. It fears nothing, and everything fears it. If we spoke of a lion in human terms, we might say its self-image is built around its fearlessness and its knowledge that it can react effectively without having to preplan its every move.

Since they are optimistic and live without preparation in the present moment, SPs cannot be timid or cautious lest they lose these distinctive qualities. They choose to be what they are. Therefore, parents engaged in the task of bringing an SP child to his knees will find they may have taken on, at best, a never ending task and, at worst, a losing proposition. Use understanding and skill, not brute force. The SPs will not bend to authority if that authority is trying to break their independent spirit or reduce them to meekness. Meekness is a word they don't understand and may even despise. It must be understood in terms of strength to be palatable. Meekness is "gentle strength," for example.

SPs must be given their rope and allowed to be themselves, but hauled in at times to teach them the self-discipline they need for life. This is a big deal in parenting them. Giving them their rope, and hauling them in when wisdom dictates, is a task an SP parent understands best (see Parenting Styles). Allow your boundaries to flex a little (but not break) for the adventuresome SP.

The SP child who is told to "look before you leap" hears "Leap!" He (or she) will leap. And then, with a broken leg propped up in a hospital bed, the child smiles and is proud of his badge of honor. Such bravery and ability to take risks is honored by the pure SP. Risk taking in an organization is, to them, a sign of activity and bravery, and they join organizations that take risks because of the basic appeal of a speculative management (even though SPs are not given to memberships and belonging). The youth department that is full of challenging activities or with chances to perform in a band (a band makes an impact on others) attracts this temperament. So does the camping experience that is more about adventure than being responsible and prepared. SPs see themselves as already prepared for life – not in need of getting prepared.

Their low tolerance for delay leads SPs to avoid complexity and concentration. A two-sided training coin is needed: first, training in accepting delay of gratification, together with training in concentration; second, freedom to be themselves without damaging the lives of others. Don't confuse their low tolerance for delay with taking their time to get ready or not keeping timely appointments. They are only on time if they might miss some excitement. To put it mildly, at all other times punctuality is less of a concern for most of the SPs. Punctuality and low tolerance for delay are two different issues.

If you want to engage SPs as children you must entertain them. They usually bring the excitement with them though. It is exciting to be where they are. Given that you must talk to them about mundane, boring things (like chores or school work) you had best bring an exciting approach to the issue if you want to be effective without having to use force. Remember, they don't take well to force either.

To save for the future makes no sense to this temperament. Spend it – now! Today must be lived, together with spending its resources.

Tomorrow will take care of itself. Training an SP child to appreciate that saving is beneficial is a task best started early in life as a contest or a game with a reward — not presented as a discipline. Don't set your goals too high, unless you want to frustrate yourself.

The SP way of living asserts itself early and never lets go. A typical SP in their sixties still struggles with saving, and still exhibits this daring, brave, impulsive lifestyle, even if mellowed a little with age.

All I have said about the SP is particularly true of the extroverted SP. The introverted ones are the same, but muted and softened by the effects of introversion. They tend to show less daring and more interest in the quieter activities, but still lean toward freedom and spontaneous activities.

Pete was the quiet version of an SP — unusual, but pleasant. He showed all the other characteristics: pleasant to meet, happy in nature, living in the moment, and impulsive. He loved to make things and showed skill when working with his hands. Music moved him, and the love of performing fulfilled him greatly. But he was reserved and quiet. Often he would sit quietly while listening to a long dissertation. He reminded me of the typical SP.

Introverted types think more deeply about things and don't display uneasiness with solitude. Therefore, they are not always seen as SPs and can fool you into thinking that they may be another temperament. If your child is introverted, yet always seems to look on the optimistic side of life and craves activity, consider him an introverted SP.

Well, enough description for now. You already show signs of fatigue. Let's find out about our parenting skills for these lovable little wonders. (Monsters?)

Parenting Skills and Tips that Will Develop the SP Child

(A quick reference guide) Most tips are repeated here for your convenience.

Why not take one of these suggestions at a time and make it a part of parenting your SP? Then go on to the next. Choose the one you consider is most needed and start there. No particular order is better than another.

- Keep them active. It's their life. Fail to do this and you will suffer, not them. They are tactical geniuses, and they will find a way to achieve their goals – quickly.
- If you don't feed them opportunities for activity they will misbehave. The rationale is easy to see. They want and need activity. If it isn't available in a healthy and acceptable way, they feel inwardly compelled to find it, anyhow. Behavior will become aberrant behavior.
- The bored SP will resort to teasing and tormenting their counterparts, since this is real fun. They don't mean to belittle others. They simply have fun at others' expense. What's the difference? They uncomprehendingly wonder about that (between exciting episodes). Others, they feel, have the opportunity to do the same to them. If they do, they will find that, usually, the SP will come alive and turn the event into a game or a contest.
- If you chase them in order to catch and discipline them, they will make the chase into a game, and will enjoy every moment until you seize them and corral them. Now you have turned the game into torture, and they will resist with all their might. This is not the way to discipline them, since they resent you for spoiling their fun. They will disconnect from you, feeling you have no sense of what they are all about or how they feel on the inside. Discipline is best effected without creating the complication of a disconnect caused by the child accusing you of misunderstanding. (See Chapter 10 under "Parenting Styles" for more on disciplining the SP.)

- The worst punishment for an SP, particularly an extroverted SP, is solitary confinement; and they will resent you bitterly for it while they tactically wait to pay you back with more challenges.
- If you send them to their room they will experiment with ways to escape and laugh about their accomplishment; or worse, they can turn their room into a catastrophic hurricane zone in retaliation. At least that was activity, if not also enjoyable revenge.
- If the task is education, SPs do best in action classes where they do things and actively interact. They learn best by doing. The technology schools attract them because so many courses are hands-on. At home, help them learn by doing. It's learning while being active.
- Some SPs are talented artists. Art is a form of creative fun. It taxes the mind and engages the body in making something that impacts the lives of other people. Excitement is one of the goals of art. If you have an SP child who loves art and shows potential, this is a wonderful way to keep that child busy and spur him (or her) on the way to making an impact on the lives of others. Encourage it!
- Turn all chores into either games or competitions. They will rise to the occasion. Why should they keep their rooms tidy? It isn't fun. It's not the content of the competition that appeals most. It is the fun of competing to win or to get a reward.
- Let them use their imagination and show you how the chore can become a game. You don't have to have all the creativity! Reward them for their creativity.
- Always praise them for winning or competing with distinction.
- Rewards that hold promise of some activity they love are very motivating. Reward can also be in the form of praise, or an item they want, or points toward some goal, or acknowledgment at the family gathering. This variety of rewards should be used for all the temperaments; but it is most appealing to the SP. The way you use rewards, and the reason for their use, changes greatly with each temperament.
- SPs have an unexpectedly low tolerance for delay. This is because they live in the present moment, and that means having

to grab an opportunity when it arises. Teach quite times in very small doses. Get them to sit still for 30 seconds to earn a small reward, and make a competition of it with other siblings. Increase the time period as you achieve success.

- The SPs are the performers. Give them plenty of opportunity to show their "stuff" to family and friends. They take to arts and crafts, drama, sports, contests, etc. Music also plays a large part in many of their lives. Their five senses are very finely tuned, and they exploit the pleasure physical things bring. If they want to show their skills, create the opportunity for them to do so.
- Watch out for the love of wheels and speed. This attraction will take hold early and never let go. In teenage, the love of speed can be fatal for some. Constant instruction to add wisdom to their daring exploits will help. At least, when doing so you are building an awareness of their need to think and reason before they act or react.
- Encourage their physical skills. Coordination, strength, and fluency with grace are worthy and helpful goals. In the development of their physical skills the SP will be coached to exert discipline and tactical skills that will help them make wise choices. (An SP child responds better to a coach than a counselor. Be a coach to your SP child.) Talent and wise decisions must go together to create a consistent winner. Teach them this.
- Their physical development and skills are important to their self-image. Seldom will their self-image sink low if they are physically able. They are optimistic, and the daring spirit seldom doubts its inherent abilities. Nonetheless, to build and maintain their self-image is a parenting task.
- Failure is a crushing blow to them. Encourage them when they fail. Show your faith in their abilities, and teach them failure is simply an opportunity to learn how to be better.
- Because they are so daring and bold, being thought of as scared by a parent is sometimes an invitation for them to prove their courage with some rash act. Don't try to build the "fear of God" into them in a negative sense because they will then feel impelled

to take God on. Avoid daring them or taunting them, unless you want them to take the dare.

- The SPs are likely to be the first to try smoking, drinking, drugs, and sex. They do so without the wisdom of experience and age. Fill their minds with the knowledge of how to keep their body operating at its maximum. Offer rewards for success in the activities they like in order to keep them focused on the helpful and the healthy.
- Scolding and punishment will achieve little. When punished, it is their goal to show you that it didn't hurt like you thought it would. They have a brave image to protect.
- They want to appear smooth, sophisticated, and cool to their peers. This often means they act defiantly and obnoxiously to any authority, including parents, to prove their prowess. They feel it is the end of the world to appear weak or scared, particularly to the face of authority. Sometimes they will be cruel and rough to animals simply to prove their boldness. Direct their feelings of pride in their bold, daring, and courageous behavior to lead their peers in daring to do <u>right</u>, which is much harder than to do wrong, or to hurt or damage other people or their property.
- They live spontaneously and don't get ready or prepare for much — unless it is the development of their skills. You will not change this. Try to modify it so that the family runs smoothly for all, even though you can't change it. Don't crush their impulsive behavior. Rather, get them to think about it; and show them the advantage of adding reason and wisdom to their long list of abilities and skills.
- The introvert will do all of these things but is more secretive about them.

Know your children and their exploits, and you will be able to help them and guide them more successfully.

Go to page 139 for a summary of key factors that apply to all temperaments.

Responsibility

The SJ Temperament in Children

The SJ is a foreign country as far as the SP is concerned. Instead of living in the present, the SJ lives in the past. This says a lot more than what you might think. We are creatures of time and space, and the basic orientation of our personalities to time casts the shell in which we live. Living in the present leads inevitably to seeking excitement. The SP is the excitement temperament — the mischief-maker, the one who challenges the limits for fun. Living in the past, however, sets the stage for caution, tradition, and a hesitancy to change which is the SJ's basic orientation to their world, and it molds most of what we find in their temperament.

Their drives can be seen when they are just infants. They can be fretful, since everything is new in those early months, and no past experience exists to which they can refer for guidance. Without something to guide them, they are nervous and indecisive. An empty past, or a past that warns them against a decision, gives them cause for anxiety. This remains true even into adulthood. When experience is the guide, the past dictates the present.

In addition to lacking a point of reference, constant change in the SJ's early days and months can easily unnerve them. So, for the SJ children, build positive routines into their lives, even though <u>everything</u> should not be routinized. It is not a weakness – this search for stability and security – as it will cause them to be the stabilizers of society. And who would suggest society is healthy without stabilization? A society in process of change is an uncertain society. Of course, change suits the SPs, but it shakes the foundations of the SJs.

They are also the "good" babies unless, of course, they are unsettled. This gives the parent of an SJ an indication of their temperament and a guide to possible causes of bad behavior. When they are "bad," check first to see whether they are unsettled. If unsettled, treat their anxiety, not their bad behavior and you will correct the behavior.

Insecurity, the SJ child's nightmare, struck in Theresa's home on a snowy day in winter. First, it was being told that the family would be moving to a new town and a new school, bringing with the move the upsetting task of finding new friends. She was an introvert, and that made matters more complex. An introvert usually has only a few deep friends in life. For them, having to start again is very depressing. "Unsettled" was a feeling that she knew only too well, but didn't know how to express her feeling to others. When her mother asked what was wrong, all she could say was, "I don't want to leave. Why do we have to?" "Because Daddy has a new job in the new town," was the answer. "But why can't he get a new job here?" she pleaded. Theresa obviously did not grasp the logic of the move or understand the situation. The disturbances in the atmosphere that were causing the storm were a reflection of the disturbances that the insecurity of moving was bringing to her little heart and causing her so much pain.

Then the worst happened. After they had moved, she was told one night that Daddy and Mommy were going to have to go different ways, and they were getting a divorce. Her whole life seemed like it was falling apart. Theresa didn't know what would happen next. She was told she would live with Mommy, and Mommy would take care of her, but she felt she could not depend on anything any longer. A negative mental pattern of worry had entrenched itself. No one could really comfort her because the one thing she felt she needed most was gone. Tomorrow did not promise to be like today. Could she be the cause of the impending divorce? Had her complaints about moving upset Daddy so much that he didn't want to stay? She had tried to please them, and, if she had, he would surely not leave, she thought. She now understood, when she thought about it, that her parents had been unhappy for a while. She had lost all her friends. Now, she was going to lose at least one of her parents, and the other might go, too, for all she knew.

Signs of a deep depression set in. Theresa spent much more time alone in her room, and it was hard to coax a smile out of her. Her unsettled, insecure world was more than she could contend with. Eating and sleeping habits changed for the worse, and she did not want to dress in the morning, which was so unlike her. Reports were coming from her new school of uncharacteristic, disturbing behavior.

Her mother was deeply engrossed in her own immediate trauma and was overwhelmed herself with grief of her own. Help was urgently needed for both of them. It did not come quick enough, and Theresa attempted to end her life. She was rushed to the emergency unit and the moments seemed like the torture of hell. Then, the news came.

She would live, and help for her and her mother would be forthcoming. Fortunately, their pastor was skilled at counseling and helping people reconstruct their lives. It was through him that her mother first began to understand that her SJ child had suffered the worst loss possible for her temperament: the perceived loss of all of her security.

A major part of Theresa's healing and return to mental and emotional health was the establishing of positive routines and the constant reinforcement that she was loved, appreciated, and valued. All sense of value disappears when (for the SJ child) the road ahead has no security, and the people around her are not reinforcing her value and showering her with appreciation for what she is trying to do to help. Her mother was overwhelmed and did not know what to expect. Now, thanks to guidance and the knowledge of how all this was affecting her daughter, she had a new understanding.

If you have an SJ child, watch for unexpected changes in behavior and ask yourself, "Does my child have cause for feeling insecure, and even unappreciated?" If the answer is yes, depression is likely, and you must start creating a stable life with much appreciation for your troubled child.

The effective help comes mainly from the parent who understands what must be done to stabilize the child. The parent also needs to be a key factor in the recovery, because that creates a bond the child will not easily forget. To start, welcome your little SJ daily to a world that appreciates him (or her), and realize that the SJ child, more than others, needs to know that what is so today will be so tomorrow. Consistency of routines gives them comfort. SJs are born to create a world that is stable, and they need the very stability they create for others.

If you are an SP parent, your love of newness and tactical challenges will welcome the fast changing opportunities of the moment. However, for your little SJ, this constant change is nothing but a mine field. They do not appreciate the change that you, the SP, meet with confidence and optimism. Instead of showing excitement, they will soon show increased fear and apprehension. You, the parent, will need to do most of the changing as you create a stable world for your child! However, don't overdo it. Yes, your SJ needs stability and consistency. But if you give them everything they want of security, they will grow up without having to flex their inner muscles and will struggle unsuccessfully against the challenges of life that can cause the instability you are protecting them from.

An SJ child who is coddled too much may become timid and excessively fearful of almost anything — a glass-house version of the true, tough, rocklike SJ. You, as the parent, do not need a home of fret and fear, nor will it bless them. SJ parents, on the other hand, tend to overprotect their children and worry about their every move, because they need secure, predictable lives as well; and they try to force each day to obey their needs.

As the story of Theresa indicates, unstable households (such as homes going through divorce) are mine fields for this type of child. They seek the security, not just of routines, but also of parental firmness, agreement, and order. And they thrive on consistent rules and regulations. As a parent, you must learn to identify the winds of either change or trouble that are very threatening to the SJ child.

An obstinate SJ child is a hard rock to move. When they refuse to budge and comply with your requests, always consider what may be causing that stubbornness. Stubbornness in SJs is often due to the fear of change, and they dig their little toes in and refuse to do what you want. Change can upset them so much that they freeze to all outside stimuli. Ask yourself, "Is there some change that my child is facing and unwilling to make?" Also ask, "Is my child's stubbornness due to the fear of an unknown tomorrow?" They want the future to be like the past. Fear can also cause them to freeze, seemingly without reason. If your SJ is an introvert, you will not likely have any communications from him or her to flag you. You must do the detective work alone. The reason I emphasize their low tolerance for fear is because you wouldn't normally expect it. They seem self-reliant and solid, and fear seems so unlikely. Remember, worry is a form of fear, and they are prone to worry.

To help you understand, remember the SJ's orientation to time. They focus on the past for guidance about their future decisions. When the past tells them that the worst always happens, Murphy's Law reminds them to prepare for the worst and to refuse and run from change. They turn pessimistic about the future, and the negative mental attitudes soon show themselves in unwillingness to obey and comply — a sure sign that something is radically wrong with the SJ child. Their worrying and stubbornness is the surfacing of their fears. If you listen closely to what worries them, you will be flagged (warned) and on the trail of a potential debilitating fear you can address. So pay attention to their talk of what worries them. Give them assurances that calm them, and they will feel better.

One parent who is strict and one that is lenient is also devastating to the SJ child's future development. Both parents must agree, or one must defer to the other each time and not switch around. If the parents take opposing sides on rules and regulations, don't think that the little SJ is not sharp enough to seize on this opportunity and attempt a takeover of authority! Traits of willing submission that you often see in an SJ child are not indications of mental dullness. These kids are sharp. If their parents can't be consistent, stable, and predictable, they feel the call to demonstrate how it must be done. Then they seize control of the household in the process as battle spoil.

What troubles SJs about house rules can also become their golden opportunity to attempt to write their own rules and firmly insist that they will live by them, rather than by your ineffective rules. Why shouldn't they? SJs need rules and structures to live comfortably, and since the parents have shown they can't agree and effectively enforce rules, what more reasonable thing to do than make up their own rules and resist the parents' attempts to arbitrarily (in the SJ's opinion) try to upset their workable alternative! If an SP parent is lenient with the boundaries, and the other parent (say, an SJ) is rigid, the SJ child will either show signs of distress or exploit the situation with skill. They do this as adults, and they start young!

So far, we've discussed behaviors when the SJ is troubled. However, when the SJ is happy and feels secure, they have delightful qualities. Even very young, the SJ makes a wonderful helpmate. SPs are playmates; SJs are helpmates; NTs are mind mates; and NFs are soul mates (as Keirsey has titled them). SJs seek to please their parents in doing what is expected of them. Cleaning house, helping with the care of other children, doing the dishes, and helping in the kitchen bring satisfaction to them. They turn out to be the ultimate babysitters, too.

To be reliable, helpful, and responsible is the mold in which SJs are cast and the mold they will impose on society. They will force this kind of behavior on their friends, as well, if they can. They will show nervousness if they can't, and may gravitate to other friends who are cast in their mold. This inborn tendency to be helpmates can make them pleasant to parent — a reward to the overworked parent.

You will, however, dampen the frequency of their help if you fail to show appreciation for what they do. Appreciation refills the tank with fuel for more of the same activity. Make your own reward! If you fail to show appreciation (this always means not that you show appreciation in your judgment, but in theirs) you will be in for some aberrant behavior. Therefore, keep close tabs on them. Talk to them often, which in itself shows them you apparently appreciate them. SJs feel important and appreciated when an adult focuses their attention on them and includes them in discussions and certainly in decisions. Include an SJ in family life and in decisions where appropriate, especially as they grow older.

The teenage SJs are getting ready to set up home for themselves. If in teenage they are progressively included in decision-making within the home, they will bond to the parent with gratitude. Far too few family meetings are held in the opinion of the teenage SJ! They want to feel valued by the adults. This inclusion will also help them learn to make mature decisions and the right decisions when they are on their own.

Rewards like gold stars for good behavior at school (when they are young) are usually treasured. An "I appreciate Mary" bulletin board in her bedroom on which symbols of appreciation are posted can be a very positive motivation. Even as adults, the SJ responds to such items! The reverse also works for the SJ. Negative criticism, if fair, can re-motivate them to do better. They want to be seen as responsible and helpful members of society, and family is their front line society. Constant feedback from adults is deeply affirming to them. Constant means constant! Of all the temperaments, I think, these are the ones taken for granted the most.

"Responsible" and "reliable" are key words that describe their temperamental drives. Throw in a need to be thought respectable, and the little SJ may comply with mannerly behavior, which delights SJ parents (who will then brag on their "good" child and await the accolades from other adults of being "good" parents). "Respectable" also means clothes are important and must bring respect!

Authority is a special issue you need to understand. The SP child resists all authority that attempts to be authoritarian. The independent nature of the SP wants the freedom to be his own authority wherever possible. The SJ, however, respects authority and will willingly accept it as long as the authority figure shows the integrity that should come along with the office. This can be a major potential cause of trouble in parenting an SJ. If the SJ child sees reason not to respect parental leadership the parent is in for a no-holds-barred rejection of their right to be the authority figure.

Apologies will not reinstate you. You have to walk the long road of proving your right to hold office again. Warring parents lose respect as authority figures, too. Parents who don't obey their own rules are demoted. Rules that are unfair, or inconsistently enforced, are cause for the SJ child to hold the parent as "fallen from grace." Boundaries that are not enforced on all siblings equally are evidence, in the mind of the SJ, of the authority figure's incompetence. You will need to explain your actions to the SJ and have them understand (if not agree) that we are all different, and rules can, at times, be unfair when applied without some consideration of the other person's temperament and circumstances.

Unlike the SJ child, the SP child will see all these actions (or lack of actions) through rather liberal glasses – not the conservative glasses of the SJ. For example, the SP will see the lack of consistency in enforcing the boundaries as the action of enlightened leadership! Are you gaining a feeling of sympathy for the parents of both an SP and an SJ child? Parenting opposites is a challenge. Children should not be treated the same. Each must be parented according to who each one is and what each needs. It's a hard lesson for the SJ child to accept.

The interplay of social development is best learned early. For an SJ to get along with and appreciate an SP is no small social adjustment. Parenting skills (or the lack of them) can set the pattern for the anger or acceptance we see in society among young people. If you do not have both an SP child and an SJ child, take advantage of helping your child relate well to their SP or SJ friends. Your goal as a parent is not simply to have a healthy, peaceful home, but to raise a child who is going to respect and love all temperaments and create a healthy society. You may decline the responsibility, but not without short-changing your children's development and forcing them to have to make these changes for themselves as adults.

The battle between SJ and SP is not the only struggle. Whatever your temperament profile as the parent, two of the SJs will try to direct you; and a battle for leadership will result. The ESTJ will want to supervise you, and the ISTJ will always inspect you and your actions with corrective intentions firmly in mind. Both can be infuriating for the parent who sees it as a challenge to authority. And it is! They are pointing out your inadequacies.

You won't win by returning like for like, either. As with all the temperaments, challenge their strengths and they will increase the use of their strengths. The principle "whatever you use, you develop" works when trying to build their strengths too. Always take a drive that exists in a temperament (like these two drives, to supervise and inspect) and teach them how to use them cooperatively in social units, not destructively. They really need this kind of teaching.

On the one hand, inspecting or supervising others can be a negative and divisive activity. Likewise, it can be a helpful and constructive re-channeling of actions that failed to meet expectations.

All the types that are blessed with directive strengths must learn to speak the truth to others in love, and learn when to withhold their criticisms.

Train your little ESTJ and ISTJ accordingly, and you may save them a heap of trouble in their adult lives. If you fail, don't blame yourself or despair, because some children resist the parent's help and are determined to go their own way. Please understand, a task attempted, yet foiled by stubbornness, is not your failure. Keep a positive attitude, be patient, and you are on the right road.

If your SJ child is introverted she (or he) will <u>not</u> tell you what is going on inside of them. The ISTJ is the most non-communicative of the sixteen types. Introversion also leads to shyness in most. Don't force them into situations that embarrass them. They must be gently led and supported. Gentleness is the greatest power for peace in a home. You may have to extract the information you need with persistent effort.

Traditional methods of teaching suit the SJ — repetition, recitation, etc. Show them something new step-by-step, and they learn very well. They pay attention to detail! Give them the details. This makes parenting an SJ less of a creative adventure. They are usually good students and do best with an appreciative teacher who takes the time to show them how to do tasks step-by-step. They keep busy and work hard to please. If all is going well, they will do their homework neatly and with diligence.

If you are an SJ parent, pray you have an SJ child. You will understand them well if you understand yourself. SJs are readable and consistent if they are not troubled.

<u>Parenting Skills and Tips that Will Develop the SJ Child</u>

(A quick reference guide) Most tips are repeated here for your convenience.

Why not take one of these suggestions at a time and make it a part of parenting your SJ. Then go on to the next. Choose the one you consider is most needed and start there.

- Encourage who they are! SJs like to be responsible with their toys and possessions and to keep them neat and tidy (remember tidy means "comparatively" tidy for a child). When they show this trait, show them you are pleased and proud of them. They will most likely do better. In this way you help them feel the fulfillment that the use of their strengths brings, and they tend to become happy and contented, giving you (and themselves) less trouble.

- SJs also like to help around the house. Don't tell them they can't help because they are not able to do the task, or because you are too busy, or because you can't be bothered watching over their attempts. Create <u>something</u> for them to do. They want to be close to you and prove that they are good helpers. They swell with pride and fill with happiness when they show adults that they can be counted on and can do what is expected of them.
- When they do their chores, show them your approval – that is, if you want them to help around the house. They feed on approval. If their efforts to be a helpmate are not approved, their self-esteem sinks and they can become a problem, resorting to aberrant behavior. Your choice!
- If you encourage the SJ and show your approval of their <u>good</u> deeds, they will, when punished or scolded, try harder. They respond to constant feedback.
- Watch their self-esteem grow when they do good deeds for others. SJs are the Good Samaritans of society, and you will want them to grow up having developed the pleasures that helping others brings.
- They will compete with their siblings for the honor of helping you prepare a meal or fix the broken lawn mower. Use competition to motivate them to help you. (But don't expect your SP or NT to compete with any enthusiasm at being helpmates).
- When they are not useful to adults, SJs can develop guilt feelings that cripple their happiness and create a barrier to their bonding with you. The barrier is not you, but their feelings of guilt. Don't ask "What has Mommy done wrong?" Simply give them tasks to help you that you know they love doing. Show them extra appreciation for their help and praise for their efforts. This helps bury the feelings of guilt. The guilt is there because they are not being what their inner drives urge them to be.
- When you want the SJ to learn something new, show them step-by-step and walk them through it. They learn best this way unless they have already learned the activity. Then, they want to show their stuff and not

have you treat them as though they don't know. That comes over as an insult. Praise their effort, and then teach them something additional step-by-step.

- Don't push SJ children to do things in public that they have not learned. This embarrasses them and makes them feel insecure – the worst feeling for the little SJ.
- The little SJ (and, for that matter, the adult as well) treasures visible signs of their trustworthiness and responsible actions. Plaques, stars, medals, and notes of appreciation are all important. Reward them with these, and you can cut down on the candy!
- Parenting SJs well means creating a home where they feel secure and can depend on the routines from day to day. Change is disquieting to them. Risk is unnerving. They thrive on consistency.
- Family traditions are important to them. They must participate! Give them a role in all such events and they will shine with their self-esteems blossoming. Not only are family traditions useful, but they connect with the past (which is, for the SJ, connecting with their roots).
- All SJs tend to worry. Some even regard a person who doesn't worry as not concerned enough and not responsible enough. Worry is, for some, their badge of responsibility. You don't want to encourage this because it turns the SJ negative. Worry is a condition that should have you, the parent, responding with teaching, optimism, and hope.
- When your little SJ leaves home on their first camp experience or sleep-over at a friend's home, he (or she) may get homesick, since even burly SJ athletes get homesick! Familiar places and routines provide a sense of security that they miss.
- Confusion, conflict, and family wars greatly disturb them. For the SP, such events can be great opportunities to show their tactical cunning and take advantage of the present turn of events. Not so for the SJ. Bad things happening simply confirm their belief that if things can go wrong, they will and pessimism becomes their default attitude.
- You are the first line of authority in their lives and they tend to trust authority, but only if that authority is (in their sense of right and wrong) trustworthy and shows integrity. Listen carefully to their complaints about your authority. It may help you to parent with an authority that meets their standards, and this, of course, keeps you in the driver's seat.

- For the SJ, rules and regulations are expected — even though they may not like some of them. They need boundaries that are consistently and lovingly enforced.
- SJs want to feel that they belong and that their family is <u>their family</u>. Introduce them with pride as important family members to visitors, especially visiting family members.
- Teach them that judgmental actions or attitudes are not responsible behavior.
- Love them and teach them. They want both.

Go to page 139 for a summary of key factors that apply to all temperaments.

Ingenuity

The NT Temperament in Children

The infant NT is probably rather solemn and likely to be a puzzle to the parents. Why does he or she not show more interest and be more active? Parents may even suspect their child is not normal.

All is well! This behavior is because the child is waiting. They want to explore their world, which is their calling. Lying in a crib is not a helpful environment to begin their lifelong passion. Once they can crawl, they will show their stuff. Light sockets may be investigated. "What happens when you put your little finger into a light socket? Or strike a match? Or throw a plate?" they ponder. They need to know! These are strong drives in their temperament.

If your little NT is constantly asking "Why? Why? Why?" you will know all is going according to plan; and the search to understand, discover, and know is healthy (if not challenging to you, the parent). Their persistence can wear you down. If you try the response "Because I said so" or "Stop bothering me," you will soon discover that the lack of an adequate answer is the start of eternal badgering. They <u>must</u> know! For the NT, life is to be lived only one way, and that is to find answers and solutions to everything that they encounter and of course find new ways of doing things.

Show them how to hold their knife, and they will hold it another way. It's often not for spite or out of disobedience, but rather, "Okay, I get it. I can hold it that way. So let's try this way, and see if that works better." It's the same with holding a pen, "How many ways can I hold it and still have it work for me?"

The NT must, in the midst of their investigations, also show their independence. Therefore, their way of holding a knife or a pen may turn out to be distinctive and identifiable as their unique style just because they must be different. Their philosophy is simple, "There has to be a better way of doing things. Just because it isn't broken doesn't mean that you don't try to find a better way!" The SJ pleads, "Don't fix what isn't broken. Leave it the way it is. It works well. Besides, I'm not into constant change." The two approaches clash. One is cooperative. The other, individualistic and adventuresome.

Time means little to the NTs, unless it affects their interest or project. Time, for them, is measured by the project at hand. "If my project is not finished, I'm not ready to move on," is the clear message. "When I finish it, I will move on, but catch me quickly or I will be into another project!" Parenting will have its challenges with an NT of whatever age. If your NT's profile ends in a P, the problem of disconnecting them from their project to meet a time restraint is greater still.

NTs live in an inner world. The outer world only holds excitement because it needs to be explored and understood. The inner world is where all of their understanding and theorizing takes place. Always thinking (the NF is also always thinking), they are, at times, lost in themselves and lose track of time and location. To remember where they left their hat is of little significance in a vast world of ideas and facts that are calling with loud voices and plaintive pleas to be examined. Parent them with patience, and don't try to make them remember where their hat is (although it helps if you can succeed). It really doesn't matter to them. "It doesn't make sense to focus on such mundane things," is the way the NT sees it.

If you focus on the small stuff, the NT will show irritation and lose respect for your concern over "petty issues." Eventually, they will also lose respect for you because you don't seem to be interested in the real issues – namely, ingenious, creative, explorations. We might add that they often need both oral and written directions. Like the NFs, they get lost in thought and lose their way easily. Ever heard of the "absent minded professor?"

Since they are explorers, the NT may talk early. When they do, you will be in for a barrage of questions. They are, as we have indicated, the masters of the word "why." The curiosity lust that drives them leads to their great talent — ingenuity. It helps to be able to communicate when one is an explorer. Communication aids discovery. You may also find that NTs become bookworms and read before others. Their minds are sponges, and they want to learn all they can. The world of ideas is a magnet to them.

The chances of having an NT parent are rather low. They have reported their childhood experiences with such phrases as: "I knew I was different," "Nobody understood me," "I seemed to be the only person like me." "Why am I different?" they ask.

This frightens parents, and they wonder what to do. First, support the NT's quest for knowledge and they'll feel affirmed. They'll also feel that their parents are at least helpful and understanding. Children do not need all of their problems solved by others. Understanding from parents is what they need. To solve all of their issues and difficulties is to raise weak children. Give them support and understanding to be the persons they are intended to be, and they will find their way to fulfillment and happiness. Their self-image is built on these traits. When they get to college, feeling like the "odd one" changes. College is filled with NTs and NFs who are there to learn and develop their latent skills. They are in their element then!

Little NTs usually do well in school and will enjoy lecture style instruction if the teacher is competent. Science class can be of particular interest, along with technology and anything that allows them to use their ingenuity and store more usable knowledge. Roll playing and unnecessary (in their estimation) repetition bore them. Seldom do they take well to drama or the performance arts. Debate, however, can be a major interest — especially for the INTP.

Independent, nonconformist, prideful – these are typical characteristics of the little NT. These independent and ingenious "agents of all things new" feel great pride when they succeed in their ingenious creativity. Furthermore, these characteristics mean they obey only if they don't care either way about the rule you are enforcing, or they think it makes sense, or they made the rule themselves. In order for them to obey, they must see that it makes sense. They will not do anything they believe doesn't make sense. Because of their dedication to ways and things that work, the

NT will, on occasion, obey simply because they know it works best that way – even though they disagree with the ruling. Reason with them, and examine your rules for the home to determine whether they stand the test of being reasonable. Then, and only then, will your little NT respect you.

The NT's thirst for knowledge also helps us understand that once a toy is understood, they will lose all interest in that toy. They move on to something else that needs exploring and understanding. I'm not suggesting that you keep buying them new toys. NTs are really made for creating strategies and working in the world of theory and ideas. A game like chess can fulfill their urges, and there is no end to the mastery of such a complex, strategic game.

Sometimes they will appear to be slow (particularly the Ps) to make decisions, because NTs are always looking at the details and fail to come to a conclusion when they feel that there are still insufficient facts on which to make a decision. Their reasoning may include the perception that more facts are still to be uncovered. Therefore, NTs want to wait to see if their theory will be substantiated by these yet unknown facts. So wait they must, while others move on. Is there something more to read? Or someone else to talk to? Can they find more details as they continue to dissect the idea or the object? Their thinking is reductionist in nature (meaning they dig ever deeper into the details to find yet uncovered truth, ingenious ideas, or simply new ways of doing things).

If you expect them to show emotional warmth or to be the touchy, cuddly child, you will likely be very disappointed. Remember, they have a T in their profile, and that means their emotions (which are certainly there) are deeply buried under a hyperactive, analytical mind. Reason trumps emotion, and emotion is often regarded as weakness, or mushy expressiveness, which is simply unnecessary (or, at worst, distasteful) to them. If they tell you they love you in a flat expressionless tone, you probably received a very warm and touching commendation. Be reasonable, not mushy, and you will be respected and sought out as a confidant and fellow traveler.

A side effect of this cool, or even cold, temperament is that the NT can be socially limited, particularly in comparison to an SP or NF child. The difference is striking. Seldom do they think to express manners. They don't intend to be inconsiderate of others, but they just don't see the reason for manners. "As long as the NT is not hurting or damaging the other person, what is the problem?" they ponder. Remember, they do only what makes sense to them.

Lost in their inner world, the NTs can be loaners and somewhat afraid of social interaction since it is not their natural world. If they are also introverted, they will draw back from affection all the more and lose themselves in their abstract, creative world. If extroverted, they will seek company more readily and show some basic social understanding – <u>basic</u> only.

How you discipline this temperament is treated later under "Parenting Styles."

Brian was an INTP teenager. He came to me because his mother and father, both SJs, were concerned that he was not finding direction in his life and was wasting his days instead of showing an interest in a career. His parents complained to me that he was spending all his time with his dreams for creating a business of his own that never seemed to get off the ground. He seemed unmotivated, suffered from mood swings, and showed no respect for his parents – particularly his mother. Brian didn't want to come to me and thought the whole idea was a waste of time and rather insulting to him. "Why did he need help?" he reasoned.

At the first meeting he was (to say the least) skeptical and not very cooperative. However, he was clearly quite intelligent and was wrapped up with himself and his importance. We talked and assessed his temperament. The first sign of his interest was when he realized the assessment resulted in my knowing him to a degree that caught him off guard. From there on, it was first a matter of gaining his respect, since he would not listen to anyone he didn't respect. Within a session or two we achieved that goal and then it was down to serious business.

Brian could not come to closure about anything, not even his dream business. He felt obliged to always keep his options open, and he displayed a serious case of de-motivation as a result. His mood swings were originating in the knowledge that he realized (in a hazy way) that his dream was not pragmatic or functional, and it stopped him from being able to fulfill his longings. His attitude to his mother was rooted in her "not making sense" and in her opposition to his being lost in thought and not (as she expressed) rooted in a sense of reality. Much learning for all parties was called for.

In a meeting with his parents, Brian's mother learned who her son really was — reserved, preoccupied, forgetful, relentless in pointing out his parents' errors and their incoherent expressions of his intentions, individualistic, formidable in debate, obsessed with analysis, and lost in his inner world of theory, using the external world mostly as a place to test his ideas. This was a person she knew nothing about and hence they had grown apart. Brian also had to learn who he was and how his actions affected the external world that he had so little use for. His arrogance over his own perceived intelligence knew few bounds.

What a journey this proved to be. Understanding by all concerned changed the attitudes, largely banished the mood swings, grounded him more in reality, and helped him realize that he needed to accept and appreciate those who provided for his care. Gaining their cooperation made sense, if only for practical reasons.

The knowledge he gained of himself helped Brian redirect his energies into starting the journey to become a learned professor in his chosen fields. For this he was amply gifted.

Dealing with NTs, if they have grown to disrespect you, is only achieved with the knowledge of how they are made and how to parent them. Brian's mother would love to have been able to start much earlier. Once he understood himself, Brian knew he must have a goal that he could move toward in small steps, and it worked for him.

If you are an SP or SJ parent and you have an INT (or, for that matter, an INF) child, pray for bucket loads of grace and understanding. Consider yourself "in school" because you are learning a temperament that is very different from yours. NT children also need help to really understand their strengths and the weaknesses they create on their "blind" side.

If you have an NT child, train him (or her) early in considerate behavior to develop social skills a little. They will need them as adults.

Parenting Skills and Tips that Will Develop the NT Child

(A quick reference guide) Most tips are repeated here for your convenience.

Why not take one of these suggestions at a time and make it a part of parenting your NT. Then go on to the next. Choose the one you consider is most needed and start there.

- The typically calm and cool nature of the NT child can be confusing for an SP, SJ, or NF parent. It is a good sign and nothing to be concerned about. They are in their own cerebral world.
- They feel that they are different from other children, so watch for signs of depression, such as an exaggerated loneness and observable sadness.
- Learn how to encourage their ingenuity and their quest for knowledge, since this is one of their main strengths and one that builds their self-esteem. Show interest in all their constructive projects. Listen patiently to their explanations of things they have discovered or built. You don't have to be better at doing what they do, just interested and a patient audience.
- Expect them to start reasoning and debating with you. It's a skill they find necessary to sharpen and develop from the earliest days. They are practicing.
- Toys such as Legos or Lincoln Logs keep NTs creating and video games can become an obsession as they pit their strategies against the software's skills. They are the technology temperament, and computers are their world. NTs will seek to understand the world of technology, and their skills may astound you. If the computer gets dismantled it may not be healthy, but your NT is.
- Don't punish this inventive, creative element of their personalities, because, if you do, you place yourself between them and their drives. Something will have to give. It is not likely that they will forsake their drives to please or even obey you. Discipline is a simple matter with the NT and is discussed under "NT Parenting Skills."
- Because they are usually mentally bright, NTs can develop an unhealthy feeling of being superior to their peers, and even to their parents. Such pride sets them up for a fall, and their social life suffers. Help them see

the reason for thinking better of others, at least in considering them as equals. It works in all social settings!

- Because they will not do anything that they do not believe makes sense, reasoning with NTs is the prime means of obtaining their cooperation. Sometimes they will obey because they think that it makes the best sense under the circumstances, and they will reverse their behavior if they think obedience no longer makes sense.
- It will be most difficult to change patterns of behavior because of their fierce independence. Again, use the discipline methods discussed under "NT Parenting Skills."
- NTs are apt to build extensive collections of rocks, insects, or stamps – anything they can analyze and catalogue. If possible, encourage the habit. It is their natural bent.
- Depression follows failure in the NT. They cannot easily conceive of failing, and it lowers their self-esteem rather quickly. Their pride is hurt. Something went wrong with their inventiveness, ingenuity, or creativity, and they are left without any support from their reason. Encouragement, <u>not</u> cuddling, can help, and a new project will do the most good.
- NTs are very autonomous; they don't like being controlled. A controlling parent will have a rough relationship with them. They have an urge to control and direct others, hence the rub. Be a supportive parent, not a controlling one.
- They hate being dependent on their parents. Encourage their efforts to achieve and be self-reliant, and they will inwardly thank you for your help. If they must be dependent on others they are humiliated. Parent their strengths. Don't provoke them to anger by forcing them to live in their weaknesses.
- When young, they can be full of fears caused by a vivid imagination. The NF is the same, and calming them when they are unnerved is more necessary than it appears on the surface because of their struggle to self-reliance.
- Rewards for the NT are in the area of support and encouragement of their passions and successes, rather than in meaningless trinkets. Reward their obedience by encouraging their strengths.

- NTs learn by experimenting and observing, and by the application of theories and principles. Don't forget, their way of communicating is abstract, and their minds are always theorizing.
- Authority figures are not automatically respected simply because they hold a position of power. All authority figures, including parents, must prove themselves. Authority and regulations limit freedom of expression and hinder discovery, so NTs react according to what they perceive as inhibiting.
- Encourage reading and learning. NTs can become bookworms and will read anything that increases their understanding. When you help build their knowledge, you help build their self-esteem.
- NTs must be encouraged to question, but warned about the negative effect of doubt and skepticism. Their skepticism usually extends even to the expert, who they will not believe until they have compiled sufficient convincing evidence. No one escapes their incessant, "How do you know that?" attitude.
- Social skills are lacking, and they destroy their own friendships most of the time. Teach them the logic of including others in order to increase their effectiveness.
- Emotions are hidden, but they are still able to be hurt by undiscerning people. Just treat them with respect, and enforce the abuse-it-or-lose-it principle of behavior that you will find in the "NT Parenting Style."

Go to page 139 for a summary of key factors that apply to all temperaments.

Sensitivity

The NF Temperament in Children

If you thought the NT was a challenge, then let me welcome you to the advanced class in parenting! However, if you have an NF, please don't despair. With understanding, you are more than up to the task. Without it you will be lost! These are the complicated little NFs that will test you at every turn. Even if you are an NF, they will still test your metal and strain your understanding. It's not as though you can't understand them. It's simply difficult, and many surprises will be thrown your way. The teenage NF needs special attention, since teenage is all about the development of emotions and social wisdom. These are the emotional giants of temperament and are affected by even the slightest upset.

Get accustomed to surprises, those "curve balls." These little NFs don't understand themselves yet, and probably won't until late in life (if ever) unless they are helped, nurtured, and educated. All the other temperaments are straight forward, with most understanding what they are, who they are, and where they are going (except, perhaps, for all the introverts who always find they don't understand something about themselves). NFs are tightly stretched violin strings who, with another turn of tension, can snap and explode (or implode) without notice.

NFs will tax your parenting skills in every area. It's not deliberate on their part (although, at times, it is). You will often find yourself, if you are an SP or SJ parent, in a state of confusion. If you are an NT parent you will affirm their interest in learning, abstract thinking, and intuitional skills, as well as their approval of logic. But you will wonder at the high emotional temperature at which they operate, thinking it to be a sign of something gone wrong, when it isn't. If you are an NF parent of an NF child you will, since you wonder about yourself, wonder about them too. This one can be your greatest treasure and your worst nightmare, all within one short moment.

Let me say it again, these are the complicated ones. Never forget that or you will despair! They will manipulate you, bless you, warm you, and anger you. Did I cover it all? Just know that they are trying desperately to find out why they act and feel the way they do. You will need to hold the line on boundaries while you give of your utmost affection in order to win and earn their respect. Their giftedness lies in their intense emotional depth, their extra high sensitivity combined with their commitment to reason, and their unusual potential at handling people (who, by the way, are the most complicated creation in this universe).

At an early age they are apt to display a gift for language. Not only do they talk early, as do the NTs, but they talk to practice talking. After all, they will need to use language skillfully, since they are the influencers of people and can feel the need to help others out of their many complicated situations. They must practice not only the vocabulary, but the way it is intoned and expressed. They say things like "I love you" with varying intonations just to note the effectiveness of their use of language and how it can make such a difference in people's responses. Talking a person into finding solutions to their problems was what Gandhi excelled at, and he is a prime example of an NF living in the powers of his giftedness.

Your little NF has a great future if giftedness is the only indicator. Sadly, it is not. Their low self-esteem may be a more certain thermometer, recording a life that could have been so much greater. Self-image is the ceiling to our performances, and this is nowhere more true than in the case of the NF. A low self-image defeats the use of their gifts since it de-motivates them. As a parent, understanding the need to lift the child's self- image constantly will be one of your daily concerns.

However, let's not paint a dark picture and forget the play of light that casts the shadows. They have a charm that attracts people. They will touch your heart with many displays of affection. If they don't, they are suffering from low self-image, or self-pity, or from an atmosphere that depresses them.

Consider this, the atmosphere in which they live constantly affects them and often creates a compulsive mood. If it is depressing, they are depressed, and their creativity is destroyed. If it is uplifting, they are motivated to higher things. All temperaments are affected to some degree by atmosphere, but none are impacted to the extent of an NF. A little NF who complains of the "feeling" of the place is flagging you of their impending depressed spirit. The way they say it, unfortunately, carries the implication that you will understand them to the same degree that they have carefully expressed their feelings. You probably will not.

They are abstract in their thinking and speaking. This causes the SP and SJ problems in comprehending. Second, they often talk vaguely and in generalities, since they know what they mean and assume you, too, have got the same picture that is so clear in their minds. Other temperaments, however, often don't get the same message. The result? Dashed expectations for the little NF. These can create dramatic explosions on their part – way out of proportion to what you might expect. They yearn to be understood, and it is true that, at times, they make it difficult (with or without meaning to). Not to be understood, and in the process to be summarily swept aside, hurts them deeply. Loving care and a real attempt at understanding will set the tone for helping them manage their emotional riches and not be controlled by them.

By "giving them love," I don't mean for you to let your guard down. Here's why. They are smart and can manipulate you skillfully with their advanced people skills. They know how to press your buttons to achieve the result they want. A parent who gives in to their every whim will be captured by their cunning and constantly manipulated. NFs are growing up to be influencers of other people, and they may be practicing on you! How do we as parents handle this? Give in to all their cries when they are fair and, in your estimation, it is the right thing to do. But never give in when you think that what they want will hurt them or is not the right thing to do. This is why standards of right and wrong are so important in the task of parenting. Standards and boundaries are your guidelines. Without them you keep changing your direction and destination.

When living in their strengths, NFs can be a great blessing. They will fight for you if you are in the right, and they will use their emotional richness to support you when you are in trouble. They always want to do what is right, and they hold themselves (and you) to the same standard. If there is a chink in your armor, they will likely expose it – particularly your emotional armor. Get upset at them and they will get upset at you – and how!

NF children need recognition that they are valued. Without it, damage is done to their sensitive self-image. As a preventive parenting measure, tell them every day that they are good and valued. And, if you believe in God, tell them God thinks they are wonderful too, since he created them and gave them all the good and noble drives that live within them. Their spiritual tendencies should respond to this with positive results if you keep it up. SJ parents beware of your tendency to say it a few times and then stop. This won't work with the NF because when you stop they discount all your efforts as meaningless. They feel, once again, that they are not any good. Stopping proves they are not worth much effort. The problem you face is not usually one of self-pity, but of a low self-esteem that shows itself in their negativity about themselves while, at the same time, they can be so positive about everything and everyone else.

The NF has a remarkable social talent. However, the introverted NF, who shares this social talent with the extroverted NFs, tires from too much social strain and can quickly resent their social skills. They will give and give until they are completely drained. Then, with flat batteries, they will fight for their own reprieve. If you badger them when they are down they will fight back or withdraw into themselves.

Because the introverted NF seems to be particularly affected by the loss of internal energy (their spirit's energy) I should discuss the matter here. Introverts get drained by too much people contact because they recharge in solitude. If they are gifted at social interaction and charm, as are the INFJ and the INFP, their gift draws them to interact and help others, and this drains them all the more. If your introverted NF child is cranky and irritable, suspect that the child's battery has lost its charge. Suggest time alone to read or play so that their battery recharges. They will reappear as new creatures. Don't forget that daydreaming is also play and refreshment to them because, in their daydreams, their imagination takes them on enjoyable flights of fancy to worlds unknown. It is one of their favorite replenishing tools for recharging their batteries. Following this simple rule will save you much stress with your NF.

All NFs are hypersensitive to emotional rejection and conflict. A home with conflict will disturb them and even stunt their inner growth. They will become withdrawn, insecure and emotionally immature – even wild – as their way of reacting to the disharmony they face in the home. Remember they are not just sensitive, but super sensitive, and all disharmony in relationships de-motivates them and dismembers their spirits. They find it hard to accept that this sensitivity is a good thing. It is! It is the source of much of their giftedness.

Parents face a challenge here. Integrity and harmony in the parents' relationship to each other is the only way to create an atmosphere that will offset this same reaction in their NF child. The NF children return like homing pigeons to their roost if they sense harmony and love. Is this an unfair demand on the parents? Well, ask yourself, "Do I want anything less than honesty and integrity in our relationship?" Of course not! We should want to model loving relationships and benefit from our efforts personally in the process. Your NF child thrives on being around loving relationships.

William, now an adult NF, told me that when he was a child of about seven years of age, he would lie awake at night listening to his parents arguing in the adjacent bedroom, and it would traumatize him. He would be fighting the urge to get out of bed and go to try and solve the issue for them (whatever it was). Or he would lie there, frozen in his fear and disbelief that people could be so disjointed – even in bed! The next day he would plague them with disguised questions aimed at determining whether they were going to split up or make up. He spent many nights dreaming of living on his own and figuring out how he would make it, since he thought they may not want him. "Why would they?" he pondered. His murky self-image clouded any positive view of his own worth. He never shared this with his parents, and it affected him for years to come.

The NFs are also blessed with an extra dose of intuition and, in childhood, can be disturbingly clear in their prognostications.

One parent I sought to help was in the back room of the house, out of earshot and eyeshot of the front door. In the middle of the same room on the floor, her five-year-old, NF son was playing with a toy. Suddenly he announced in a placid voice, "Someone's at the front door." Astounded and suspicious, because the boy could not have known if anyone had come to the door, she decided to comply and went to see if someone was indeed at the front door. Half-way there he called out, "He's gone now." She was about to throttle him for "pulling her leg" when she decided to check it out. She sped to a window and there, to her amazement, was a man, just leaving down the driveway. Racing back to the room she exclaimed, "How did you know?" He simply replied in a monotone, "I don't know." (It certainly sounded like a classic case of childhood intuition. The experiences could be multiplied in my experience as a coach and counselor.) *She picked up the phone and, in a frightened voice, asked me for an appointment – immediately!*

Do premonitions scare you? Don't be amazed if they do. Intuition is like a tall antenna that penetrates the unseen world and receives messages, seemingly at random. What is received is information that our five physical senses – sight, hearing, taste, touch, and smell – can't detect. Because it is mysterious and eerie, we either discount it or try to explain it away. Such measures are escape mechanisms. We don't need to be afraid of it.

Amazing as intuition is, it acts like a sixth sense and is part of human experience. I have found it particularly active in the sensitive NF temperament. Being private and cautious about revealing their thoughts and inner experiences, an NF can often have premonitions and not report them. If they do, be thankful that you are in their trusted circle. And, if they are troubled by it, help them yourself, or seek someone who can help them to an acceptance and understanding of their intuition.

Intuition is a gift, especially effective in the individual who exercises it regularly. Exercise causes our muscles to develop, and to exercise our intuition and develop it we simply need to pay attention to it. Awareness and attentiveness increases any pathway in our minds. Much attention to "mindful awareness" is being given by neuroscientists who have researched its powers. Mindful awareness can be thought of as meditation, too. Extrasensory perception is another term used to explain things that are beyond our senses and our physical world. I think that this increased ability, as found in the NF, is an intense sensitivity in the virtual world of their minds that enhances their ability to intuit. Sometimes they will talk about their intuition as "having a feeling about something." A very good question is, "What best explains this astounding ability to be able to know something without the use of the physical senses?" I have my answer. What's yours?

Imagination may be a distant cousin of intuition. The NF child lives in a world of imagination. Each toy and object is likely to take on a dual identity — its real identity, and an even more real second identity in the child's imagination. A teddy bear can be a prince, or a princess; a truck can be an interplanetary transportation device, personally created by the child's imagination. Remove or throw away these toys and you also destroy the imaginary being. To make matters much worse, that toy may have been (in your child's imagination) himself! And you had the nerve to throw him away? Trouble should be expected under these conditions.

If they are little, they don't know how to explain to you this dual identity. If they are older, they won't explain for fear of being made a laughing stock. They identify with characters in the stories you read to them, and these characters become, in their minds, the princess or prince their toy represents. Because of their search for their own identity, they can live in the world of fantasy and imagination as a way of exploring their real selves. They are the most likely among the temperaments to have an unseen imaginary friend to talk to. Don't forget, their personal possessions can become an extension of themselves as well.

Leslie lost his cap during a gust of wind while traveling on a commercial boat to a distant tourist destination. He was inconsolable all day because he had, in a way only imagination can tell, lost a part of himself, which could never be truly replaced. No offer of a new hat sufficed, of course, and without his hat he was less than himself.

Dismissing the reality of an NF's imagination is tantamount to denying his inner kinetics (the inner powers that drive our systems), and he is not only offended, but hurt and wounded by such apparent insensitivity and thoughtlessness by his parents. Note that, to him, this is clear evidence that the parent just does not understand him, and he is all on his own in his little world and without love and companionship!

This imagination can also get your little NFs into trouble of another nature. They can be accused of lying when they are really only imagining with a sense of reality that overpowers the real and the actual. Do NF children do this? Yes! It is so real in their minds that they believe it to be real. Is it, then, lying?

Their imagination is one of the NF's most valuable creative gifts. Squashing imagination can ruin one of our most valuable qualities as humans – valuable in all of our endeavors. The parent walks a tight-rope between trying to encourage the child to live in a world of reality and not discourage the child's valuable imagination. Much great potential has been known to get crushed while people are still children. Balance the preservation of imagination with a training that respects the need for responsible behavior. It is not an easy call. However, whatever you do, show that you understand them, or they will disconnect, and you may lose them.

Janice, age seven, was lying (according to those who favor reality) and imagining vividly (according to those who value and encourage imagination). The two realities meant Janice must learn to live in the real world while preserving her imaginative creativity. Wouldn't you agree? How did her parents solve the problem? One parent was an NF, the other, an SJ. The SJ parent was somewhat appalled – moreover, mystified – at this explanation by her counselor. How could Janice imagine so vividly that she actually believed what she imagined was real? The mother was incredulous – and, for an SJ, understandably so. She wondered to herself, "Is there something wrong with my child?" She favored some kind of discipline that would make her child understand, imagination or not, that in reality she had lied, and this behavior must be corrected pronto. She was also afraid that her precious Janice might grow up dislocated from reality, and live in a fantasy world (or worse, become mentally deranged, if she wasn't already). SJs wonder about the mental health of such people.

Her spouse, the NF, was more understanding as he recalled incidents of his own when he had lied but believed it was real. However, he too shared the concern that Janice should grow up in the real world, and not in fantasy and delusion. He had made this transition and still held on to some of his imagination. The rest he had lost in the process. He wasn't sure what to do.

They discovered the issues were not opposite alternatives. If Janice's imagination was first affirmed she would be on board for an explanation of the facts that denied her story. She must not be made to feel she was odd or strange, but gifted. And she needed to understand her gift. It was explained to her that imagining to the degree that it seemed to be real, when it was not, was nothing to be ashamed of, it was a creative gift. Imagination could lead her into creative exploits in her life. Of course, what was real was equally important. When it was clear that she had told a false story, she should accept the facts, apologize, if that was needed, and recognize she should not deny the reports of others when her imagination may have been involved (unless she had evidence or an overwhelming conviction that her story was indeed real). Janice was convinced it was real, but others were persuaded to the contrary and had facts to prove it. Imagination is not damaged if it is affirmed. But it must, by necessity, then bow to the facts. Its real purpose is to discover things that the facts themselves can't reveal and to create a world of values and wonder. Janice warmly accepted this, and apologized to her parents. The SJ mother showed her delight, and expressed her pride in a daughter who had the qualities of a vivid imagination she so envied. Amazing how we can make U-turns, isn't it!

NFs read early, love stories, and want them read over and over. They also tend to love detailed illustrations with many rich colors. If encouraged, they become bookworms. The INFJ, in particular, becomes a lifelong student because learning often becomes an obsession.

NFs don't crave competition with others. They have been known to lose a foot race just so their friend could win. They are as hypersensitive to other's feelings as they are to their own. To compete against themselves is fine though, although it often becomes a painful struggle due to their high self-imposed standards. Self-judgment is the all too certain result.

I think we all agree that condemnation is a negative force and is not helpful in positive parenting. NFs condemn themselves, perhaps more than others condemn them. It all stems from their low self-esteem. Building their self-worth should become a major concern of the parent of an NF child.

You may notice (and you probably will if you are an SJ) that NFs tend not to focus on the details initially. They tend to see the big picture first, resorting to the details only after they have understood the whole. Contrary to this, the little SJ will go straight for a detail they can't understand and want that explained first, before they go on to figure out the big picture. Both are valid approaches to understanding issues. Speed is on the side of the NF, and careful attention to details is what the SJ brings to the table. The NF can become impatient with the explanation of details when they have already seen the big picture that is involved in the issue. It can also result in an argument during the process of understanding, since they both misunderstand each other. The SJ wonders why the NF seems unconcerned with the details, while the NF wonders why the SJ can't see the big picture and is bogged down in a "minor" detail.

When all is explained, agreement can be reached, but the process can be turbulent. The teacher or parent, who slowly goes over the details as though the NF cannot grasp it without a laborious explanation, bores the NF. They keep wondering what they have missed, since they have already processed the big picture and can see where everything is going. Add to this that the NF is abstract in language and the SJ is concrete, and you realize that understanding and appreciation of each other hold the key to harmonious relationships. You, the parent, may end up being the arbiter in many sibling spats.

If introverted, the NF can be painfully shy in youth and seem sensitive to the slightest rejection or gesture. Usually, they sit at the back of the class feeling different, anxious, and lonely.

Justin, an INF, sat at the back in school, ". . . because he liked it," he said. Later he told me it was because he didn't feel comfortable with others watching him. Although this was the real motivation, he also found that from the back he could watch the girls and admire them. This caused a warm round of daydreaming, and when the teacher noticed him staring into space she asked Justin a question. Embarrassment followed, and Justin was mortified. The girls giggled, and the humiliation ended all happiness. He hated going to school because he imagined all the students were making fun of him (and some were). His only solution, because he wouldn't tell anyone (not even his mother) about this, was to withdraw further into himself and be "in school" while he was really hidden in his mind. His grades suffered, and he began to think of himself as awkward, unintelligent, and a misfit.

No more than two percent of the population are INFs, and this compounds their feelings. They lack a natural defense against the insults and off-handedness of others. As a result, they can suffer quite intensely. Understanding parents are very helpful to their development and to their happiness. In fact, they are a Godsend. Don't force them to sit at the front of the class. If they are reserved in the presence of strangers, let them warm up at their own pace. Embarrass them and you too will belong to their disconnected "has-beens."

NFs can do very well academically due to their abstract mental functioning, love of learning, and their inner intensity, although introverts may not do well until they enter college or university. Passion drives their learning, and they usually develop a linguistic fluency, which is a talent well worth encouraging. Languages, written or oral, can be their forte.
Keirsey, following Plato, calls them *Idealists*. Although that does not capture all of their major traits, it clearly describes the heartbeat of their passions. They love the world of ideas, and they fashion their lives on possibilities. However, they are emotionally ill-prepared for the crumbling of their ideas and sink into self-blame for whatever falls from the pedestal of their lives or imaginations. Their lives are a continual search for self-worth (as one might expect from people who hold high ideals before themselves), and they raise the bar constantly – even when they fail to clear the bar the first time! Some of them are tormented by feelings of inadequacy. Given this internal climate, it is hard for them to hold their self-image high for long. Almost every NF will confess to low self-esteem. Parents should not feel responsible for matters beyond their control, but can contribute greatly to their well-being and feelings of worth with a few simple practices.

Although I will say this again at the end of the chapter, I want you to hear it in this context also.

- Tell them you love them daily — even several times a day. This should not be hard.

- Let them know they are wonderfully made on the inside, as this is an area of personal concern to them. Do it daily! Positive reinforcement can do wonders. Pride is not their default attitude; self-depredation is, so don't worry too much that you may be encouraging a prideful attitude. Remember, humility is not thinking less of one's self than what is in reality true. That's false humility, and is not healthy. Pride is thinking of one's self as greater than you really are. Humility, then, can only be defined as thinking of one's self up to your true worth – not less than or more than your true worth.
- NFs love to be touched. Physical closeness is extremely warming to them. They are the big responders to affection. Cold, they are not, unless angered – in which case they turn frigid! Their huge range of emotions extends from intense love on one end all the way to raw hate on the other. However, once they warm up again their sense of inner integrity makes them feel bad, and they take the blame regardless of whether they were wrong or not. You will often find them saying they are sorry – repeatedly – and they mean it. Talk about complex personalities! In this case, complexity also means fragile.
- Endeavor to keep harmony in the home of an NF because this temperament thrives in the peace and love this offers them, and it encourages good behavior.

The NFs' complicated personalities, which you can easily notice in childhood, seem to aid them in understanding complicated problems, particularly people problems. They can grow up to be excellent advisors, counselors, and consultants.

You will think you know them until they surprise you with some unlikely response. You will never <u>really</u> know them. Social skills often hide their complexity and privacy. Because they are skilled at making you feel good, you would not believe they are hard to get to know.

Anger and hurt are real problems and surface as parenting issues. Let me help you understand this in a real life story.

Jamie was a treasure of a child when he wasn't angry. Unfortunately, he was angry most of the time, and it was getting more frequent and more intense. His parents were at the end of their wits and had tried all measures of discipline to control his anger without success. In true desperation they came to me and asked if I knew what they should do. I told them, "Go home, and the next time he gets angry (you say you won't have to wait long) immediately go up to him, put your arm around him, and, in a really caring, loving voice, say, "I'm so sorry you are hurt. What can I do to help you?" Then call me and tell me what he does. His mother called soon and exclaimed, "It was amazing!" "What was amazing?" I asked. "He broke down in tears," she replied. I asked them to return to see me so I could explain to them what they could do to help him further.

When they came, we used the child questionnaire to identify Jamie's temperament, and he turned out to be an INFJ. I had expected him to be an NF and had remembered what seems to many a strange piece of advice that Paul used in his letter to the Ephesians. It reads:

> *Be angry, but don't do the wrong thing… and don't let the sun go down on your wrath.*

Paul was also an INFJ, as his personal letters reveal. This was what a little NF could use. You see, an NF has no shield (so to speak) against getting hurt, so, when they get hurt, they automatically get angry. Strecker and Appel, in their book *Discovering Ourselves*, make a convincing case for the unavoidable nature of what they call an automatic reaction of getting angry when you get hurt. Try hitting someone on the toe with a hammer and see whether anger results from the hurt! <u>Imagine</u> it. Don't do it!

Anger is the instant response to hurt – so fast we can't stop it. I thought this little NF might be getting hurt and, as a result, was getting angry. When the hurt is repeated often a sore spot inside of us develops. The more tender it is, the more reactionary we become. Jamie had developed a very tender spot, and he was reacting – sometimes even before the hurt occurred. Explaining this to the parents, I suggested they use a three-point plan to help their son gain a way of handling his hurt – confessedly an ancient plan.

Here's the formula we used that resulted in a peaceful household and a changed, healthy child.

1. Teach him it is OK to be angry when he gets hurt. Even God understands that, but the parents had not! As a last resort they were sending him to his room, and heatedly telling him, "Don't you come out until you have changed your attitude!" He was feeling that his world (and, in particular, his home) was a cruel, horrible place. First, you get hurt. Then you get punished for getting hurt! It was becoming unbearable for the little boy. Where was the fairness? It is all right to get angry when you are hurt! That knowledge alone created a new feeling and a sense of fairness for Jamie. He could accept this.

2. Teach him that it is always to our advantage to do the right thing when we are hurt, not the wrong thing. Punching the other boy who hurt you is only going to result in a fight and a lost friendship. Into the bargain, repercussions are possible from discerning or non-discerning adults. Teach him he will gradually reduce his possible friendships to a pitiful level if he does the wrong thing. Also, show him there is a way to win even when someone has hurt you. Do the right thing, which will often be to do good things in return for evil. It is not weakness to return good for evil. Try it, and you will soon find that out. It is what strong people do who are in control of themselves, and of others!

   The parents themselves first learned how not doing the wrong thing was best accomplished by doing the right thing and the winning thing. Then they taught their son. We all need this! Jamie understood many more things as he discovered the different feelings he could create inside of himself by doing good things in return.
3. Teach him how to control himself and become strong by going to bed thinking happy and positive things – not angry and negative things.

   This was also a revelation for them. They began creating the last moments of the day as happy moments for him. Their son soon learned to be happy before the light went out so he could go to sleep happily. In two to three weeks he was a different boy. In

> three months he had all kinds of friends and was enjoying his new-found super status as a boy who, instead of losing it, was in control of himself and largely in control of the reactions of others.

All of this happened because we understood how Jamie was made on the inside and, as a result, knew how to diffuse his anger and replace it with some winning strategies. The same formula can be successful with an SP, for example; but with different emphasis and application.

Remember, NFs have no shield against hurt. They try to please and are deeply offended when they are treated with disdain. They even get hurt over what is <u>not</u> done as well as what <u>is</u> done. Their super-sensitivity makes them surge quite violently with anger before they can even think about it, while other temperaments would shrug the same offense off with responses like, "Who do you think you are? I wouldn't listen to you for anything," and they move on to the next stimulating opportunity for pleasure. That's it. The NF can't move on as fast and has to wait for the temperature of their emotions to drop to bearable levels. The above three steps help them do this. They must know how to handle their anger and their hurt so that they can reenter the field of relationships again.

If you have an NF child, pray for wisdom, and watch out for the unexpected. If you want to win them, love them lots and lots and lots, and they will be yours. Did I say "lots" enough?

<u>Parenting Skills and Tips that Will Develop the NF Child</u>

(A quick reference guide) Most tips are repeated here for your convenience.

Why not take one of these suggestions at a time, and make it a part of parenting your NF. Then go on to the next. Choose the one you consider is most needed, and start there.

- NFs are the enthusiastic, passionate ones. Passionate is not the same as, for example, the excitement of the SPs. NF passion shows itself as enthusiasm for a cause, a dream, or a hope, while excitement in the SP is purely excitement over the moment's activity. Although the distinction can be blurred, the NF is focused on imagination and the future; while the SP is focused on the present and the real. If you dampen the NF's passions you will find he will become irritable and a problem, and may even resort to unacceptable behavior, acting and living in his weaknesses.

- ENFPs, in particular, have an intense passion for life and an urge to experience all of its offerings. Guide them into non-damaging fulfillment of this drive. By that I mean things that do not damage them or others. If they are not guided by a set of values, they can follow the passion of the moment and not find real direction along with its reward in their life.
- As babies, the NF's alertness is more an inner itch to express emotion, and anything that pleases them (or displeases them) will release those emotions. This is the indication of a rich, emotional future.
- You must remember that this emotional depth can be expressed in love or hate that lives "just under their skins" and is readily triggered. They earn the phrase "wearing their hearts on their sleeves." But watch your NF carefully. You can be fooled. These explosive emotions are sometimes expressed with a vehemence that shocks you, and at other times it can be hidden as repressed anger.
- Of greater concern is the child who holds anger inside and fights the hurts resulting in her own damage. The external eruption of anger may hurt their relationships; but the inner repression of anger will destroy their self-esteem and have other damaging effects.
- Emotions are far more difficult to handle than facts. We all know that. The heart is more complicated than the head. Therefore, they will be, at times, very difficult to parent – particularly when their emotions are erupting or their inner emotional temperature is hot. Their emotions are quite unpredictable, too! Always take the safe route of giving plenty of love and care, and you will not hurt them further. Keep your volume down, and you will help calm their emotional storm. Keeping the volume down is a key skill in dealing with all temperaments, but particularly the NF.
- A flower, a color, fluttering aspen leaves, or the song of a bird can send them into inner raptures. Everyone can enjoy these things, but the NF becomes even euphoric at times. Inside they are either appreciative of

or are repulsed by everything they encounter. Developing this sensitivity to beauty and awe (not suppressing it) is your task, since many of them become authors or artists of one sort or another, and sensitivity is a key element in all creativity. Develop them to be what they are! Do this, and you are a very successful parent.

- Especially if your NF is an introvert, watch out for the internalization of their emotions, because they also don't want to tell you about their inner pains and are not open communicators as compared to the extroverts.
- Physical closeness is comforting to them. They will often cling to you and not want you to let them go. In the comfort of these moments, their imaginations are also often in flight, and they are in a world of their own, soaking up the love and feelings of pleasure. They are intensely happy in the warmth of your acceptance. They bond closest with those who take time to give them much love. At times, you will admit, this can be exhausting. Your reward is the loving attentions they will heap on you and your knowledge of the great help you are being to the development of their self-esteem. Remember, the SPs are smooth in relationships, and the NFs are warm (at times, irrepressibly hot).
- When they turn frigid on you, you will know that they are hurt and you are the probable cause. Again, you may be puzzled having no idea what you could have done to cause them hurt. If you can't think of anything you have done, it is probably something you have <u>not</u> done – some expectation they had that has been disappointed, and disappointment is a real cause of hurt to them. You may hear, "You don't love me," or "You don't care." So, say you are sorry first, then ask, and explain if appropriate. Of all the temperaments, these are the ones that respond most to a little honey before they feel the bite of correction.
- Even the introverted ones will take off on a talking tour, practicing and finely tuning the art of speech. They enjoy the process of communicating because it is an outlet for their ever present and sensitive emotions. They talk early and talk a lot. Give them the floor when they are talkative (they will grow up with the potential of being influential communicators) and you will develop one of their strengths. It also builds their self-esteem for them to feel that, with practice, they are becoming good at this art.

- Most of them will also find they have a skill in written communications. Reading, speaking, writing – encourage these skills if they are present, since these may fashion their lives.
- Their verbal skills can result in punishing, hurtful tirades when they are in the mode of self-defense. Their loving nature turns to intense hate or deliberate hurt. And when their emotions have returned to their normal simmer, they are smitten with guilt that makes them apologize over and over. What they are really after is the assurance that they have not caused irreparable harm to a treasured relationship. Once they feel all is well, they are off on another adventure in their minds. They can also take the blame for the disturbance, whether it was their entire fault or not, since this is a way of atoning for their sins.
- We have noted the tendency they have to be hurt, and the way to handle it is in the comments above about Jamie. Use the method suggested whenever you feel they are hurt. Your best indication of their being hurt is their anger, which, if suppressed, is seen in their depressed spirits. Most of their anger is the anger of hurt.
- In the case of bad behavior with the NF, be sure to first determine whether they are hurt before you punish or correct them, since being fair is a huge factor in their moral standards of right and wrong. They will reject a person who is unfair in their treatment of others – or of them, of course.
- If they are punished for being angry when their anger is the anger of hurt, they feel the world is a very cruel place and they know of no other way to handle things but to get angrier still. Soon they feel there is something wrong with them, and they then plummet into aberrant behavior and low self-esteem, if not dangerous depression. Why behave in an acceptable manner when you are not worth anything anyhow? Crushed, they settle for a life of despair. Many potential greats are crushed in this fashion as children. They may find their way back, since they feel responsible for their actions and reactions; but the path could be a long one.
- You may be puzzled at the introverted NFs, because they are often very private and non-communicative. They are harder to get to know, shy, and can be hurt more easily than you may imagine. If you are an SJ parent you will find them, at times, most difficult to understand and a

real mystery, because although you, too, get hurt, the depth of their hurt produces behavior you find extreme.

- They are abstract in their speech and with an active mind they often don't finish their sentences because their mind is two thoughts ahead of where their tongue is.
- Ideas and possibilities will fill their virtual world, and they will be examining the logic and the emotions of all they mentally entertain. Hence you can also find them lost in a kind of daydream that is, in this case, really mental processing.
- Give all NFs (the introverted ones in particular) time to make decisions, since they are thinking in depth and, at the same time, processing their emotional responses to the issue. That can take time. Be patient!
- You will know their inner life is healthy when they play at being what their main strengths are calling them to be (such as teachers, advisors, healers, champions, little diplomats, and influencers of all sorts).
- They should show evidence of emerging people skills early as they tenderly interact with others to make sure harmony and warmth is maintained. Sensitivity and empathy is their normal healthy state, and if you observe them treating others insensitively something is wrong. They are either hurt or living in their weaknesses, not their strengths.
- Encourage the NF's studious habits since the INFJ, in particular, is the lifetime student and learner of new challenging things.
- Build their self-esteem by helping them maintain and create positive, intimate, and harmonious relationships. Their theme song for life could be "I'd like to teach the world to sing in perfect harmony!"
- They can be super sensitive to their environment. Surroundings often create feelings that deeply affect them. In their early years they may react strongly to the dark or the fear that some creature is under their bed. You need to react with love and tender assurance, not with scorn or mockery. Sometimes, the room they sleep in can be made more pleasing to them, and this will definitely affect their behavior. Physical punishment can be deeply hurtful – more for the perceived cruelty and the loss of a relationship than the pain. They even hurt when their siblings are punished. Remember that along with sensitivity comes a real dislike of physical pain also.
- Develop ways they can keep score in competitions against themselves. They are always assessing themselves against their own high standards,

and this can be very motivating for them. Help them set some goals, especially the ENFJ and the INFJ, and get them to keep track of their progress. This will develop their self-esteem and give direction to their strong inner drives. You are teaching them self-management and more importantly teaching them a certain amount of control over their emotions.

- Like the SJs, they have a respect for authority and they trust authority, unless that authority is unfair and unkind. Be the fair and kind parent, and you will have little trouble with them.
- In a home where the voices are raised in anger and frustration, the emotional level of the little NF skyrockets, and you are in for their turbulent addition to the already rowdy home.
- Because of their well-used intuition, their decisions will often be based on a gut feeling, and you will find it hard to dislodge them from this feeling. Reason with them, and don't make them feel bad for having this gut intuition if it happens to turn out to be wrong. Their intuition must be encouraged to grow. It will serve them well in future years.
- Tell stories with a happy ending before bedtime, unless you want to get up often during the night to calm their fears and respond to their nightmares.
- Respect their fantasy world.
- They are the spiritual temperament, so encourage their interest in spiritual things and spiritual heroes.
- They want the answers to the big questions of life and their world. And they may, as many do, turn out to be philosophers or deep thinkers.
- Above all else that I have said, give them plenty of love. Tell them <u>often</u> that they are good and special, and you will build their self-esteem and create a more peaceful and happy home for you and them.

For All Four Temperaments:

Now that you know some key factors that determine or describe the four temperaments, you will be able to use this knowledge to:

- Make your child feel understood.
- Better teach and train your child.
- Resolve conflicts with understanding.
- Assess your children's friends, and understand the dynamics of their relationships in interactions with your children.
- Avoid damage to your child's self-esteem and create a healthy self-understanding and confidence.

Memorize and use these five objectives to structure your parenting. You can keep it simple by adding one skill at a time to your parenting abilities. Expect to see some real changes in the atmosphere of your home. Of course, a change in your home's atmosphere is not your main objective. You want to parent your children to be the best that they can be. As a result, watching the growth of their strengths will certainly give you great pleasure and confidence.

PARENTING STYLES

Chapter Nine ♦

If you would judge, understand.
~ Seneca

Dad, Mom: Your Temperaments Are Showing

The parenting characteristics of each temperament are strikingly different and exist in the preferences each temperament displays. Others, particularly our children, readily see these characteristics. In the next chapter you will discover how your child and others see you as a parent (with, of course, the uniqueness of your individual history and conditioning giving you a special touch).

These special touches that each of us display — the environment and culture in which we were raised, and the changes to our values and beliefs that we have adopted along the way — have stamped us with our own distinct fingerprint. However, our conditioning does not change our temperament or erase it. Every original human being is governed by drives, and the drives common to each temperament identify that temperament.

Although they can't be changed, all temperaments can be modified. We can, therefore, modify our own drives and the resultant parenting style to satisfy the needs of each temperament. If an SJ parent has an SP child, the parent can, and will need to, modify his or her approach to parent their SP child successfully. Modifying the way parents express their strengths (or preferred drives) enables the parent to be all things to all their children. Does this mean that the parent must study some kind of manual to be able to parent a child of a different temperament effectively? No! They simply must be aware of the differences of their children and have the basic knowledge that the section on "Understanding Your Child" and the next chapter present.

Although this book will, perhaps, also give you more information than you can remember about each temperament, plus many notes on parenting, a basic knowledge will guide you in most parenting situations.

The following sketches of the different parenting styles seen in the four temperaments will introduce you to what I hope will be a rewarding study of your own temperament and its tendencies. An added benefit will be seeing your temperament in light of other temperaments. A common set of drives will lead to a recognizable parenting style, and this will round off your parenting knowledge and clear the way for those effective skills you long for.

Not only do our children see us through our temperaments and the preferences we follow, so do the parents of our children's friends, and this "free advice group" (known as our friends) will surface with their observations for sure. The latter can be a source of irritation at worst, and a gift of wisdom at best. We do well to know the style of parenting that we likely employ, so as to understand the comments we receive and the judgments we may endure.

It is beyond the scope of this book to show how each temperament in a parent affects each of the different temperaments and types in children, nor is it necessary. With four temperaments, each with four distinct types (making 16 types in all), it would require a massive volume to give detailed accounts of all possible interactions of all types. Not only that, but when all the possible reactions of one temperament to another, and the differing circumstances of those reactions are taken into account, we would extend our discussion to many volumes. If you are having difficulties, or need more help, see a coach who has knowledge of temperament psychology and how it plays out in parent-child relationships.

As an extra insight into parent-child relationships we will include, after the discussion of the four parenting styles, a look at the effect of E-I, S-N, T-F, and J-P interactions on our relationships with our children. All of this will be enough for you to handle your child effectively.

Friendship is love with understanding.
~Unknown Source

Chapter Ten ♦

The Parenting Conflict — Different Solutions to Common Parenting Issues

Each parenting style – SP, SJ, NT, and NF – is summarized here by its main characteristics, not described in full detail. Full details are not necessary. The major characteristics of each temperament's parenting styles will cover 95 percent of our interactions with our children. The remaining 5 percent will either be insignificant ultimately, dealt with successfully by intuitive parenting, or can be discussed with a knowledgeable coach. Get 95 percent right and you are very close to perfection!

I must also remind you that each temperament has four types. For example: the SP temperament is made up of the ESTP, ESFP, ISTP, and ISFP. You may be familiar with this up by now. Each of the types will be slightly different to the degree in which their basic characteristics reveal themselves. I have described the characteristics in what I would call their most distinct, or potent, form. Please understand that your particular style may or may not be a more muted version of the temperament than I describe. Nonetheless, it will be the style of an SP, SJ, NT or NF, and your child may see you as the "potent" version when you know you are, in actuality, less potent. When your children are upset with you, they may well see you even more dramatically than I describe here!

Read through the total description to get a feeling for the "atmosphere" of your temperament. Then read it again to focus on elements you may wish to address in your own life. Finally, think through how your child will respond, and is responding, to your parenting style.

Please read through each temperament (SP, SJ, NT, NF) since your temperament will appear in the discussions of other temperaments, particularly in comments about contrasting behavior and opposite parenting styles. Reading other temperaments and their parenting styles also sets your style in a more realistic context.

Self Expression – SP Parents

Likable-Liberal

This temperament in a parent is "likable" and "liberal." Not necessarily liberal in the political or philosophical sense, but likable and liberal from the child's perspective. An SP parent could wear a tee shirt saying "Kids vote me likable" with a disclaimer saying "most of the time!" SP parents tend to create wider boundaries and judge less severely if the boundaries are broken, believing that self-expression explains much of the child's challenging behavior.

Self-expression is a goal of SP parents for their children. Is it a bad goal? Of course not! However, as with all goals for our children, it must be tempered by other equally important goals. Self-expression can lead quickly to aberrant behavior, and when it does it offers no remedy. The remedy is in self-control, not self-expression.

I have noticed that SJ parents will jump on this statement, and affirm it with vigor, because a sense of personal responsibility is one of their major concerns. Then there emerges, in some SJs, a tendency to impose control on the child with the belief that parental control teaches self-control. They have that wrong! While external control does teach inner self-control, external control imposed by the child is not the same as external control imposed by the parent.

In a famous study, children were offered a second marshmallow if they didn't eat the first one before the instructor returned. They were faced with external control to teach inner self-control. That works. However, parental control can, and usually does, teach rebellion (when harshly enforced) because a human being resists being controlled by another. It is amazing to me how many parents just don't get this. You can often encourage a child to impose self-control and avoid the need to impose it yourself. Try this wherever you can.

Children really long to be self-controlled, because self-control (when understood properly and when exercised in the context of care for others' rights and needs) leads to the enjoyment of freedom. Teach this and give opportunity for it. A certain amount of tactful, loving, parental control (observed as loving in the child's estimation, not the parent's mind) can help a child develop self-control. But too much raw parental control encourages children to fight back and establish their own rules. Of course, enjoyment of true freedom is not the only benefit of self-control. It leads to successful self-management and enriches love, joy, peace and a host of others virtues and provides boundaries for children. For example, love without self-control will soon become a dangerous virtue, violating the rights of others.

The NT views self-expression similarly to the SP. But the NT defines self-expression as being independent and self-reliant.

The NFs are fans of self-expression, but only if it serves others as well as themselves. They aim to please, and this helps curb their use of it. They will also agree with the SJ's sense of personal responsibility, but they will tend not to parent their children with control measures unless they have been angered (at which time all restraints are off).

So, children who are always after more freedom favor the SP's parenting style with its more liberal boundaries and liberal ideas of self-expression.

Carefree and in Search of Excitement

SPs live in the present and want to make every fleeting, present moment count. Life is to be enjoyed. Therefore, every moment must be lived optimistically and with pleasure. Pleasure is often found in exciting events, adventures, and things. The SP parent has a natural bent that favors sports, theme parks, discovery, and the expression of the arts. All enjoy these things, but the SPs are the kings and queens of excitement.

I remember an SP groom who was arranging his wedding and, in typical dashing style, he planned to arrive on a white stallion, sweep his bride up off the ground, gallop to the front of the assembled well-wishers, and there he would dismount with flair. He had overlooked one matter. His bride was of a more cautious, sedate temperament. She was an SJ, and his plans fell into a pile of dashed hopes as she took control of her wedding with the iron grip of traditional values and appropriate decorum. His wedding was a lesson in the less exciting world of fashion and convention – a world he found alien to his impulses, but relevant to his future happiness. What SP child would not want to have viewed this groom's idea of a wedding? The SP parent stimulates a child's thrill-center.

In order to fully enjoy the moment, it is disastrous to carry into it any worries from the past or concerns about the future. "So, live the present moment carefree, as far as you are able," says the SP parent. Children of SP parents are likely to have a rich diet of carefree excitement dished up on their plates as often as time and circumstance allow. Most children will love this. "Carefree" is a quality that makes the most of excitement and pleasure, don't you think? Carefree is excitement devoid of worry.

The SJ parent is more concerned about possible danger, trouble, and pain. Therefore, they advise caution and care, and plan for "safe" enjoyment. "Safe thrills"? Even the sound of those words kills all enjoyment for the SP.

One SP parent felt the call to help with the local Boy Scouts camp. He left, however, after only a few concerned days. All the fun was carefully choreographed to be "safe" and to avoid possible danger. He couldn't stand it. Where was the daring and the adventure? Differing definitions of pleasure had collided.

Likewise, the NF parent (who is always concerned about the future) dampens the enjoyment for the SP. The SP parent approaches the future with abandon, impulsively, while the NF approaches it in search of its possibilities and cautious of its pitfalls. Again, where is the carefree attitude? So the SP parent opens up Pandora's Box and dashes through the contents in search of something exciting, while the NF warns of the contents and secures the lid.

The child of an SP parent is not likely to grow up without an optimistic outlook on life, even if it is muted by his or her own temperament.

Although joy and happiness are essential ingredients in the mix of a healthy life, they can, perhaps, best be dished out with some concern for all the other ingredients of success, such as planning and preparation. Caution and considered risk can be successfully mixed with impulse and can add to the enjoyment. I can see you (an SP) frown!

The SP parent who gives liberally of the essential ingredient of excitement is perhaps best partnered with an SJ to temper the quest for excitement and prepare ("be prepared" is an SJ's motto) the child for life's pitfalls and serious challenges. The two often end up marrying each other since opposites attract and, if the parents can agree on parenting issues, the children grow up with a balance that fits them for the world of SPs and SJs. Conversely, the SP parent will temper the SJ parent's tendency to see the worst and operate on Murphy's Law, which is to most SPs one of the silliest inventions born of the demon worry.

Impulsive and Daring

SP parents take pride in their children exhibiting a brave, daring spirit. All of these SP traits almost feel like a repeat of each other, don't they? They do, because they arise out of the same spirit that is the trademark of an SP. They are, as Ezekiel saw them, the lions. Lions are impulsive, brave, daring, and if they take no risks they bag no meals. So the SP parent releases to their children loads of freedom to test their wings and do what they want when they want to do it. If they are going to be successful as SP parents there is a drive in them that says "I must encourage my children to take risks and test the limits" so they can develop the SP's distinctive self-image: namely, bold confidence. When SP parents see a bold, confident spirit in their child they are very proud.

If they are partnered with an NF, the SP parent who uses the argument of self-image improvement will find a ready response! "Let them explore the boundaries, and even what is beyond, and let them risk and fail a little, since they will learn from the hard knocks," says the SP. The NFs buy in only if they can be convinced that it will gain for the child a confident self-image. NFs yearn for their children to find a confidence that they themselves have longed for all their lives.

The NT welcomes a lion-like approach if the impulse is tempered with reason and sense. In contrast, the SJ shudders at all the possible dangers.

If the child is an SP, this way of parenting develops their strengths and they emerge as brave, bold adults, with all the confidence they will ever need. However, if the child is of a more timid temperament (which is likely since we do not necessarily pass on the same temperament to our children), they find the freedom frightening. The risk-taking can make them grow inward and seclusive. It is simply more than they can handle.

"I'm afraid she is going to kill herself," a nervous SJ parent complained to me of her SP child. Nervous was not the word. "Beside herself," as our English language humorously has it, would be more accurate. "These kids who scream down the road racing each other are not only dangerous, they are deadly!" she exclaimed. "What do I do? I've tried everything from urging to punishing, and the reports still come back about my daughter. In fact, they seem to be increasing. 'Your child is a daredevil and a danger to others. I won't let my child ride with her if I can help it,' was the urging of an irate friend. What can I do?" the mother pleaded.

What <u>did</u> help was the following prescription:

- Help her SP child understand who she is and why she is doing this. Understanding how she is made will be the first step, and an important one toward self-management.
- Help her to see that her daring spirit can be satisfied in more beneficial ways and endanger her passengers less.
- Help her discover those ways, and actively encourage them.
- Teach her that strengths, when used without wisdom, are destructive. Unwise use is wrong use.
- Reward her in a way she will appreciate for any reliable reports of her more restrained driving habits.
- For other reports, use the NT method of discipline (described under "Independence — NT Parents"). Quietly, and without emotion, take the car away for a period that will help her learn what is best for her and her passengers.

I'm sure you can think of other things that will help, but whatever they are, they must meet the following requirements:

- Help protect her life and the lives of others.

- Cause no damage to the strengths of her temperament, but use them constructively.
- Avoid destroying her self-respect which would lead to loss of all confidence and a depressed life (which only results in further destructive behavior).

Parental Control

The freedom given and the seeming lack of control that marks an SP parent's style raises the question of how effective they are at disciplining their children. SPs don't like to dish out punishment of any sort. It's not fun. Their belief, which comes from their drives, is that too much restriction and the use of inhibitions make for fearful children. Being afraid (a "scaredy cat") is not at all what the SP parents want for their children. They can't admire fear!

The danger? One SP parent, who was forever coaching his son to be bold and daring, noted with grave concern his son's timidity and growing fear. His son was a cautious little SJ. What concerned the father most was the increasing feeling of disdain and dislike he had for his son. The natural desire to have our children grow up like us is a very powerful force. He found himself becoming pessimistic about his son, and that (for an SP) is a sure sign that something is malfunctioning in them.

He redoubled his efforts at encouraging his son to risk and dare, and the results decreased in proportion to his efforts. He was embarrassed. His son was freezing up with fear. He spent less and less time with his son. Occasionally, words of disgust would escape his lips and whip his timid son. His embarrassment became obvious. The relationship was, for now, lost. Both suffered. So I taught him the damage of all Pygmalion projects.

He learned to set his goals for his son's lessons in daring much lower, to encourage every tiny success, and to show pride – real pride – in a boy who was in every way as good as he was, but different. He also learned that the most effective method of teaching confidence to a child (and an adult for that matter) was to model confidence and allow the child to modify his temperament slowly by the influence of example. SJs will be SJs, and even the persuasiveness of an SP will not change them. It will only modify who they are. To modify the SJ's caution with confidence was no Pygmalion effort. The SJ son did not become an SP, but a more daring SJ.

So how do they discipline? First, in clever ways, manipulating the limits in order to entice their children to test them and show courage, but also not to let their children get too far from the required boundaries – a skill other temperaments find hard to emulate. An SP's boundaries are much more liberal than those of an SJ, or even an NF parent, to begin with. Second, they discipline by unexpected bursts of anger. This comes as a surprise from the pleasant, fun- loving SP. It seems out of character, but a little thought will reveal its sense. The child is surprised nonetheless. Here's the rationale for the SP's anger. The SP parent gives liberally of freedom, but comes down hard on backchat and unappreciative behavior, since, having given so freely, they expect the recipient of their gifts to return a degree of respect and obedience as a show of gratitude.

They can speak with damaging words and spank without caution when they suspect their child is ungrateful. They can be tough parents, but you will find they are seldom strict. Strict belongs to the SJ and the NT parents. *Tough* belongs to the SP and the angered NF.

The saving grace for the SP is the way they recover from their anger. Surprisingly, in a few moments they act as though the whole affair didn't even occur. Punishment is fast, furious, and short lived. The SP is favored above all the temperaments at being able to forget the easiest. The NF forgives the quickest, but finds it harder to forget because of the longer lasting emotional hurt that must heal.

Summary of the SP Style

The SP parenting style has much to commend it. Perhaps the greatest contributions it makes to the development of a healthy adult are the building of self-confidence and the application of much joy (which is an essential nutrition for the happy, healthy human spirit).

The avoidance of worry is a definite plus, and the development of optimism should be envied and emulated by all temperaments. Courage is also high on the list of benefits that are encouraged by the SP parenting style.

The areas of negative impact have been touched on. Parenting "SP style" can be overwhelming for some temperaments and can create more fear and cautiousness instead of less. The SJ parents want me to mention the need for more responsibility. I just did.

Rules and Regulations – SJ Parents

This is the serious parenting style. It is the opposite of the SP style. Instead of "likeable" and "liberal," it is known as "responsible" and "conservative."

Two Styles within the SJs

Each of the temperaments has four types that can be subdivided into two slightly differing styles. In the case of the SJ temperament, though, there are two noticeably distinct variations that need to be mentioned. The four types that make up the SJ temperament are the ESTJ, ISTJ, and the ESFJ, ISFJ. You will notice that two have a "T" in their profile, and two have an "F". The parenting style of the Ts is firmer and more demanding than that of the Fs. The Fs, being softer, can form a friendlier bridge with the SP style of parenting, but they are still insistent on their children being, above all, responsible for their actions and good conservative citizens. In the SJs, we have a distinctly firmer and softer SJ style. That being said, let's note the overall characteristics of SJ parenting.

Raising Responsible Adults

It is hard for an SJ parent to conceive of dissident and wayward children. "Obey your parents" seems only to make basic sense. So parenting, for the SJ, is all about making this happen if it doesn't happen naturally. Society, for which an SJ exists, must be guarded, molded, and constantly recreated by adding responsible little models of reliability and dutifulness. Nothing makes SJ parents happier than to see their children display to other adults a responsible attitude (which also includes a display of good manners). Why anyone would think this is not basic to raising good children an SJ parent cannot conceive!

I've seen it and I guess you have, too — a child that shows manners and "place," as it used to be called. This child has most likely been raised by an SJ.

> "Mary, this is Mr. and Mrs. Visitor. Say hello."

> "Hello, Mr. Visitor. Hello, Mrs. Visitor. May I get you a glass of water or tea?"
>
> The visitors smile warmly, and Mary's mother swells with pride, even sits up straighter and makes out that her daughter is always this courteous and good.

Also, I have often noticed that the SJ mother doesn't complement her daughter later . She sees it this way, being good should not be rewarded. We are supposed to be good "for nothing." When this attitude is taken, especially toward an SJ child, you will have made a self-fulfilling prophecy. She will be "good for nothing!" She will let you know that a lack of <u>expressed</u> appreciation results in undesirable behavior.

For the SJ parent, they believe that if you are going to raise responsible children, then you must teach them to be prepared for the possible troubles of life. So the focus in much parenting by SJs (not all, thank God) is the trouble and how to prepare for and avoid it.

Is there anything wrong with parenting to protect the child from trouble? No! But overprotecting presents problems. There is, also, a real failure if it is the focus of our parenting. Parents must be focused on the positive issues and concerns, not the negative. Focus is singular. Our main emphasis should be on the positive, not on scanning for and avoiding trouble. Just as we can only think one thought at a time, we can focus on only one thing at a time.

Parents should view potential and actual problems positively – not with the focus of avoiding them, but rather to build the solutions and, as a result of this, avoid the problems. Parent so that you are continuously focused on encouraging and improving the good, rather than avoiding the bad. Raising responsible adults is a noble goal, but raising positively-minded problem-solvers is even more productive of good behavior and of productive adults.

Children who grow up with the model of having to focus on avoiding trouble do not readily lift their eyes to possibilities either. NF parents are, by nature, always looking for the possibilities and they model what the SJ needs.

Pilgrim's Progress used to be regarded as a classic piece of literature, but has grown out of fashion because of its moral plot. It is skillfully weaved, a tale of a pilgrim on his journey through life, who learns how best to live. The author (who writes from prison, having been jailed for his beliefs) paints this lesson in a memorable scene. A man, with rake in hand, is busy scratching for something of value in the scattered refuse of a dirty street. He constantly looks down at the muck and the trash, searching. Above his head is a crown of precious jewels that he does not see because his focus is on the problem of avoiding starvation and extracting a living from the trash. His whole future would be solved, and his poverty avoided, if he would only look up. Parent your child to look up. Model success for them – not primarily to avoid trouble, but to find possibilities.

Tradition Is Important

If society is important, traditions are necessary. Traditions are what culture and society are largely built on. Tradition means tried and proven values and customs. The Boy Scout law sums up the SJ parenting agenda well: Be trustworthy, loyal, helpful, friendly, courteous, kind, obedient, cheerful, thrifty, clean, brave, and reverent. Without this agenda our society will, and does, suffer. Tradition is a way of honoring the values of respect and goodness that impresses the little SJ, and when that happens, it thrills the SJ parent. It is also important because it helps keep the connection with the past, like being reminded of your roots. Therefore, SJ parents make a big issue of birthdays, anniversaries, national days of remembrance, as well as religious traditions. All these keep values and the SJ's ceremonial traditions alive. There is much good in the SJ model of parenting that the SP would do well to consider. The stability it brings is not to be lightly dismissed.

This message of SJ parenting particularly reaches the heart of the little SJ (and the NF to a slightly lesser degree), but falls on otherwise occupied ears for the SP and the NT. Its influence can be lost in the tug of the passions of the present, whether excitement for the SP, or strategies for the NT.

Worry Is Expected

When we focus on the problems and their possible outcomes, we can become rather negative in our emphasis. SJs, when they fall into their weaknesses, can become pessimistic about anything and everything. This pessimism in them can, and does, destroy the good they do. Remember, it is not part of the strengths they so nobly display in their true temperament. It is the result of a reversion into their weaknesses which creates this pessimistic approach, this negativity. Therefore, the true display of the SJ temperament – which champion's responsibility, reliability, and a "do your duty" attitude – is not to worry. SJs who live in their temperament's strengths bless their children immeasurably.

Because worry is the SJ's most common weakness, we need to explore the damage of the negative and let it highlight the health of the positive. A negative mindset is not the normal or healthy state of mind we were created to enjoy. Negativity produces damaging chemicals in the brain and the body, carving deep highways of thought that become the default pattern for all worriers. These worry highways demolish, for want of use, the positive highways of faith and hope. Worry is a fear, and fear takes over when we become obsessive worriers, immobilizing us. Worriers damage their health and the health of all who are infected by their contagious disease. Your child may be the victim of fallout from this behavior. Have you noticed that it takes much effort to stay positive in the presence of a veteran worrier? They can dampen the faith of the best optimist. That's why we are often advised to avoid negative people.

Nothing I have just said suggests that there is value in worrying. Parents who model this mindset certainly leave their children with a mountain to overcome in their adult years if they wish to become positive.

Of most concern for parenting is the tendency of the worrier to look askance at optimists and label them as not caring enough for their children. Worry, for many, is a sign of care. That is a huge distortion of the reality. On the contrary, it is, however, the indication of a parent doing damage. Worry is a slippery rock on the edge of the precipice of depression. Keep your little NF away from worriers, if possible, since their tendency to depression will be realized all too quickly. Not much good can be said about a negative parenting pattern for the SJ, either. Worry is not an SJ strength but a sad caricature that is too common, an easy trap to get tangled in.

Tough Love

SJ disciplinary style is firm and strict. Not just tough "at times," and not really "strict," as in the typical SP parent. *Tough*, to the SJ, means *strict*. Physical punishment is more likely to be enacted by an SJ parent than any other temperament. And, in their defense, SJ children who receive physical correction usually do better as a result of it. This is a classic case of parenting by the methods that you, yourself, respond to and you know work.

Where SJs run into trouble is when they apply a method effective for an SJ to all temperaments equally. NT children will resent it deeply. SP children will scheme a way to pay the parent back – usually by more misbehavior until the parent has run out of punishments. NF children will be deeply hurt and terminate the closeness of the relationship.

What must be kept in mind with these serious parents is that they love their children with the same dedication to duty and sense of responsibility that they demand. A child who wants love can find it in abundance with an SJ parent, provided the love they seek is of the practical and sensible variety. SJs coined the phrase *tough love* so that their children would be made to live good and honest lives. Their love is also seen in their selfless provision of the child's needs, both physical and spiritual. They will even forego their own comforts and pleasures for their child's perceived needs and wants.

Too much tough love promotes stubborn rebellion. When the child feels that the tough love isn't love at all, he senses a discrepancy and wonders about the lack of tender love. Love is tender and kind. Kindness is its practical expression. I understand why the phrase was formed, and with what meaning, but once it becomes a parenting method, it must defend itself and its integrity, which can be lost in its choice of words. I find the use of the word *love* in the teachings of the greatest moralists of our world to be the tender expression of respect, kindness, and gentleness in a practical manner and with an attraction that I find the phrase *tough love* violates. If your child is rebelling, and you have been using *tough love*, ask yourself, "Am I, in my child's mind, known for my tender love toward him or her, or known for a rough love, hewn out of feelings of anger?"

Also, with that warning in using tough love in mind, you must also watch out for over-providing and the dangers of spoiling a child. This practical love can lead to spoiling. Doing things for the child when it is best to let the child provide for his or her own needs, or protecting when the child must learn to self-protect, and shielding from harm and hurt when the child must grow strong, inner muscles in order to rebound from hurt and harm, only steal from the child the very thing that good parenting provides — self-reliance. Over protection also become controlling, and this is something the SJ parent must avoid or he will do damage to a growing and developing life.

Summary of Style

What would society be like without an emphasis on responsible, reliable, trustworthy, caring behavior? The SJ parent who models the lessons taught in the story of the Good Samaritan is priceless. If they have overcome the tendency to become an inveterate worrier, they are even more valuable. Their rock-like, stable character is worth awards in a shifting society. The SJs, who comprise approximately 46 percent of our population, steady the ship of life with tradition, concern, and a lifestyle that likes closure. They tie up the loose ends of uncompleted tasks and build solid routines to perpetuate today's lessons into tomorrow.

For this serious parent, the challenge is to "lighten up a little." Enjoy! Joy is a nutrition the SJ needs more than any other temperament. Their children need joy. The trilogy for a healthy spirit is love, joy and peace. SJs give love to their children abundantly in actions of care and provision, the peace they seek, and the joy they struggle to supply. We will never change their cry that "work comes before play," but we urge them to play a little for their own and their children's sake, or they will undo all the good they so selflessly provide.

Avoid all Pygmalion efforts to make your children like you. SJs are made wonderfully. They strongly desire that their children follow in their footsteps, but they must let their children do it with the drives of their own temperaments that won't, I warn, seem (in the eyes of the SJ parents) like the child is following in their footsteps.

Your task, if you choose to accept it, is to appreciate and respect the other temperaments for the strengths they bring to society, and develop them in their own pattern.

Independence – NT Parents

We now enter a different world with the NT and the NF. These temperaments do not gather their information from the world primarily by means of their five physical senses. They see the world and happenings through the complex operations of their intuition, imagination, and sensitivity. The NFs do this more than the NTs who, governed by the influence of the T in their profile, use their five senses more in the pursuit of science and engineering. It is to these occupations they gravitate, and they interpret intuition, imagination, and sensitivity almost exclusively through their analytical and rational functions.

If you study the intuition of both the NT and the NF you may come up with the conclusion that they are two, almost distinctly different animals. Intuition in the NF is a matter of reason and emotion, but mainly emotion. In the NT, reason trumps everything, and emotion is buried (though not absent) under reason's considerable weight. The use of reason and emotion, respectively in the NT and NF, is key to understanding their intuition.

Imagination and sensitivity are affected by the same elements. The imagination of the NF is particularly loaded with emotions, the NT with reason. The emotions are often the seat of the imagination for the NF. The use of reason with emotion, in the NF, probably accounts for the artistic creativity so often found in them. Perhaps, these notes will help in sorting out the sharp differences that exist in two temperaments that begin with the same orientation to their world, the use of intuition.

One other factor will help us orientate ourselves to the NT and the NF. The NT, like the SP and SJ, is what I call a straight-forward temperament. This means they understand themselves easier than the NF and are less complex in emotional makeup. This complexity in the NF is brought about, in large part, by their emotional depth and sensitivity. Emotions are complex – more complex than reason. Tactics, logistics and strategy — the world of the SP, SJ and NT — can be very complex analytical exercises. But add emotion, and you have added the most complex operation of the human system. Where emotions rule complexity abounds. The NT can be thankful for avoiding this complexity although it has its benefits. Now, to the "all-about-my-head" NT.

Self-Sufficient, Individualistic, and Independent

These are the NT parents' goals for their children. The goal is rooted in their belief that a child who has learned to contend with difficulties by himself is able to face anything in life and will, in turn, respect others and further the goals of humanity. "What better way to parent?" is the NT's defense of this much-needed goal. The SP and SJ argue likewise about their parenting styles and, to a point, each is right.

To help their children achieve this self-sufficiency, NT parents are not likely to interfere with their children's decisions unless absolutely necessary. "Don't interfere with the natural struggles of the child," they maintain. "The child is meant to find his (or her) own way, and when he or she needs information or help they will ask, and you will be able to help." Their claim is that self-sufficiency leads to healthy independence. Children are taught to accept the consequences of their own actions in the process and much interference from the parent can be avoided. If you rescue children when they misbehave, you create a weak individual, and weak children are a disgrace to the NT parent and a burden on society.

Children should be held responsible for the creation of successful lives, responsible to themselves alone. If they choose not to be self-sufficient, let them learn from consequences. It should change their ways. "Therefore, raise them to be self-reliant by making them face consequences," is the cry of the NT parent. The NT parent will proudly supply all the necessary support for this journey.

This interesting discussion (as near as I can remember it) occurred between an NT and an SJ parent.

> *SJ parent: The parents know when to interfere and should interfere wherever they feel they can help the child.*

> *NT parent: That will make the child dependent on the parent when the child should be self-reliant.*

> *SJ parent: How will it make them dependent? Aren't they dependent anyhow? A parent is the crutch for children to lean on while they are not yet adults and need support."*
>
> *NT parent: I'm hearing that you want your child to depend on you.*
>
> *Sensing a trap, the SJ replied: No I don't, but I feel better when my children are supported by me and I have input into their decisions.*
>
> *NT parent: Control you mean, not input! Control is a limiting factor in the child's growth!*
>
> *SJ parent: I never want to control my children!*
>
> *NT parent: But you do when you interfere. Children need help only when they can't make a decision, or need information to make that decision. Even then, the parent (if asked) should interfere in the child's decision-making process as little as possible. Let children learn from their mistakes. They will add this knowledge to their toolboxes, learning not only what to do, but through the experience, how to do it. Children are better equipped this way.*

I think you can see that some SJ parents hold on tight to the reins of parenting, while the NT gives the child the rein. If you are a horse-lover the analogy will be clear. Perhaps an NT approach is too loose for the SJ to feel comfortable, but the NTs do hold a valid point — children must learn for themselves.

Discovery and the Use of Ingenuity

As soon as NT children can explore the world, they seek to discover everything their senses can detect with great curiosity. The more they successfully discover, the more their self-images rise, and pride in personal ingenuity and achievement fills the mind of the NT child. NT parents support and encourage this adventure with enthusiasm, since it has paid dividends for them in their discoveries.

Reading for discovery, investigating how things work, and pursuing the labyrinth of science is the best education for a child (according to the

NT). "Educating a child in this world's wonders and functions is a parent's sacred duty," says the NT parent, not least because it involves the NT parent where that parent is most skilled and finds most satisfaction. An NT parent shows obvious pleasure in a child who wants to learn. Therefore, the action-packed SP is less likely to get the NT parent's attention. The sober SJ child, who wants to be a helpmate, is under the NT parent's radar and may suffer a little. The introverted INF, who is an avid learner, will spike the attention of the NT, and the two are a match in their logical pursuits and love of learning, until the NF's emotions flare. Then the NT parent is nonplussed and somewhat repelled by the display. The other NFs suffer the same fate. The NT parent is cool, and the NF child is warm. One irritates the other somewhat.

The NT parent offers an excellent style for achieving goals. But there are other goals, such as the drive to be loved and find warm acceptance. The NF who struggles with a wounded self-image is not best parented by an NT approach. The NF will feel hurt and rejected. The SP child will revolt against the NT parent in an attempt to cross the boundaries for personal freedom and to "do his own thing" simply for excitement and motion. Again, an NT approach works best for an NT child, but not so well for the other temperaments, except in one arena: the challenge of discipline.

No Fuss Discipline

No child is perfect, and correction is inevitable. The NT parent knows this. Physical punishment is not, however, their norm, nor is an angry attempt to belittle and humiliate the child, thank God. The method most used is simple. **Quietly, take away the privilege (or another like privilege) that the child has abused for an appropriate period, with no fuss or bother.** The helpful addition to this removal of privileges (which all temperaments practice to some degree) is the quiet, no-fuss way of doing it.

For the NT parent, "no fuss" means not raising the voice and not exhibiting anger or degrading the child. "You asked for an extra thirty minutes before you had to go to bed and I gave it to you. You then made out you were going to bed, and here you are, an hour later, with your light on playing with your Legos. Abusing a privilege means you lose it so you must go to bed on time for the next month and surrender to me your Legos when you go to bed each night." Conversation ends there and the parent walks out with no response to any complaints.

This method soon shuts down the complaints and the child finally chooses what is good for him.

When correcting a child, emotion is only stirred more destructively by emotion. A no-fuss method of imposing discipline saves the parent stress and delivers the measure with *quiet power.* All temperaments could advantage themselves by omitting the anger and delivering the verdict with calm, unbending deliberation.

Of course, for other temperaments it might not be that easy. Easy maybe, for the NT, whose cool, calm nature lends itself to the control of emotions. The SP can erupt in violent anger and then cool quickly, but the discipline is enacted during the spate of anger. If damage is done, that's when it takes place. The NF is known for volatility and can flare more often than any other temperament. The NF is also ashamed of this, but finds herself aware after the fact and needs a special methodology to gain control. Since the NF is prone to a longer period of cooling than the SP, damage may be done during the slow cool down – not only to the child, but also to the NF parent. Having intense emotions can be very challenging.

The SJ may apply the discipline with calm emotions at times, but is usually emotionally affected if the child remains obstinate. SPs can easily rattle the calm of SJs, unless the SJ is in control of himself and his intentions. Anger arouses anger or fear. Do we want to do that to our children? Of course not! But children can be very frustrating at times; and who has not been guilty of discharging their discipline in anger – sometime. They can play on our nerves with constant whining and then push our emotional buttons before we know it. Suddenly, even with all our good intentions at remaining calm, those whom we do not want to provoke have provoked us, and we lose it. The fact is we have complicated the situation with our anger, though it was not our intention.

To suggest that parents need training in self-control under extreme circumstances of child aggravation usually does not sit well with an adult. Macho as we are, we resist the thought of a child being able to get the best of us. Others are more in touch with reality. They know they can be tempted to lose control, so help is accepted. Your goal is to manage your children and not have them manage you, and to do this without hurting or damaging them in any way. The wise learn, and the foolish resist help. Nothing is more important than learning how to keep your cool with children and keep the control in your hands.

I haven't emphasized fear, since we see anger as more of a problem than fear. But are we afraid of our own children? Is this the reason we get emotional? Of course not! That's what we want everyone to know, including our children. Have you noticed that a parent, frozen in fear (not only of her child's attack, but of the lack of knowledge about what to do) is not an uncommon scene? Most fear is dissipated by knowledge – the knowledge that comes from understanding and from experience. Before you decide to get experience, get understanding. It smoothes the path of experience and avoids many hard knocks. If you are finding the no fuss clause difficult, then think hard about this paragraph.

All parents need to learn to control anger and fear before they can administer this method with skill. The NT's method sets this down as a prerequisite course.

Keep the volume down! I have mentioned this elsewhere in this book. To me, it is that important. Volume and emotion rise and fall together. This fact reveals a secret, but few understand it. Talk in a loud volume to your children, and they will talk back to you in a louder volume. Talk to them softly and quietly, and soon their volume will drop and their emotions with it. A low volume not only calms your emotions, it calms theirs, and you will now be able to administer whatever justice is required without emotion blurring the interchange. Their emotions may rise again once they hear that they have been grounded, but at least you did not provoke their anger by your emotion.

Also, consider that, at times, anger is appropriate. Or is it? There may be a time when your anger is appropriate. If so, keep it under control. An adult broadside can do great damage to a developing child's mind. Think carefully before you decide it is justified.

No Conditions – No Comment

In addition to no fuss, some NTs perfect their method even more by making sure the punishment is unconditional, with no bargaining room, and by making no comment on the child's behavior. The "no comment" is as much for the parent as for the child. Parental stress, and the danger of a loose tongue (I call it a "loose cannon"!) are avoided. Unwise and degrading statements that contain not only a berating of the action, but an attack on the child's self-image cannot then ravage the child.

Can we do this? Can we control our emotions as parents? Can we be distant enough from the infringement and from the child to be so calm and detached? It's not easy, even for the NT temperament that is said by some to have ice in their veins because they rely on logic without consulting emotions. Though not easy, it is certainly worth the struggle. Yes, and it pays well. I whole-heartedly recommend this method with the NF the addition below.

Here is the no fuss, no comment NT method in brief:

1. The child abuses a privilege.
2. The parent imposes the removal of the privilege for an appropriate period.
3. The parent does this in a restrained manner, quietly and calmly stating the way the child will lose the privilege. (No loose cannon allowed!).
4. The removal of the privilege is not negotiable.
5. No criticism of the child, only the direct or implied criticism of the behavior is allowed.
6. Afterwards at some unrelated time, if further teaching is needed, the task of education is completed.

All temperaments can benefit by using this method with their own heartfelt style of application.

Special Application of this Technique

The NF is perhaps the temperament most negatively affected by this method. As it stands, it is not altogether acceptable to them. They argue that the child's self-esteem can be hurt by a lack of love in the communication. They mean the kind of communication that does not express the parent's love for the child. They want a method that does not disturb whatever bond they already have established with their child. This may sound impossible; but read on. For the NF, every encounter, even discipline, with the child must somehow deepen the bond between them.

The first caution to this desire that needs to be expressed is that, as parents, we are not to see parenting as creating a friendship with our children – a bond, yes; a relationship of friend-to-friend, no! The child will have many friends. The parents are supposed to be the parents. The child needs both parent and friend; but an honest understanding of parenting and friendship uncovers the fact that they are not synonymous. We really can't be both at the same time, and we shouldn't try – at least until they have left the nest. We must bond with them as parent to child. Accepting our role as parents and realizing its limitations, we can create the bond that is unique in their lives – parent to child – and function with love in that role. This is what the NF addition attempts to do.

The second caution is: What about the potential damage to their self-esteems – particularly if they are NFs? We want all self-esteems to flourish, but especially the ones made tender by intense emotional sensitivity – the NFs. Therefore, I think we must add a step to the NT's method that will in no way adulterate it or its effectiveness. I call it the "NF addition."

The NF addition to the NT method of discipline:

After step one of the NT method, add:

2. Assure the child of his or her personal worth, and express your love (since love expressed during a disciplinary action that is *calmly* administered contains the feeling of integrity that the NF parent wants it to have).

You may also insert the above as point 6 in the NT method.

Other temperaments can benefit from this addition as well, and I suggest it with confidence.

The final NT/NF method for administrating discipline:

1. The child abuses a privilege.
2. Assure the child of his or her personal worth and express your love (since love expressed during a disciplinary action that is *calmly* administered contains the feeling of integrity, even if the child objects).
3. The parent imposes the removal of the privilege for an appropriate period.
4. The parent does this in a restrained manner, quietly and calmly stating the way the child will lose the privilege. (No loose cannon allowed!).
5. The removal of the privilege is not negotiable.
6. No criticism of the child, only the direct or implied criticism of the behavior is allowed.
7. Afterwards, at some unrelated time, and if further teaching is needed, the task of education can be completed.

Or:

1. The child abuses a privilege.
2. The parent imposes the removal of the privilege, for an appropriate period.
3. The parent does this in a restrained manner, quietly and calmly stating the way the child will lose the privilege. (No loose cannon allowed!).

4. The removal of the privilege is not negotiable.
5. No criticism of the child, only the direct or implied criticism of the behavior is allowed.
6. Assure the child of his or her personal worth and express your love (since love expressed during a disciplinary action that is *calmly* administered contains the feeling of integrity even if the child objects).
7. Afterwards, at some unrelated time, and if further teaching is needed, the task of education can be completed.

Summary of the NT Style

I think the best thing we learn from the NT is their disciplinary method. If the NT taught us nothing more, this is a gem of a contribution.

The emphasis on parenting our children to independence is, perhaps, the second most impressive contribution. The SJ and the NF parents need to pay special attention to raising their children to independence and self-reliance. We have failed in our parenting task if we release children into this adult world without having allowed them to struggle enough to develop their own self-reliance through self-control. Sometimes, with an obstinate, troubled child, he (or she) will leave home before this is completed. The parent then needs to bear no blame or guilt for not having completed the task. The task is an 18-year-long task if it is to be completed with full graduation honors.

NTs could learn to use their latent emotions more, and respect emotion more, thus giving their children a greater feeling of love and warmth. The NT parent's method works well for the NT child, but not so well for the NF who they don't understand. Both the SP and SJ may fare well with the NT style. The key, even for the NT, is to understand the differences of the temperaments and to parent with knowledge, all the while watching for needed adjustments. Skill follows.

Bonding – NF Parents

Of all the temperaments, this is the complicated one. SPs, SJs and NTs are straightforward temperaments. Being complicated is no blessing when it comes to parenting. Every possibility is thwarted with difficulties. Even the NT's method of privilege removal in a quiet determined manner is destructive of the deep relationships NF parents want to form with their children. So, with this challenge, NF parents must pay particular attention to their disciplinary methods. They must realize and mold their thinking to include the inevitable sense of loss, as well as gain, in every decision they make.

Emotions – Always Present and in the Way

A sense of loss affects us all. Few decisions will excuse us from this inner pain. Why is it that the temperament which focuses on the future feels a sense of loss so acutely? Because all things past, present and future are scanned by the NF's sensitive radar and loss is loss, no matter where it is spotted.

Let me digress a moment. The NF's sensitive detection is very much like the radar a bat uses to find its way around objects and to its food while flying in the dark. The NF flies by the radar of sensitivity. They will discard any visual evidence if their sensitivity contradicts that evidence. They read the feelings of people and, if the facial expressions belie the evidence of their "radar," they put it down to the facial expressions trying to hide the true feelings. They trust in this because they are skilled at hiding behind their own expressions that belie their own true feelings. Empathy, intuition, and sensitivity are all a part of this sixth sense, and it can be as astoundingly accurate as a bat's radar.

Therefore, NF parents know that if they discipline it means they must prepare themselves for the loss of closeness with their child, particularly if the child is an NF, too. The matter is not as critical with the other temperaments. They don't react with the same emotional loss and withdrawal, although in their own way the little NF can surely test any parent's heart with their manipulations.

An NF child is a bomb ready to explode with the slightest slip in management. And they do! The NF parents, who also wear their emotions on their sleeve, can easily explode in response. Instead, they should see this as a tender opportunity to love their child all the more, since their child is probably hurt, too, and reacting to that hurt. The struggle is with the control of the parent's own emotions – more so than with the child's emotions – when they discipline. The way to unnerve an NF parent is to get to their heart and make them feel the loss of harmony. Children soon find the path.

If the child betrays the parent's love and trust and uses it against the parent, or rejects it, the NF parent can extract severe penalties, since this is the rejection of all the parent has endeavored to do. Expectations have been dashed, and love has been trampled on. So the loving approach of an NF parent has with it some very real dangers lurking at its borders. An SP child may very well take advantage of this kind of parenting. If SP children step over the boundary and experience loving guidance and correction, they may well, at first, be confused and lost about what to think. However, soon the tactical SP will figure out the advantage and exploit it further. The NF parent's love has been spurned and manipulated, and the child now stands in the path of the NF parent's wrath. Watch out SP! There is nothing like the fury of spurned love!

To add to the confusion, the SP (whose anger flares and fades fast) is now at a loss to understand why the NF is still distant and cooling very slowly when he (the SP) has all but forgotten the matter. Living in the present, SP children can quickly forget, because the next rush of adrenaline or promise of excitement distracts them. Life must move on for the SP.

NT children will reject the closeness that an NF parent will want because they feel smothered by the love and care. NTs also see the love as too sentimental – a feeling that is beneath their dignity. When the NT child rejects the warm affections of the NF parent it is the parent that suffers, while the child simply disengages and continues the exploration of his or her world.

Jean, an NF mother, was pitting wills and powers with her NT son and finding she was turning up on the losing side. She wanted to be obeyed because she felt her cause was important for her son's welfare, but the son felt she did not deserve his respect. This was because she yelled at him (a mark of weakness to the NT). She also demanded that he do things, another mark of weakness to the NT. "Why do you have to yell and demand if you are requesting a reasonable thing?" is the way the NT sees it. Her demeanor told him she must have a weak case to resort to such unreasonable methods. He hadn't even heard her case yet, merely her emotion-filled demands. If her request made sense, all she needed to do was explain her case and if he saw the sense he would obey. "One is always willing to do what makes sense," reasons an NT.

Furthermore, it is hard for an NT child to obey an authority figure who does not, in his or her opinion, deserve respect. Jean's emotional behavior caused her to be filed with the "unworthy authorities" in his mind. Most of the time he would stand motionless while waiting for the storm of her anger to pass. He would not comment or flinch. This nearly drove her to drink, or escape to some other land of forgetfulness! This NF mother was infuriated with her son's calm dismissal of her passionate appeal and demand for obedience.

Failing to get results this way, she used her strength – love! She would approach him lovingly (touching him, asking him to sit close to her) while she explained her case. But NTs don't take well to displays of tenderness and love either. He would not sit close and would tighten at her loving touch. If she hugged him, he would freeze. Love, her potent strength, was not getting it done. This behavior mystifies an NF. The matter got worse. On occasion, he would even smirk and laugh at her – a display of the NT's disdain.

A steep learning curve lay ahead for this mother. She had to understand the cold mysteries of the NT's world and how an "I love you," spoken in a low, toneless voice (an expression of love that would hardly warm her heart) would warm an NT's heart! She had to appreciate the unappreciable. Reason and common sense were the tools she needed to use, not emotion, command, or even love.

When she changed her approach, and reasoned first, she found she seldom had to do anything else. That raised, emotion-packed voice of hers was now occasionally used on her husband when her son was not around (the latter fact reported by her husband). He was familiar with it. An NF will always have passion, but it is best used in the expression of love toward her loved ones (in a muted style for an NT child), not in anger or frustration, unless she needed to scare off a burglar.

One helpful thing resulted for her son. He began his education in appreciating, and eventually welcoming, loving expressions and tones that would prepare him for a more rewarding marriage. The NT can be an extremely cool and remote lover, and can do with being taught some warmth. STJs run a good second in their toneless communications when they are focused on a task or choose to be remote and non-communicative.

An SJ child will usually be much blessed by the rich emotions of an NF parent. The balance of another temperament in the parent mix can make this helpful to all children. The NF parent will love the ingenuity of the NT, the optimism of the SP, and the responsibility of the SJ. In a remarkable way, the NF parent will be all things to all temperaments when, and only when, they understand the strengths of both their own and the other temperament. After all, this is the "people-people" temperament. Emotions and empathy, used passionately to connect with others, can and does win, in most cases, for the NF. Therefore, the NF is in command when solving relationship problems, unless the other person steals themselves against their love and passion.

Parenting Is Relationship

The style of parenting that is so loved by NF parents is to bond closely with their children, providing for them a relationship in which they can take refuge. Their love knows no limits, unless it is spurned. There is much touching and cuddling, with a constant flow of encouraging words from an NF parent. The child is encouraged into maturity with a steady, conscious eye on the task of lifting and strengthening the child's self-image. In this desire to bond with their children, NF parents feel the power of their own love and believe that mutual love is the strongest connection and the greatest leverage to help struggling, developing people. To the NF, parenting is a matter of establishing relationships.

Commands, rules, and all other matters are subservient to relationship. They believe that with a bond you can do almost anything as a parent.

Since parenting is relationship to the NF, and a relationship is leverage, they commit themselves without further thought to this path. Wherever they can establish what they call a meaningful relationship (NFs are the masters of relationship), they parent with life-changing success.

As I typed the previous sentence, my word processing software flagged me that "meaningful relationship" was an overused phrase, and I should consider a more precise phrase. That's just it! NFs overuse the phrase all the time and have a deep connection with it since it conveys this all-embracing and accurate (to them) definition of their behavior and passion. Relationships must be meaningful. If not meaningful, they are discardable. The bond they seek is as much for them as it is for their children. They believe their children want a meaningful relationship, and if and when they don't effect one, as in Jean's case, they persist to eternity in trying to establish it. If not knowledgeable of temperament differences, they pursue their beliefs blindly and finally disconnect when they hit consummate resistance. The "finally" is usually a long way down the road of struggle and persistence. Meaningful relationships are hard to define for the NF. They require supplying whatever the need is. To the NF, relationships are the direction for our lives that encourages us to lean into the tough times and overcome them. A meaningful relationship with their children is undefined because the NF will define it, and redefine it, as the need to do so arrives, and as many times as required. Their intuition will guide them. It happens almost miraculously. The NF suddenly senses (probably by way of an overactive empathy and alert sensitivity) what to do and excitedly, with their nose to the scent, they track with fervor the child's (or adult's) feelings and needs.

Meaningful relationships are always in a state of flux. Therefore, it requires making constant progress toward them and making already existing ones deeper. NF parents never tire of seeking and developing closer bonds with their children. This may alert you to their being the least likely to embark on a Pygmalion project. They want to develop their children in the fascinating molds that unfold before their eyes. If the child is different – with a different temperament, interests, and passions – they bond over the glue of encouragement (at which they are particularly skilled). There! That will teach my word processing software! I have used the phrase "meaningful relationship" seven times in three paragraphs!

Another way to understand the NF parenting style is to see it as the development of a partnership. The child's progress is the parent's challenge and progress too. They grow with every advance the child makes. Their inner world is constantly changing to meet whatever needs the child may have. It is a passion of all NF parents to partner with the child in discovering and realizing his or her potential. It is also a passion to enjoy the shared experience. To have found their way into the heart of their children, and to have been welcomed to share the journey, is the NF parent's ecstasy and meaningful reward.

The timid child (or the needy child) benefits greatly from this partnering. Just out of gratitude for all the help and encouragement, a child will often be more compliant. The parent is being paid back for his or her efforts. Such results only spur the NF parent to closer and more meaningful engagement. Whereas the SJ parent is the child's helpmate, the NF parent is the child's soul mate. "May I bond with your spirit?" they seem to ask the child.

NF parents talk to their children a lot. They talk abstractly about fear, bravery, love, hate, and all the virtues that they want their children to possess in ever–increasing measure. For some, it is not too far from the truth to say that parenting is talking. What is for some temperaments an overuse of touching and words, is for the NF the main track to success. Humans have developed language to a high level of communication. It is not only words, but choice of words, cadence, subtle intonations, voice quality, pitch, modulation, inflection, emphasis, pace, rhythm and repetition that the NF skillfully uses and does well to practice.

When young, a little NF often speaks incessantly, just for practice. Language is a complex tool, and, since when they grow up it will become their main tool, they must perfect its use early. Their liberal use of emotion in their voice is their key to success in much of their persuasiveness. They show that all success is linked to the effective use of words.

Much of their encouragement moves on to become persuasion. They also have an understanding that motivation is achieved through words, and they are right. Words create images in the mind which can then form beliefs. Since we all act on our beliefs, motivation can begin effectively with words.

Self-respect Is All-Important, Too

Children must feel good about themselves to develop into the best they can be. The NF, as another noble task of parenthood, accepts being positive and developing a child's dreams, hopes, and ambitions. How can you do that if you don't have a door into your child's heart? Gaining entrance to the heart is the NF parent's road map. Begin with relationship, then proceed to lift the child's self-esteem. From there, help them build their dreams.

Building self-esteem is not like building a tree house for your child. The materials are abstract and ethereal, making the task of creating the "mind-house of self-esteem" an exercise in fashioning unseen feelings and thoughts for the person's good. Not an easy task, or one that the other temperaments are naturally enthused about. Once the house of self-worth is built, you can then successfully help them structure their dreams.

Dreams begin in imagination. The mind of an NF is full of imaginings (daily and hourly), and they live in the warmth of its promise. Children are more comfortable dreaming than most adults who, if they daydream, don't want to admit it. Therefore, the daydreaming NF parent connects with the child's dream world, and the child explores more freely and confidently the wonderful world of imagination.

Dreams, if they are constructive, can be used as goals that give direction to life. The NF parent knows this and exploits it early, using it to deepen relationships and enrich the child's development.

Not all children welcome this emphasis on the inner life, certainly not the SP or SJ whose interest is in sensing and experiencing the real world. Their self-image is lifted by external success. The NF parent's attempts at developing the inner world of the child may result in the other temperaments being impatient with this behavior, but accepting it most of the time because of the love the NF parent exudes.

For NF parents to be really successful at parenting all temperaments they must obtain knowledge of how the other temperaments differ from their own in acquiring self-esteem, and they must understand their world of sensing, too. The S is so different from the N. They look at each other across a canyon of misunderstanding. This knowledge the NF parent is usually happy to acquire if they know where to turn for help. NFs are the ultimate coaches, since they are always optimistic about potential and undaunted in their efforts at self-improvement.

"My child is saying she is no good," an NF parent complained to me (and the pain was written all over her face). For some parents the statement would merely be regarded as a "bad inner weather report." For the NF parent it is a "thermometer" that is recording an "extreme drop in temperature" in the tender world of the human spirit – a real cold front. To many concerned NF mothers, this is critical. They are right! It is! Cold feelings about one's self lead to unhealthy, negative minds and spirits, which – well, let me tell the story.

David was nine. He had been having disturbing dreams lately and something had changed his normally bright, outgoing personality. His mother thought the dreams were depressing his lightheartedness. Her friends said, "Don't worry. It will change. All kids have these doldrums." Debbie (David's mother), however, couldn't let it go so easily. It was affecting their relationship, and she worried it may develop into something worse – maybe a loss of self-worth, was her instinctive thought.

To an NF parent that thought can border on being scary. Healthy humans must have a sense of worth (and the higher the better, they rightly feel).

As Debbie watched, her son become morose and sad in a way he had never been before. He lost all interest in things that had given him pleasure, and he became irritable and sassy. She also noticed he was complaining about being tired. She would occasionally find him sitting on his own, slumped over and crying. Her husband, who was of a more earthbound temperament, had taken the matter into his own hands and scolded his son for being lazy and (as he put it) only "half a man," thinking the shame of his words would snap him out of his stupor. That made matters much worse. He increased his statements of worthlessness, and the sadness deepened into what was now obvious depression.

Debbie asked me what she could do to help him feel better. We focused on his self-image and the reasons why he had lost his sense of worth in the first place. Sometimes, for a child, the least little insult can start a downward spiral and plunge them into depression.

It had all started when a little girl he admired told him she hated him and gave him several reasons why he was less than admirable. It toppled his sense of worth. He told no one. Other comments added to his fall, and his own failure at a sporting event confirmed his feelings. Rumination on these things magnified the effect, and he fell into a negative cognitive pattern that he could not shake.

Debbie, who turned out to be an NF (but a puzzled and insecure one, living in her own feelings of worthlessness), had an opportunity to parent her son with her own encouraging style and lift her self-esteem at the same time as she partnered with him. The way out of depression is often the way you came in. Minds circling in negative thoughts were, for David and his mother, the downward spiral, and positive minds, spinning just as obsessively in a self-created, healthy atmosphere, were the way out. Overall, the NF parenting style was ideally suited to helping David.

What could she do? Focus on his inner world, and bring him loads of love and comfort as she encouraged positive thoughts. She did. It made her feel like a worthy mother. That spurred the rise of her own self-esteem, too. She also took him to places she knew he enjoyed, and they played together, recreating the bond they had before his self opinion had started to tumble. For David, the loving attention and encouragement (together with a mind that was turning positive again) worked wonders.

His mother had warned his dad that he had better follow suit by showing pride and respect for his son. They had better play together and have fun together, or else. Being the smart man that he was, and knowing it was not healthy to mess with his wife's plans, he found himself part of the solution. A family, working together through pain and emerging from it, became an example of the worth of the NF's parenting strengths.

"Deepen Their Spiritual Connections," Says the NF Parent

Spiritual connections with God and with other people are second nature to the NFs who are functioning in their strengths. NF parents strive constantly to reduce disharmony. They are made sick by disconnectedness, wanting that soul-bond with their children and the peaceful, loving home it ideally creates. This desire for harmony extends, often quite deeply, into the world of unseen spiritual forces. A soul-bond with deity fascinates and exercises their inner world. Encourage the connections of the human spirit with beneficial beliefs if you have an NF, since this steadies their spiritual gyroscope.

The NF parent is often in tune with a child who experiences strange, extra-sensory happenings (ESP). Spirituality, far from being confined to the NF temperament, is perhaps nurtured more intensely since they are focused on their sensitive inner world. They also know that the inner values of life, such as integrity and gentleness, are best fed by a spiritual connection and positive beliefs. Hence, spiritual organizations are natural homes for the idealist temperament who seeks a better world with more fulfilled people. Life is more than material things and more than a material universe, as humans from the beginning have accepted. The pull of faith, and of ethics rooted in more than reason or convenience, has driven the human heart in all cultures both East and West. The NF parent simply has an activated consciousness of this, and naturally nurtures its contribution to society, no matter what form the faith or ethics takes. What I am saying here is that the NF temperament is, most of the time, drawn to things spiritual.

Discipline? I Hate Being the Bad Guy!

NFs hate handing out discipline so much that they almost prefer to be angry with the child because it is easier then to level the boom and be hated in return for their actions. Furthermore, their desire to be closely bonded with their children can make it all the harder. "I hate to discipline," moans the NF.

Therefore, you will often find them acting as mediators over their own firmly introduced boundaries. Not a good idea. A smart child soon pokes holes in this behavior because it reeks of weak intent. However, NF parents are diplomats and peacemakers of the first order, and the child is not always assured a victory in spotting this obvious advantage. Mediation over breaches of mandatory rules makes them "negotiable" rules. Is this what you really want them to be?

Perfection Is a Setup for Failure

The task that NF parents set for themselves of a perfect home that is built on harmony, peace, and mutual respect is a setup for failure most of the time, and they incur much grief as a result. Perfection cannot be reached. A lesser goal is more realistic and can also reduce tension caused by repeated failure. NF parents must consider their goals carefully and ask whether they are reachable in a world of imperfect people. And if not, are they willing for a sense of loss as well as a sense of gain if they attempt them?

However, being enthusiasts with boundless imagination and passion, they can often surprise everyone by finding a way to achieve their lofty goals with their children. They have learned that their creative resources (intuition, imagination, sensitivity, and powerful emotional motivations) fuel their hope and eternal optimism, and they can trust in finding the way to their goals even when the goals seem impossible. Therefore, they often attempt the impossible with people. Who would want to bet against these potent forces at work in a heart of love and a mind of faith?

The goal of not having to discipline is only sometimes achievable. When it is, trust an NF to reach it. For most of the time, the NF had best use the NT/NF method of correction. (Refer to the NT parenting style.)

Summary of the NF Style

Just in case you have forgotten, NFs are complicated, and we need to make their methods and goals more understandable. So here is an over-enthusiastic attempt at simplification.

- Parenting is relationships, and the NF teaches us not to forget that. "Protect your relationship with your child," they say, "since you will need it. Bond with them."
- Parenting is not controlling, nor is it letting children do as they please; nor is it all rules and regulations; nor is it all learning by consequences or cool disciplinary measures. Parenting, to the NF, is developing children to be their best.
- Parenting is constantly developing this relationship and growing the partnership of parent with child. The tools for such a project are respect, love, insight, and understanding – all of which fuel a bond of trust.
- Emotions, if you have them in large quantity, can both bless and curse your efforts. Try to control them, or pay the price of sabotage.
- Self-esteem, if not in place, will produce aberrant behavior. The building of it is a needed parenting goal to develop your child.
- Spiritual values anchor the life and ward off much inner despair.

This is what the NF parenting style teaches us.

Now this. Lots, and lots, and lots of love, respect, and encouragement make for a healthy child. Dish it up at every meal!

Develop Your Style

Your temperament's parenting style may need modifications. Living in your strengths, and not your weaknesses, will reestablish your true style to begin with. Learning from the styles of other temperaments and paying first attention to how your child has been made on the inside will help you perfect your parenting style.

You need to develop <u>your</u> style since this is "you" and becomes your natural default method. Taking the other temperaments into account, and adjusting your style to meet their needs, will also benefit both them and you. Start now, and adjust your style for the benefit of all!

The highest activity a human being can attain is learning for understanding, because to understand is to be free.
~ Baruch Spinoza

Chapter Eleven ♦

The Clash of Opposites And The Opportunities Opposites Present

Understanding the four temperaments is your easiest and least complicated method of understanding your child and yourself. However, if we look with more detail into the four letters of your profile we will receive even more help. This chapter investigates some of the common issues that arise when Es and Is, Ss and Ns, Ts and Fs, Js and Ps clash. We will also discover the opportunities such encounters provide.

Paying attention to the differences in the four-letter profiles of yourself and your children will flag you and **help you diffuse some very upsetting situations that can occur.** These letters can guide you in a myriad of different ways and you will be able to turn them into opportunities for the personal development of you and your children.

Extrovert versus Introvert – The "Space Invaders" and the "Territorialists"

The differences between extroverts and introverts account for many of the clashes and disturbances that occur in a family.

The introvert wants his space and is disturbed when it is invaded. The extrovert is attracted by people and invades the space of the introvert at will – meaning no harm, just seeking the company of people. The introvert feels violated at this intrusion and reacts in defense of his territory. Neither can understand the other. Both resent the other, and wars start.

There is a deep-seated reason for this resentment. For an extrovert, the energy of the human spirit is charged by interaction with other people and things, but for the introvert, their spirit is drained by the same interaction. This means the introvert must seek out solitude to refresh, while the extrovert needs people to recharge their batteries. When the introvert, whose battery is flat, suffers an invasion of his space (his solitude), he reacts – sometimes strongly – to protect his wilting spirit from being submerged in the draining experience of yet <u>another</u> person. Let's see how some scenarios for interactions, both helpful and not helpful, work out.

- The introverted mom is worn out and seeks a little solitude in which to recharge. The extroverted child finds her and shouts, "I've found her!" and her three extroverted children converge on the spot, invading her "space." She reacts with annoyance. The children can't figure out what she is annoyed about and feel they must somehow be distressing her. We can see where this can lead. Solution? The mom must educate her children about her needs. If she doesn't, she will become more irritable and her children more wary of her presence.

- Extroverted parents are prone to invade the space of their introverted children. "Why are you up in your room? Why don't you come down and be a part of the family? Come sit with us." They wonder why the introvert is so antisocial. The introvert's behavior worries the extroverted parent a great deal. Since only approximately 25 percent of the population are introverts, you may have only one introvert in the family, and they will feel the odd one out, the strange one. Be careful not to reinforce this feeling in them. A seemingly harmless question of "What's wrong with you, why don't you …" can disturb them more than you think.

- Even the well-meaning query "Am I bothering you?" can be very disturbing to an introverted NF. The child may just be recharging a flat battery, and the parent hurts the child with this line ("Am I bothering you?") which implies a backhanded accusation. The parent has provoked the anger of the introvert. The NF introverts will feel this hidden accusation more intensely. You should not be surprised if they show irritation at what <u>you</u> feel is a minor infraction at most.

- Consider this: "Why don't you come down and have fun with us?" is a frustrating lack of understanding that the introvert is having fun – quiet fun! "Why does fun always have to include others?" they ask themselves.

- Introverts and extroverts predominantly live in different worlds: the extrovert in the outer world of people and things, and the introvert in the inner world of thought and imagination. Don't try to force one to be happy in the other's world – except for brief periods. Each world is a valid way of living. On occasion, they will cross over and show that they want the opposite environment. But don't confuse this with their natural world. The introverted NTs and NFs compound this inner world issue. Their inner world experiences are far more intense since they live there more often.

- Extroverts aren't usually good listeners, unless they are extroverted NFs. Even extroverted NFs are not as good at listening as introverted NFs. A family must have good communication. So extroverts need to act deliberately to listen to their introverted members, and introverted members need to make more effort to communicate fully since they also tend to abbreviate their thoughts or keep them to themselves.

- Introverted children are usually more timid and shy in new surroundings. A great idea (for introverted children) is to walk them through new surroundings prior to the time they must appear there with others. Introduce them to people they may meet there, and let them "feel" the surroundings. Among the introverts, the NFs need this most, as they react more to a change of atmosphere.

- Introverts are usually slower to do things than extroverts because they are thinking about it more and processing the scenario to (among other reasons) protect themselves from possible hurtful situations. The speed at which they process is determined by the state of their inner world and how ready it is to accept new information. If that inner world is already full and busy processing highly important, imaginative or actual matters, it may not be ready for new thoughts. If the parent insists on a speedy answer or action, they should not be surprised at an angry response, or even a lie that tells them "I wasn't ready, so you get whatever I think of first!"

- Extroverts seek to be approved by others, since their world is composed of others. If you don't give approval liberally to your extroverted children, they will distance themselves from you and seek approval elsewhere. Watch out for this – particularly during their teenage years – because you don't want them to focus their lives on peers and exclude you as a parent. If you don't like repeating your approval of them and their achievements, you will likely not meet an extrovert's standards for approval (or for that matter, of all NFs). They need to hear continually that you love them and approve of their contributions.

- The introverted child often will not acknowledge the presence of others when they enter the room. This is particularly true of the SP, SJ and NT introverts. It is not a crime. Draw their attention to others if the circumstance warrants it. Otherwise, let it pass. The other people in the room have probably met introverts before!

- An introverted parent will often fail to recognize a child's presence. If the child is an extrovert this can be a cause of friction in a parent-child relationship. The introverted parent can also be less affirming and affectionate than the extroverted or NF child will require. You will usually hear complaints about your coolness, which is helpful in alerting you. If you don't heed the complaints it can lead to problems. Furthermore, an introverted parent might be less likely to treat seriously the ramblings of an extroverted child. The blow-by-blow descriptions of an extroverted child, or of the SP and SJ temperaments, are a display of their capability to recall the details well. They should be encouraged, not offhandedly dismissed. I say this because a blow-by-blow description can irritate an introvert, particularly one whose profile ends in a J. However, these details are important to the extrovert who will feel you don't relate to their needs.

Sensors versus Intuitives — How Information Is Received

Sensing people primarily gather their information from the world around them with their five physical senses because they live mostly in the outside, real world. Intuitive people, on the other hand, primarily gather the information that they pay attention to with their intuition because they live in the inner world of their minds. If you add to this that the sensors speak concretely and the intuitives speak abstractly, you have a recipe for family confusion – at least in communication. Communication is a big problem between Ss and Ns.

As you can imagine, sensors speak with exactness and preciseness. "Please clean up the kitchen" means what it says, no more and no less, and sensors can't conceive that others don't "get" this. But the intuitive child will see the words as pregnant with possibilities rather than details. The first utensil they touch activates their imagination. It is filled with potential to them, and they may immediately begin playing with it, weaving imaginative stories around its use. The opportunities presented by a sink full of soapy water can only be imagined, and the parent may return 30 minutes later to find that nothing seems to have been achieved. The kitchen is still a mess or messier from the sensor's point of view. But to the intuitive child it has been transformed into a rich mine of ideas and imaginative play. Sensing children would not have misunderstood the command "Please clean up the kitchen." So what do you do if you have an intuitive child? Provide step by step details.

> *Please take these utensils and put them in the sink. Wash them. Dry them. And put them away. After you have done this, you can play. The sooner you do it, the better.*

The intuitive child's mind has been filled with details to follow, instead of possibilities to explore at will.

Intuitive children will talk to you abstractly and vaguely. They will tend not to complete their sentences, since the rest of the sentence is vivid to them and their minds have already gone on to other parts of their virtual world.

Their minds are very active, and one thought racing into another causes all kinds of confusion for a concrete-minded, sensing listener. The conversation may not make sense to you, but it does not mean they are scatterbrained – just always overloaded with thoughts – and you will need to ask them to tell you again – slowly, please!

Intuitives can also get bored with the details of a sensing parent's blow-by-blow descriptions of their exploits. Once they have grasped the drift of the conversation, they want to go on and explore the significance of the event, not the concrete details which tell them little more than they have already understood. They may seem disinterested when they are not. They are just unconcerned about details when they have all they need to understand the situation.

If you insist that an intuitive child clean up his (or her) room and put things away, you may be asking the child to destroy the field of possibilities that all these things have already generated in his mind. Be prepared. You may be met with anger and stubbornness that you don't expect or understand.

As I said previously, consider what you may be doing if you pick up a toy and throw it into the closet. The toy may have been (in the child's imagination) transformed into a prince, and the little intuitive put it where it had to be in his story. Now he is upset because you have hidden the prince and destroyed the story. Worse still, the prince may have been, in his imagination, himself; and now you have thrown him away! How would you like to be thrown into the closet? Parenting an intuitive, especially NFs, can be a minefield for an S parent. You destroy or interfere with their imaginary world at your own risk.

Effective communication can make for a much more peaceful house. So talk to them. Be patient. Ask them to tell you again, and try to understand. This is the path to good communication.

Remember, intuitive children live largely in their minds and create worlds you can't see. If you talk kindly and approvingly of their creations they will open up and tell you more. Don't you want to know them? Please, whatever you do, don't criticize or make fun of their imaginative efforts. They will seem to you as if they are not connected with the real world, and it may bother you. But don't forget what Einstein said, "Imagination is more important than reason."

If you are the intuitive parent of a sensing child:

- Don't be disturbed at your sensing children's lack of imaginative exploits. They live in the real world where imagination plays a more down to earth role!
- Encourage their use of imagination, of course, but don't expect great things.
- Don't give vague instructions like "The kitchen is a mess. We need to do something about it." The "we" will likely be you.
- Listen attentively and patiently to their blow-by-blow descriptions. They are good at details and want to talk about them to show you their skill in remembering them.
- The sensing child is always seeking *specific* instructions and directions. The vague instructions of an intuitive parent can leave them feeling lost and strange, and thinking of their parent as not very helpful in showing them how to live in the real world.

- A sensing child is usually willing to throw things away. (An intuitive child doesn't want to throw things away since the items still may have possibilities, and they do have memories and meaning.) A sensor will say, "We haven't used this in ages. Let's get rid of it." The intuitive knows that it will be needed the day after you throw it away – or even sooner now that you have drawn attention to it. You never throw a possibility away – particularly what is a "possibility" to an NF.

Someone who has an E and an S in their profile can be very demanding and always want to see immediate results in the real world. A child with both an "I" and an "N" in their profile translates everything into inner experiences (introspective geniuses), reflecting on them and feeling them. They do not want to let others see their inner life being waved about in the real world. Most of the time, they don't want to have their rich inner world seen at all. When the ES demands to see results according to the way he sees it, he can threaten the integrity of the IN's inner world and create a self-image crisis or a standoff battle between them. The IN often thinks he is inferior to the ES (although he is not), and he tries to be demanding and authoritarian like the ES. Both simply practice their skills in different worlds.

Sensors want to see their children advance to university and learn in order to get a good job and earn a rewarding salary. Their intuitive child, however, will want to go to university to learn, often with no real goals at translating study into a real job. For him, that will come later. Fights can result. Intuitives live in a theoretical world and thrive there. Understand that. They will reward you in their own way by getting a job where they can use their skills. There are fewer jobs out there that are ideal for intuitives.

Thinkers versus Feelers – Expectations in the World of Decision Making

We noted in Chapter Seven that even the task of making decisions is problematical in a family with both Ts and Fs. The T will look at the facts (the data) and make a decision based on that data. Not surprisingly, they will usually do it quickly and decisively, with no second thought. To them the task is easy and straightforward. Consider the facts. That's all there is to it. For the F, however, it is much more complicated. One must consider the facts, and then adjust either the decision to one's feelings, or one's feelings to an undesired decision – a difficult and, at times, lengthy process.

For the Ts, decision-making is a cool, calm, and logical process, void of emotional disturbances.

Not surprisingly, the F's process is fraught with emotional trauma. First, they must consider the facts and process the data. They can do this just like the Ts. However, processing facts calmly, when feelings are bristling in every fact, is a stressful – sometimes volcanic – experience. They can get angry, worried, and fretful, and a T parent is not only confused, but also angered by his child's lack of cool, quick processing. The T parent is likely to make scathing comments and show impatience and concern over whether the F child's emotional sensitivity is healthy.

If the child is the T and the parent the F, the child can lose respect for the "irrational" parent. The F parents are upset when their children do not understand, and can even begin to doubt themselves, lose confidence, and withdraw. This amounts to abdicating their leadership role.

First, understand what the T or F in your profile causes you to feel and do. Then respect the differences. Teach your children to understand others if they are Ts. And help them modify their emotional surges if they are Fs.

Js versus Ps – Hurried or Relaxed?

I have not used the Myers Briggs terminology for Js and Ps because it is so misleading. A J is not a "judger" anymore than a P is. And a P is not a "perceiver" anymore than a J is. So let's call them, simply, Js and Ps. We will fill the J and the P with their real meanings.

Lifestyle

This is the element of temperament that governs lifestyle. Instead of focusing on various scenarios in family life (as we have with the other letters) I think lifestyle is best understood by focusing on the elements that make for the differences and their opportunities.

Our lifestyle is either hurried (wanting to get things done) or laid back and spontaneous. Of course, this can cause many conflicts since the J wants to be on time – in fact, hates to be late – and the P seems to have no concern for time and is not in the least upset about being late.

Timeliness

A J parent who is blessed with a P child will tear their hair out trying to get the child to be on time. The P parent with a J child will find the child upset at the parent's lack of concern and timeliness, and will become very irritated at the parent. As the J parent becomes more demanding about being on time, the P child is rattled even more or simply falls further behind the schedule. To the P parent, the J child seems stubborn and insistent on his own way, wanting things immediately and getting upset when it doesn't happen. These are not stubborn, disobedient actions. They are simply lifestyle differences showing themselves when you wish they wouldn't.

SPs are motivated more by the excitement factor. If the event is exciting, and they don't want to miss it, they will be *almost* on time – a really rare blessing! If it holds no fun value, they will let other interests in life govern their timeliness. What to do for the J parent? Offer the SP some exciting activity as a reward for being no more than five minutes late. It can be more play time, or a visit to some park, or a game with you that they enjoy for the competitive value. Make sure you stick to your promise.

Try always to allow them a small grace period. This they interpret as your acknowledging their temperament's urges and parenting them with understanding.

Stress

Stress shows in lifestyle. Js are what used to be called "type A" personalities. They stress easily and sail closer to a heart attack. Stress is both beneficial to them and damaging. Too much negative pressure can stress the SJ more than the SP.

Just because the SP does not show himself to be stressed as frequently as the SJ, it does not mean they are not stressed. An SP will stress if they are fearful or failing to meet their goals. Fear itself is so repugnant to them that to be fearful is a stress in itself – let alone the issue that is causing their fear. Fear, in an SP and an NF, is notably compounded by the fear of fear itself.

Control

Js also like to control anyone and anything around them (but some Js more than others). An SJ parent is always unconsciously trying to control the P child, and even feels they <u>must</u> do so. An SP parent will soon feel the J child's attempts at controlling him (or her) and, as they grow older, the J child feels the need of directing the P parent's life. Watch out for eruptive reactions on either side. If you are a P parent of a J child you will not need a timepiece!

Requests

With a P child, requests can come at the last minute. "Mom, I forgot to tell you. I told the teacher I would bring the drinks," says the P child as you leave, already late for school. Calm down. They don't mean to frustrate you. They just forgot to tell you on time. Time is not their prime motivator. Remember? Make yourself a note to ask them, when they come home from school, what they are to take to school the next day, or you may be frustrated or embarrassed.

Routine

Js like routines. Routines bring a sense of comfort to life and a feeling of security. SJs particularly like them. What is today had better be the same tomorrow for the J. The P, on the other hand, is irritated by routines. They rob life of the spontaneity and freedom to execute last minute desires. Try to give each his preference. But remember, everyone must have some routine. Too much routine harms the Js, since they lose all spontaneity. Too little harms the Ps, since they need more in a world where routine is used to keep chaos at bay.

Parents on Parents

You will often hear a J parent saying that another parent "let's her child get away with murder" or "is not raising responsible kids because they are never on time." That other parent is most likely a P. They simply parent on a "need" basis.

The P parent will complain that the J parent is "uptight for no good reason and can't relax." "What's the hurry?" says the P to the J, "You'd think the world was ending tomorrow!"

Parental wars and slights are not going away any time soon. You had best simply be secure in your own method of parenting and in your understanding of your children, and of yourself.

Language

A J child's language sounds like this:

1. "Hurry! We will be late!" ("Kiwinglish": "Come on mate. Rattle your dags!")
2. "It's supposed to be done this way."
3. "You can't do it that way."
4. "Why did you change? We were supposed to go to the cleaners."
5. "Why can't you do it the proper way?"

A P child's language sounds like this:

1. "What's the hurry?" (Australian translation: "What's the hurry, mate?")

2. "Anyway will do." (Australasian: "She'll do.")
3. "I can do it any way I please."
4. "Why can't we change?"
5. Ignore.

(Pardon my "down under" comments.)

Tricky Differences

Understanding how each of the letters (of a temperament profile) can report and predict your child's behavior is helpful. But remember the all important temperament factors that will change the meanings of the letters slightly.

Here are just a few examples:

An E is not exactly the same in each temperament. Remember that. An "I" is quite different when observed in the NF than in the other temperaments. A T in the NT is more intense than a T in the other temperaments.

An "I" followed by an "S" is very, very different from an "I" followed by an "N". The reason for this is that the S is more closely related to the outer world of people and things, while the N is connected to the inner world of intuition. The IN is more intense on the inside.

All these differences among us become easier to remember the more we think about them. In your own way, become a student of yourself and your child, and your lives will dramatically change for the good.

Strengths and Weaknesses

Chapter Twelve ♦

When a man begins to understand himself he begins to live. When he begins to live he begins to understand his fellow men.
~ Norvin Mcgranahan

Hello, Strengths and Goodbye, Weaknesses

Tell Me How!

So far, we have been ignoring an important element in the mix of temperament. Temperament is strengths, or drives, which create the inner forces that mold us. However, what if we don't use these strengths or overuse them? What if we are trying to be someone we are not? If we develop weaknesses how do they affect our temperament?

I live in Colorado. To learn that the state is half mountains and half plains, and then to become familiar with the main mountain ranges, the beautiful forests, and the gin clear rivers, gives you an overall view of its features.

But on a closer look you may notice the devastation caused by the pine bark beetle that has turned beautiful, green forests to brown. You also may become aware of the scars that avalanches have left and the erosion caused by floods and fires. These features altar the landscape, it is true. But the state is still a beautiful state, and the forests gorgeous. Damage has been done by the negative impact of destructive forces, but to focus on them is to miss the true image of Colorado. Colorado is still Colorado, despite the scars.

Are the scars expected when certain features are present? Yes! Rugged snowcapped mountains are likely to feature the scars caused by avalanches. Lodge pole pine forests are likely to be attacked by pine beetles. Erosion is more likely on steep grades. We can expect certain scars, since we have certain geographical features.

So it is with our inner selves. Strengths determine the overall picture – our temperament. Weaknesses that we create detract from it, and certain ones can be predicted because of the "geographical features" of our temperament. To focus on the damage caused by weaknesses is to miss the beauty, but to ignore them is to give free expression to their destructive purposes.

This chapter is going to help us understand how we function in our strengths so that we can better guide and help our children (and ourselves) to live in our strengths and eliminate weaknesses.

Weaknesses Confuse Identification

Weaknesses can create confusion about the identification of our temperament. When weaknesses predominate the picture of our temperament is hazy at best. For example, a passionate NF who is not using that attractive strength makes the identifier say to themselves, "I thought this person was an NF, and NFs are usually passionate; but I can't see it in this person. Who are they, really?" Knowing what weaknesses do to confuse the identification helps us avoid the confusion of seeing both the true beauty of our temperament and its opposite, and being misled.

We can learn to identify the true strengths by seeing their opposites when we realize that all weaknesses are negative and all strengths are positive.

One is the reverse of the other. When a person is living in their weaknesses they are, essentially, malfunctioning.

Where did our weaknesses come from? And what can we teach our children to do so that they do not become victims of their own weaknesses? When they do, undesirable behavior is certain, and they lose sight of how they are made and what fulfills them. To understand weaknesses we must first understand strengths.

Strengths

Where Do Our Strengths Come From?

One of the first things we need to understand before we can deal with strengths is their origin. We are born with them. We don't choose them or even make them our strengths by repeated practice. We can, however, develop or strengthen them with practice, but only if they are part of us in the first place. Strengths (which make up our temperament) are given. They are inborn.

These strengths, gifts, temperament become obvious soon after we are born, and they exist as drives (or urges) in our nature that constitute, at the most basic level, who we are. They determine what we can most effectively become.

Our strengths are what give us our abilities. When developed, they can be seen as talents or special gifts. For example, if a person has a talent with people, behind that talent lies a temperament (a strength) that aids and drives the gift. A desire to please, sensitivity, and empathy would be strengths that support and produce this talent or gift.

Strengths are our temperament! We can call them drives, or strengths, or urges, but we mean the same thing. These give fundamental direction and purpose to our lives. When we use them we are fulfilled. When we don't, we are empty and depressed. We can even feel guilty at times.

Strengths and Weaknesses Operate Like Light and Darkness

This is where I differ from all those who see temperament as an expression of both strengths and weaknesses.

How can a person be given a weakness? A weakness is the failure of a strength in some way. We can't be given a failure. Weaknesses are something we produce. Perhaps we could understand it better this way: being a negative, a weakness can't be given. We create negatives by not correctly using positives.

We can't create shadow without light. As the light fades the shadow takes over the landscape until no light is seen. Weaknesses and strengths, you will find, are related to one another as light is related to darkness — one is the negative of the other. In the picture of life we choose to live in either our strengths (the light) or our weaknesses (the shadows). Strengths dispel related weaknesses like light dispels the shadows. We want to help our children live in the light and dispel the shadows from their lives!

Someone said to me, "Now I get shadows! When I am living in my strengths I am full of light, attractive, and purposeful. When I am living in my weaknesses I am not using my strengths, and my life becomes progressively darker and unattractive." True!

So, for now (more later), my strengths are given, and my weaknesses are created by the lack of the true use of my strengths.

The "Purpose" of Having Strengths Is Purpose

Because strengths drive us, they must have a goal. They must be driving us somewhere. In fact, an examination of our strengths goes a long way in determining our purpose or our goal in life, and in discovering who and what we are. Therefore, strengths equip us and empower us to be what we are intended to be. Failure to know our strengths leaves us with a sad omission in the discovery of who we are and what we are best suited to become. Our children will be helped on the road to success, and to a clearly defined purpose, by being led to the discovery of their strengths. Know your child's purpose in life, and you can guide your child without remaking her (or him) into your own image. You know their purpose when you know their strengths.

Talent is not the same as strengths. Talent is a giftedness to do something. Strengths are the driving force behind our talents. Strengths shape and determine our talents and gifts. If you don't have an inner drive to do something you are usually not good at it, nor do you even desire to do it. The drive of your strength also empowers and fashions your talents and your desires

Purpose Is Direction; Direction Is Purpose

A child or an adult who does not have direction is purposeless and powerless. Any gift, talent, or power that they may have is then easily scattered by the winds of circumstances, and they can wander aimlessly through life. How sad that is.

I have had the privilege to help many who had lost their way in life. Sarah was a bright and rarely-gifted young girl who went to university to study and learn. Parents, take note: she did not know what she wanted to be or do in life, but she had a thirst to learn. That's a good reason to go to university! Because she had never taken a reliable temperament assessment, she chose what others felt best for her and decided to become a graphic designer. She did have observable creative talent, so it seemed right to her and to others.

After receiving her degree, Sarah got a job as a graphic designer. She soon hated every moment of her chosen career. The depression she felt at work (where she was confined to her table) journeyed home with her. Finally, she answered the questions in the Temperament Key, and the result was, to say the least, interesting. Her strengths lay in the area of working to help people and, in particular, to help them reach their potential. Helping someone with their life design is a far stretch from helping create graphic designs. She changed her direction, reentered school to get a degree in counseling, and found her happiness in the direction her strengths were leading her. Her strengths also led her directly to her happiness.

Don't let your children make major decisions in life without knowing who they are and how they are made on the inside. A temperament assessment, and knowledge of their temperament, will identify their strengths. If you start while they are young to help them develop their strengths you will have prepared them for later decisions and developed their talents. By the time they enter college they should know what their drives are and where their temperament is leading them. You will not be manipulating them in any way by developing their strengths since their sense of fulfillment, or its absence, will confirm to them whether the chosen path is right. If they listen to their inner sense of fulfillment they will not be fooled by anyone. Helping them become what they are intended to be, and not some other desired pattern of our own, is our task.

Where Fulfillment Comes From

By now we should fully understand that the use of our strengths also fulfills us. What drives us and what we love are the same as what fulfills us. An unfulfilled child is a problem to himself (or herself) and to others. They misbehave most of the time out of frustration of being molded into something they aren't, or because they have lost direction in their lives. To avoid this loss of direction, encourage your children and develop their strengths. Parenting is all about teaching your children to live in their strengths.

Perhaps the connection of fulfillment to happiness is now no surprise. We cannot be truly happy if we are not feeling fulfilled. Furthermore, since our fulfillment comes from the use of our strengths, it means that we are responsible for our own happiness. That's hard for a child to swallow. They naturally feel that other people or their circumstances are responsible for their happiness or their sadness. It seems heart-warming to blame others for our negative state of mind because it frees us from the feeling of responsibility. Even grown adults fight the idea of taking full responsibility for their own happiness. It may be partly because they were never taught to take full responsibility as children for their happiness.

Teach Them to Recognize Their Fulfillment

Every one of us wants happiness for our children. We can't be happy for them. They must find happiness inside of themselves if they are to be truly happy in all circumstances. We can help them find that happiness if we will help them live and experience the fulfillment and personal high of living in their strengths.

Show your children how using their strengths makes them feel good, and they will have a path to return to when they feel bad. It will be their "recovery" path.

When, for instance, the excitement shows on their faces as they use their strengths, ask them, "Does that make you feel happy?" Pointing out to them where their happiness is coming from helps them find it again. Do this often until you can see they are finding their happiness by using their strengths. When children feel happy, they do not necessarily make the connection of cause to effect. You can help them see what is causing their feelings of happiness. Just seeing your children happy should prompt you to ask them what is making them happy and to guide their thoughts to its source — the inner satisfaction (not the material object, toy, or circumstance that is the superficial cause).

Potential Lives in Our Strengths

Potential also lives in our strengths. Our "best" is the best our strengths can produce. Many of our strengths are not developed because they are lying latent in our makeup. They need encouragement, training, and exercise to grow to their potential. Once you know your child's strengths, use the growth trio that a coach uses for the development of those strengths and find direction. (A good life coach uses the same.) You will give your child a great start in life, and loads of confidence as a bonus.

The growth trio is encouragement (when they use their strengths), training (where training and education can help), and much practice at using their strengths.

You will be paid back for your effort with good behavior by the child who is feeling happily fulfilled.

"What are their strengths?" you ask. The section on the identification of their temperament's strengths – what they are and how to live in them – is in the next chapter.

Now that we understand the nature and purpose of strengths, let's understand our weaknesses.

Weaknesses

We have ourselves to blame for our weaknesses! Sorry, we can't blame our temperament. We are responsible! By the way, don't say "blame." Blame, to me, is a dangerous word. We should not "blame" ourselves for anything since blame is condemnation. To condemn ourselves results in negative judgments against ourselves and can be very damaging.

We should, rather, hold ourselves responsible for our actions. We don't want to blame our children because it lowers their self-esteem. And one of the temperaments (the NF), in particular, is strongly affected by continual inner judgments against themselves. We cannot afford to encourage these inner judgments. We should not let ourselves off the hook when we are responsible either. Blame is condemnation, but accepting responsibility points us positively in the direction of change. Being accountable, without the negative impact of blame, is our goal. We simply are responsible for all of our actions and reactions, and that means for all of our weaknesses, because I hope to convince you that you really are responsible for your weaknesses – as I am for mine.

Weaknesses are the negatives in our lives. We have already said that we can never be given negatives. Positives, yes! Negatives are the malfunctioning of a healthy system. They result in and are caused by mistakes, failures, wrongs and hurts. Weaknesses come from the wrong use or nonuse of strengths. Here's how…

The Three Ways We Create Our Own Weaknesses

My observations have taught me that all weaknesses are a negative reflection of our strengths and we create them in one of three ways:

1. When we don't use our strengths, we create weaknesses in our lives. This should be obvious.

2. When we overuse our strengths we create weaknesses. The overuse of any strength creates a weakness. Overuse creates a negative (not a positive) force.
3. When we use our strengths for wrong purposes (that is, to hurt ourselves or others – any others) we develop weaknesses, and we soon feel the pain of guilt flagging us that something is wrong.

Here It Is in the Real Life Experiences of Each Temperament

The SP Temperament

One of the strengths of the SP temperament is the urge to act freely. They lead the charge in society for individual expression and personal rights. It starts when they are very young and never lets go. The feeling of being inhibited and bound by rules and regulations irks them greatly.

Behind their testing of limits and boundaries is this passion for personal liberty and the sense of self expression it promotes. We should all know that freedom is a drive because we all want freedom for ourselves and others. But the SP wants it more intensely due to their dominant desire for self-expression. Being bound in any fashion can be frustrating to them.

- If the SPs **don't use** their drive to be free, they fall into the unbearable condition of slavery to others who want to rule over them and use them for their own selfish purposes. The SP can then give in to abuse and into being a "nothing." Abuse and lack of freedom destroys the self-image of the SP and plunges them into despair and depression. So nonuse of the strength creates a condition of weakness.
- SPs can also **overuse** their freedom. This can result in license – the license to do whatever they want to do. They then can tread on others and become the abuser instead of the abused. Overuse of the drive for freedom is a self-developed weakness that is destructive to society. It is

also destructive to the SP's own ability to function without guilt and exist peaceably in society. This overuse of freedom also relates closely to a wrong use of the strength, which is the third possible weakness.

- SPs can **wrongly use** their strengths without any respect for others or for others' rights and freedoms. We've just indicated the damage such behavior does to society and the individual. In this case, too, they have used their strength to create a weakness.

The nonuse, overuse, and wrong use of the drive to be free create weaknesses. All are related to the strength, but each is different in nature and in the damage it causes.

Children will exploit the use of this noble drive for their own ends. Freedom seems like candy to the SP children — always enticing them to buck the rules and show pride in their daring, with no remorse when caught. They must be taught to treasure and use their strength in a positive and helpful way. If the SP's drive is suppressed by the parent (who rightly sees the possible damage caused by the wrong use of this strength and is determined to stamp it out of their little SP), the parent will suffer from the SP's inevitable rebellion. Direct it. Don't try to eliminate it. They will eliminate the rebellion when they rightly use their strengths.

The SPs will not be the only ones to use this strength. They merely lead the charge and often teach their friends to act for their own advantage as well. The SP is a formidable leader among children and adults – and a formidable foe if opposed. Monitor the leadership of your child's peer group when you can, and you may see where some of your problems are coming from. If you do, refusing contact with a child who is badly influencing your child is not the only alternative, nor always the most advantageous. Your child will be exposed to this kind of thing as an adult and needs to learn early the wisdom of making the right choices. Encourage your children to take action and change the attitudes of the group where appropriate. Alternatively, show them that the bravery to quit the group is a better alternative than to submit to the group and have the group control you.

The SJ Temperament

Let's observe the nonuse, overuse and wrong use of a strength in the SJ temperament. One of their strengths is careful, cautious behavior. They constantly check the past – theirs and other people's – to see whether it is prudent and safe to do something; and they will lean to the side of caution.

- If they **don't use** their finely tuned "caution antenna," they give themselves cause for worry, and worry damages them and others around them. Nonuse of their caution antenna that is sensitive to past experiences quickly develops the weakness of worry.
- If they **overuse** their caution, they create a case of frozen nerves, and they cannot bring themselves to act. As a result they miss opportunities and are overwhelmed with fear. Again, an overuse of caution creates a weakness, this time stronger than worry – a case of immobilization. For the SJ in particular, either nonuse or overuse of their caution creates a fear of sorts.
- Then there is the **wrong use** of care and caution. Caution is intended to be a pause in action in order to consider the right or wrong of an action, but not to be a tool for getting their way. When they use caution to delay a project that (for selfish reasons) they do not want to happen, they wrongly use their strength.

Nonuse, overuse, or wrong use of care and caution creates weaknesses in our character and our lives, and it affects others around us. You may have already noted that the nonuse or overuse can also be wrong uses of the strengths you posses. It makes sense that nonuse, overuse, or the wrong use of our strengths is somehow going to damage us or others. Help your children to healthy living. Teach them to use their strengths positively.

Children of an over-cautious spirit become timid and afraid of almost any move. They become the butt of the SP child's jokes and taunts. "Where is the daring?" says the little SP. The NT child also resists caution because, in their case, caution inhibits discovery and the urge to make all things new. The SJ child's cautious attitude remains intact most of the time, since the urge to make sure and certain of each move is forceful.

As the parent, are you modeling a too-cautious behavior that is encouraging fear in your child? That's a question for the SJ parent that is too important to neglect.

The NT Temperament

For the NT temperament the same is true. One of their strengths is their insistence on not doing anything that they consider doesn't make sense. Their analytical, or rational, brain is always in gear, and they use it as their prime strength.

- If they **don't use** this strength (which is also a prerequisite to the use of their ingenuity), they develop the weaknesses of shame and a low self-image, and they feel the loss of personal integrity because they are not acting in a way that their inner drive insists is worthy and essential.
- If they **over use** their reasoning powers (a condition they think is impossible), they ruin their relationships because "ice forms in their veins" due to the absence of any consideration for the emotions of others. As a result of this overusing of their rational powers they see themselves as the ultimate judges of right and wrong. However, like all humans, they don't have the knowledge to be ultimate judges. The weakness of pride emerges. The NT's overuse of rationality and reason is probably the main cause of their having difficulty in maintaining healthy relationships. When you keep cooling the emotions of others with reason the relationship fire is put out.
- If they **wrongly use** reason or logic to confuse or frustrate others when truth is not on their side, they show weakness of character. They may be trying to escape embarrassment or avoid admitting they are wrong. This brings a lack of inner integrity and damage to their self-image and to other people. Pride strikes and does its damage, unnoticed until it has corrupted the NT's self-esteem and destroyed other people's trust in them.

Again, nonuse, overuse, or the wrong use of a strength has created a weakness.

NT children often do not seem to notice what their rational, cold approach is doing to themselves and others. They create aloofness and, at times, even an arrogant spirit. It shouts, "I am better than you, and I do not respect your weak mind." They often relate better to adults, but only the adults that win their respect. If your little NT is a lone ranger and seems to be becoming more seclusive, this could be the reason. When they are little, they need to learn to appreciate the other temperaments or they will suffer from the segregation their pride creates.

The only way to reach them and help them is to make them see that to fail to appreciate the other temperaments is to lessen their opportunity to influence others and lessen their success in relationships. Show them it makes no sense to feel they know everything they need to know because they, too, are limited beings like the rest of us. No human can logically assume superiority over all others. Point out that to believe that they are superior doesn't make sense. Other temperaments excel at things the NT does not do well. It takes reason, emotion, tactical skill, and cautious logistical planning to deal with life and its problems. Reason alone seems to be the way to reach them. An emotional appeal is, to them, a resort to weakness – which, of course it is not.

The NF Temperament

For the NF temperament, the same pattern for the development of their weaknesses is obvious. Each temperament has more than one strength. It is hard to choose which is the dominant strength of the NF. Sensitivity, perhaps, rates highest, but for this exercise we will choose an emotional strength related to their idealism.

Passion is one of their strengths. Whatever is ideal to them they are passionate about. This is what makes them so influential because they can present almost any thought or idea with compelling power, skillfully using both reason and emotional appeal. Package reason with skillful application of emotion, and the persuasive power that results is hard to resist.

- If NFs are inwardly passionate about some injustice and they don't express it (**nonuse**), it churns within them, increasing in temperature, and they soon explode over the first thing that irritates them. The suppressed tension must find an outlet. A child can feel that the parent has been unfair and if denied the opportunity to express the pent up passion, the child will implode. They will either heap unreasonable hurt on themselves or seek to hurt the parent in other ways. It provokes obvious weaknesses.
- If they **overuse** their strength, they can overpower others. If in their overuse of their passion they meet resistance from others, their passion can quickly degrade into what appears to be unreasonable anger. Overuse of passion invites, or incites, division.
- Passion can, for many reasons, easily be **wrongly used**. Passionate expressions can be used to overpower and get their own way. It can also become a repeated outburst in search of revenge that creates disconnectedness in relationships. Passion can also be used to defend what they know is indefensible. You can probably think of many other reasons where passion can be wrongly used.

Watch carefully for the use of passion when your children clearly know that they are wrong. They are simply trying to get their own way or appease a wrong application of their emotions. NFs are tender of heart and because they have no defense against being hurt (especially the introverted ones), they often get emotional and passionate in self-defense.

It is easy for the NF to transfer the success that their passionate outbursts can achieve into using their passion falsely to get their own way. Don't let them fool you although, with this temperament, it is best to give the child the benefit of any doubt as to motives and purpose. If you end up treating them unfairly you may bring the house down on yourself. For the NF child, more trouble can brew in the kettle of unfair treatment than you can imagine. Treat them fairly, and expect the same in return.

It will be most difficult to do the right thing all the time with the NFs. They are secretive and private, and full of people skills that they can use freely to manipulate adults. They actually find out that most adults do not have the same highly effective intuitive skills that they themselves possess. I don't want to give the impression that they are little "manipulative demons." Mostly they seek to please and love, and they find their fulfillment in these strengths, but in their weaknesses they can be manipulative. Parent your NF with loads of love and approval, and you will not have them frequently living in their weaknesses.

I hope I have demonstrated that, in all temperaments, the nonuse, overuse or wrong use of our strengths creates weaknesses.

How to Get Rid of Our Weaknesses – Quickly!

Wouldn't you love to know how to get rid of your weaknesses — fast? I can tell you how. Since our weaknesses are self-made, and since they are the nonuse, overuse or wrong use of our strengths, we can dismiss them with warp speed. It's all a matter of what we focus on. Sit on the edge of your seats for this one.

Focus on Your Strengths, Not Your Weaknesses

We must learn that when we focus on our strengths we magnify them. Anything we focus on we magnify.

When we focus on our weaknesses we magnify them, too. Moreover, we give them the power to control us. Then we can never get rid of them, because the more we focus on them the bigger they get and the stronger they become. We wrestle with them, exert a gigantic pressure from a strong self-will (if we have one), or even pray for their disappearance. But they stay to haunt us because we continue focusing on them. We were not built to function well when we focus on our weaknesses, or on any problem for that matter. We are built to focus on our strengths and on solutions. Our true powers are in our positive abilities, not in our negative actions!

It seems contrary to common sense not to focus on what is bothering us. We instinctively want to focus on the problem and get rid of it. Children do it automatically because what is bothering them gets their attention. Without consideration, they focus on what is irritating them. However, remember the principle "Whatever we focus on we magnify." Whatever we give our attention to is granted more space in the brain. Blood flow increases to that area and the negative emotions that are produced by the weakness are also stimulated. If we continue, obsessed with the removal of our weakness, we, in effect, make it impossible to remove it.

The children who throw tantrums are often focusing on what they don't have, and the focus magnifies the feeling of loss. They quickly become obsessed and overwhelmed by their negative feelings. Whatever they focus on, they magnify. They throw themselves on the floor and wail bitterly as they obsess over their loss. Change the focus! Yes! As parents, one of our successful tools in dealing with tantrums (for the NF, in particular) is to change the focus. Distract them. Attempt to change the focus: first with love and in positive ways. Resorting to condemnations, punishments, and attempts to shame them renders all positive methods, if you choose to use them later, ineffective. We, unfortunately, resort first to the opposite of love to gain control, since love is the last thing we are feeling or thinking about in the seismic waves of their tantrums. We are embarrassed (if others are around) and determined to fire our most potent ammunition first for a quick victory. Negative ammunition turns out, most of the time, to be the least effective ammunition.

What is the best thing to focus on? Answer: Focus on the strength that is the opposite of the weakness that we are observing in their behavior. In other words, focus on the strength that they are not using and that created the weakness by its absence in the first place. This is why knowing the strengths of the temperaments is the easy way to guide us to the right place for our children's focus.

The correct focus is always upon the strength that belongs to one's temperament, the one that they are clearly not using. Since this is so important in the success of parenting, both for the child's benefit and for the parent's stress reduction, let's see it in a few examples:

- An NF is easily hurt and can lose friends, becoming lonely because anger (either externally expressed or internally suppressed) results from being hurt. Anger does not win friends. They are the temperament that loves with a passion, and love is the opposite of anger and revenge. However, when they are hurt it turns to anger, and it may then become clear that the NF is acting with revenge (not love) and repelling their friends. Anger and bitterness, in this case, is the weakness caused by not using their loving nature to build successful relationships. Learning to love those who despise you is a hard lesson, but the one that will make your little NF into a master of himself (self-control) and the envy of all who truly love goodness and kindness. Furthermore, people love to be loved, and love is a power that can turn the tables in even the most spiteful situations. This is not an easy fix, but it is a *certain cure* for a little heart that is turning bitter and resentful because it is hurt. Teach them to use love and kindness in return for hurt. When NFs do this, they live in their strength and it strengthens their relationships.

- Let's say an NT child is defying your authority and refusing to do things your way. Let's also assume that what you want makes sense to you and is a good thing. The NT's strength is for them to be reasonable and do what makes sense. Sit the child down and explain how what you want makes sense for them, not for you. Perhaps you can show them that the world has other people in it beside themselves and, if they want their freedom to be ingenious and creative, they had best (at times) do what makes sense for others. Being cooperative is the way to be given more freedom, which makes sense, even if the task might not. Teach them that their freedom depends on other people and the restrictions others can impose, so why not try for the greatest amount of freedom by considering others and their rules — rules that make a society run smoothly. Remember that, with an NT, it is reason alone that reaches them. With an NF it is reason plus love and approval.

- Let's surmise that your SJ is being disobedient and stubborn. Since their strength is to be responsible, reliable, and cooperative, what you are observing is clearly the opposite. Help guide them back to their strength. Show them what they are doing to themselves and others, and remind them they will never be happy if they don't live in the reward of their strengths. Why are they being uncooperative? Find out what is causing this behavior and address it. Then lead them to use their strength again. Give them an opportunity to be responsible and to show you that they are your best, most reliable helpmates. Let them feel the inner happiness of doing what they do best.

- Perhaps your SP is sad, morose, and appears depressed – an unlikely condition for an SP and, therefore, one that should get your attention. The opposite of sadness is joy, which (together with excitement and optimism) is a strength of the SP. They are obviously not in their strength. Ask what will make them feel happy and seek to restore their joy. Take them to places they enjoy. Let them live in the excitement of the moment and show what they are made of. Encourage their impulsive tendencies in a way that will be constructive and bring joy. If they show signs of happiness again, you have succeeded; and the sadness has proved to be easily dispersed. If they still don't snap out of their depressed state, persist. As with all temperaments, if they do not come out of depression, get help, since their depression may be deeper and require more care. The parenting skill to remember is to help them to use their strength. The lack of use or wrong use of their strength is the way they have fallen into their weakness.

In all cases, you must focus on the strength and get them to focus on it, allowing the weakness to fade on its own.

We can also simply try to distract their attention onto something else other than their strength. This helps, but does not cure. It helps because it changes the focus from the weakness to some other thing that interests them. However, the weakness remains, and will, until they return to their strengths. Its power lurks and waits for another opportunity if they continue to entertain their weakness. However, if we focus on the positive strength we magnify it. Remember?

Magnifying the Strength Weakens the Weakness.
We have, in this case, doubled our effectiveness. First, we have changed focus; and second, we have focused on something that diminishes the weakness.

Gustave, a young man in his mid to late teens had lost direction in life (a weakness). He had no knowledge of his strengths or his purpose and, as a result, became easy prey for life's downers. Depression, drugs, and the increasing urge to check out of reality and into a state where he didn't feel the ache of emptiness were now his reality because his emptiness was too much for him to bear.

When I first met him, I was impressed with this seemingly pleasant, socially composed individual who gripped my hand confidently and smiled to assure me of who he was not. He was hiding, even in his social encounters. The mask was an example of his desire to please everyone. It was also his ability to be whoever he desired to be — ". . . all things to all people." But I was to learn that he wasn't happy with who he was. My reaction was to wonder why he had come to see me. What could I do to help? He told me (from behind the same mask) that he was addicted to alcohol. Usually I have some kind of feedback as to who is talking to me, but this young man had painted an impressive facade that fooled me and had fooled others.

I asked him to answer the Temperament Key, knowing that I could get a better glimpse inside of him, so to speak. He was an introverted NF. Introverted NFs have good people skills and can be very private people who don't want others to know who they really are. Gustave's temperament explained his social skills and gave me a clue to his hidden life. His parents, two wonderful people in their own right, had simply not understood how to help him find himself. Not knowing his own strengths, he had no knowledge of how they were his natural boost. His parents told me they had provided, even over provided, for his needs, but they did not know that they had failed to realize that he had no understanding of what he should be, who he really was, and how to find his own satisfaction. This lack of understanding was his downfall.

We can't go through life successfully without knowing ourselves. If we do, the journey can be a disaster. The earlier we begin to learn our natural strengths, the better able we are to find our way to success, happiness and fulfillment.

Gustave was focusing on his every failure and weakness, and stressing over them. He would sit alone, with his negative feelings flooding his mind while he ruminated on them excessively. Soon, the pain of being nothing in his own eyes overwhelmed him. Then he would feel compelled to find relief in the alcohol he didn't even like, but which dulled the pain and wafted him into a clouded world of tingling nerves and pleasant softness.

If only he had learned as a child that he had strengths, and that the exercise of those strengths would make him feel great. They were the natural "high" that he longed for. They could fulfill him and give him a true feeling of worth that he could activate whenever he wanted. Those great feelings were the payback for using his strengths.

Children must be taught to focus on their strengths because, when they do, they feel the payback and learn the path to finding these feelings that bless them. Life must have meaning, and meaning banishes emptiness. The ancient philosopher who wrote the book of Ecclesiastes understood this when he said, "All is emptiness under the sun;" emptiness, if you haven't found your purpose, that is. If we focus on our emptiness, our worthlessness, our failures, we will reap the result — a magnified world of hurt. (It can become a form of brain lock.) When you first meet a person, you may have no idea of what is inside the cover that protects their fragile self-esteem. That cover is never the true person. It never tells you the full story.

The ability to help ourselves is learned best in childhood, and it should be in place by the teen years to save the teenager from excessive swings of emotion without the ability to self-control. It was a long road, at this late stage of childhood, to lead Gustave back to meaning and purpose, and the use of his natural highs: his strengths. But we succeeded, and he started a new, promising, self-controlled life.

Don't focus on their weakness or their failure or their loss. Whatever we focus on, we magnify. Remember, that also means, whatever we don't focus on, such as a strength, is not in the conscious mind, and we are operating without it — out of mind, out of power.

For something to control your mind and actions, it must be in your conscious mental vision. Your weakness is, at that moment, gone when you focus on the use of your strength. Even if it lies quietly in your subconscious mind, it can be dismissed again with equal speed if it happens to invade your consciousness again. Teach your children to focus on their strengths. They may not get the theory behind the action, but they will learn something more important: namely, it feels good to use their strengths rightly.

One more example may help. If you use your strength – let's say, for an NF, the drive to be kind – then unkindness is not operating in your life at that moment. You are being kind and thinking kind thoughts. Then, let's say you have an urge to lash out at someone who has just irritated you. If you focus on your irritation with that person, your weakness which you have now created is fed and fueled. It grows, and you may not be far away from trying to hurt the cause of your irritation.

Suddenly, you become aware of your irritation and identify it as a weakness that you don't want to control your life. So you call up the drive to be kind and focus on returning good for evil. This confounds your assailant and shows him that his irritating actions have no effect on you and that you (not he) are in control of this situation. As long as he can't hurt you, you are impenetrable and beyond his reach. He is the weak one, not you. As you focus on these thoughts your desire to hurt diminishes, and your desire to be in control of yourself and to be kind has magnified. Your weakness has gone. It works as long as you can focus on the good and not the bad.

That's the point. Develop your strengths so that, when you need them, they are healthy and ready for action. When you focus on them, they are at your service.

Teaching our children the experience of returning good for evil is the starting place. We then need to help them learn how to understand what is really going on when we maintain control of ourselves and exercise our positive strengths. Model it for them. Their mirror neurons will help you be an effective teacher.

Positive Reactions Lead to Our Strengths

Your strengths are positive, and your weaknesses are negative. Positive reactions to whatever happens to you will naturally lead to living in your strengths, while negative reactions lead to living in your weaknesses.

This is another easy way of understanding how to live in your strengths. It's easy to teach people that all they have to do is to be positive. If you don't know whether your children are living in their strengths or weaknesses, watch their reactions to the pressures in their lives. Ask yourself, "Are these negative or positive reactions? Do they see the silver lining or the black cloud?" This will give you a workable guide.

Always lead your children to positive actions and reactions to help build strengths. If they have been negative for some time, it will take a while, but consistent help and encouragement will persuade them to try and, when they make the journey, you both will be forever thankful. The SP is easiest to teach to live in a positive lifestyle. The SJ is the hardest. The NT is comparatively easy, and the NF is difficult if they have not yet learned to control their emotions.

Wilma, a teenager, had a compelling and well-practiced urge to make herself pay for the things she thought she had done wrong, and even things that she considered were only wrong thoughts in her mind. Whatever was a weakness or a failure, she atoned for with self-punishment. She cut herself and, in other ways, physically damaged herself to inflict this punishment. Perhaps her most common way of punishing herself was to deprive herself of something she was longing to get. She did not think she deserved pleasure, and removing it would somehow (she believed) teach her a lesson.

Wilma's parents had no idea that she was cutting herself. She had segregated herself from her family to an extent that screened this behavior from notice. She loved her family, but, unknown to her, she was on a slippery slope that would cause everyone hardship. The parents had not detected, even in her early childhood, that she was withdrawing and living a hidden life of self- punishment. It had been a pattern of hers as long as she could remember. All concerned simply did not understand what was going on in their lives or what to do about it.

Once it had surfaced (which it did, of course, when her mother noticed a cut and pushed to find out that her daughter had many, apparently self-inflicted, cuts on her body,) she was immediately sent to a psychologist who treated her. But, due to her non-cooperation, he was not able to help her significantly. When she came to me she was withdrawn and resistant.

I have often thought that a coach's number one quality should be the ability to win the confidence and the respect of the client. So, having gained her trust and confidence, she opened up and the inner story of her self-atoning actions spilled out to me. We were then able to freely talk about them. She answered a Temperament Key, which revealed an INFJ who was very protective of her privacy and, as is typical, given to low self-worth, self-blame and the nursing of a lot of hurt.

A low self-esteem opens the door wide to self-blame and to a slew of weaknesses. Wilma was very gifted, but gift alone is not able to quell the feelings of uselessness that low self-esteem causes. We started a pattern of positive responses to teach that using positive responses to pressures brought healthier and more fulfilling feelings than using negative responses. A long history of hurt feelings, produced by negative reactions of self-blame and worthlessness, had dug a deep trench in her mind and required a strong effort to fill the trench and dig a new path of pleasant feelings and thoughts. Understanding her temperament helped her understand where her feelings were coming from, and that gave her an immediate guide to recovery.

Every positive reaction on her part led to the use of her strengths. When she felt she had failed again, she would now say to herself, "Failure is an invitation to step up to a new level of performance. Thanks for the invitation!"

Two of her strengths were seeing the possibilities in her future and searching for her full potential. In this response, she found herself striving for her full potential and loving it. It was a complete reversal of her mental attitudes, and it changed her whole life.

Let's remember, positive responses lead to the use of our strengths. When we use our strengths, we are not in our weaknesses. We are where the road slopes upward, not downward into worthlessness. Our strengths also develop and grow stronger, and we can even feel the positive difference in our own spirits. For a growing and developing NF, this feedback is essential to being able to reinforce their optimism about themselves and others.

Getting rid of our weaknesses is a positive game, not a negative struggle with our thoughts and our sickly habits. Again, let me say, this game should start early in life, teaching our children to be positive. Parents, it is our charge.

Actions Reveal Our Inner State

When parenting our children, we often excuse ourselves (from our failure to notice what is really happening inside them) by reminding ourselves we can't see inside. That is a real fallacy and a common excuse. Actions are the product of inner thoughts and feelings. We, as parents, should accept it as our prime responsibility to ask why our children are acting in a negative way. Why is she depressed and sad? Why is he not doing better at school or at the things he loves? Why is she spending so much time on her own? And then we should ask, "What inner belief or pattern of thought could be leading to these actions and non-actions?" If we don't know, we then need to ask a life coach, a counselor, or a wise friend. This book will help us learn what to look for in temperament – which is our best guide.

The same principle that is observed in the world of physics works in this search for an answer to what people feel on the inside. Every effect has a cause. The effect is the action you observe with your five physical senses. The cause is an adequate thought pattern that results in the action or non-action you observe. Ask yourself what pattern of thought could be the cause of such behavior: "What might my child be thinking?" Better still, "What might have caused this change in the way my child thinks or believes?" Most of the time the answer will be easy to find.

In Wilma's case you might have asked, "Why is she so withdrawn and sad?" It could be because she had trouble with her friends. Maybe she was depressed. Or maybe her friends had upset her. You could have gathered the reasons you could think of and gone to talk with her. You could tell her you love her and were wondering if she was sad because of this reason, or this, or this. She would then know that her condition was being diagnosed and that you cared enough to try to help her.

Most temperaments (except, perhaps, the NT) will be touched by this and will most probably tell you at least a little of what is bothering them. Continue helping them make positive responses to all their issues (including a root cause like "I'm not worth much, anyhow.") Help them change their thoughts. Reinforce their worth and shower them with love, and they will begin to be positively affected. Temperament will also play an important role in recovery. All you have to do is to focus on the strengths of their temperament, knowing that the more you can get them to use their strengths, the more their weaknesses and downward spiral will reverse. Their strengths will do the job for them, and you.

I can't emphasize this enough. The way out of our weaknesses is to use our strengths.

Weaknesses Frustrate and Destroy Our Strengths

When we don't use our strengths they atrophy.

One of Sid's strengths was his people skills. He cared for others and always tried to be helpful. Another strength was the sensitivity he used as a kind of "radar" in social settings. He would always be super sensitive to what he saw was happening and what he sensed intuitively that others were feeling (and even thinking). He felt it was uncanny for him to feel this way, and he often wondered if he was normal since he certainly was not like the other boys. They took pride in hurting other people and showing bravado and speaking demandingly and coarsely to others. (They obviously felt it was a display of their maleness and their strength.) Sid was only fourteen and his kind treatment of others (especially girls) had even stirred some derogatory statements about his manhood from them. This really hurt him, and he was at a loss to understand this. He tried to avoid the girls, and avoidance became a passion.

Boys would also test his courage and would find Sid had a temper that, when it flared, was something to avoid. He didn't like his "soft" image, and he determined to toughen it up. His father encouraged him to learn gymnastics and boxing, and he started reading books on self-defense and body building. At some of these he even excelled.

But for some reason, his mother (although she didn't say anything about it) was less enthusiastic than his father.

Sid's ego had been seriously hurt. He lived daily with the pain of who he was (and wasn't) and he determined to change it. The urge to please was so strong that he reacted automatically with care and concern for others. But then, realizing his kindness was showing, he tried to be "tough." Kindness seemed too soft for a male. This was his observation, sharpened by the actions of his friends.

He finally completed his new image to the best of his ability. He would not care about the girls, and he determined to simply ignore them, making sure he wasn't caught in their company. That would be easy, he surmised. The words of mockery from the girl who hadn't appreciated his soft caring attitude still tormented and deeply hurt him.

Sid decided to enter more tough sports to show that he was a force to be reckoned with as far as boys were concerned. So he added football to his agenda. He developed his muscles (for which he won a medal that he wore to deter criticism of his kind nature) more. He needed a macho image and found anger helped to isolate him from talk of his being too kind or soft. So he set his jaw in public and appeared angry and distant. Finally, Sid practiced being inconsiderate and, although not coarse, at least gruff. Somehow he couldn't bring himself to be coarse. He at last thought he had succeeded in making the man he felt he had to be. If only someone had noticed earlier and taken him into their confidence.

Boys who have an F in their personality profile are in the minority of males and swim against the current of popular expectations. Males are expected to be "masculine" and tough.

There was, however, one noticeable problem of which Sid slowly became aware. He did not feel happy. Whenever he went out in public he had to put on his "tough" image, and it felt both good and bad. He wasn't happy, since he was sort of angry when he was with others. The anger certainly did help him wear his uncomfortable mask though. Something was happening to him that was unseen and undetected by him but obvious to others. He wasn't the boy he used to be. He had lost his helpful demeanor. What some thought to be his strength of personality had been replaced by what they thought was a weakness, but no one told him so. In the meantime, his strengths were atrophying from a lack of use and attention.

Sid's enlightenment came from an unlikely source. A skinny, short male (who he had once tried to help and be kind to) actively sought his friendship. Jack was the opposite of masculine bravado and Sid had been kind to him because he felt the pain of Jack's being avoided by other teenagers. This was a complication he had not planned for, nor did he recognize it. Now he had to be Dr. Jekyll and Mr. Hyde. His new friend was needy and mentally stimulating, both of which attracted Sid's attention. They would study together. He recognized new feelings when he was with Jack. They were pleasant feelings, and Jack (without knowing what he was doing) encouraged the sensitive, kind, loving nature of Sid to resurface. As Sid used the strengths of his temperament again, they began to grow, and he felt the fulfillment that using our strengths always brings.

Certain side effects of Sid's return to being Sid was a loss of respect for his father who was still trying to make his son a "man after his own image." The respect vanished, because the evidence of who he was on the inside was too compelling to ignore, and because living in his strengths was so rewarding, comfortable and peaceful.

Unfortunately, his father did not know who his son was; nor did his mother. But at least his mother welcomed the old Sid in his reincarnation. If only they had known. If only they had encouraged him to be what he was, the painful loss of his strengths and hurtful wallowing in his weaknesses would have been avoided. His long struggle with his self-image would have been, for the most part, avoided. He placed no blame at their feet – only at his own for not being what his inner guide and conscience had told him to be. A low self-image made him blame himself instead of others.

Parents, let me suggest that if only Sid's parents had made an attempt to intervene when Sid's behavior changed so dramatically, they and he would have felt a deeper bond. His mother could have, even without understanding, supported him, and his father could have avoided his Pygmalion goals. However, hindsight is usually not fair. And Sid's attempt to take responsibility for himself was, for him, both the right and helpful path.

The story that is unfolding in your child is complicated most of the time, and you may shrink from the task of dealing with it. It is not so difficult. Ask questions. Follow the leads you get and you will, without much effort or foreknowledge, uncover the facts about your children that will endear them to you and solve the rest of the problem. If you have discovered their temperaments via the Child's Temperament Key in this book, you already have your best guide to success.

Lessons We Have, Hopefully, Learned

- Focusing on our strengths feeds them.
- Our inner life needs nutrition just as our bodies do.
- Starve your powers and you become weak and listless of spirit: a false, malfunctioning, lost identity.
- Our happiness is dependent on exercising our strengths and feeling their effects on our spirit.
- Living in the fullness of our strengths is living to our maximum potential.

Chapter Thirteen ♦

I want, by understanding myself, to understand others. I want to be all that I am capable of becoming.
~ Katherine Mansfield

Developing Your Child's Strengths (Yours, Too!)

Becoming a Super Parent

Our main goal is to prepare our children for adulthood.

Parenting is preparing our children for adulthood – something we often forget in the stress and strain of the task. This means understanding their temperaments and helping them develop their strengths. We don't want our children growing up and living in their weaknesses.

We also want them to face difficulties in their journey to adulthood, and learn to exercise the right strengths to overcome their troubles. Developing and honing those strengths will help them grow into their best. Whichever is used most —strengths or weaknesses — will become strong. We must parent our children to become the best they can be by focusing on developing their strengths, thus saving ourselves and them heartaches on the way.

It might occur to you that if we are to prepare our children for adulthood we may choose to make a few adjustments to our own self-development, as well. "A little child will lead you" seems to come to mind!

In this Section We Will Ask: What Are Their Main Strengths?

Understanding Primary and Secondary Strengths

A question I often get is, "Do we have any of the strengths that are listed as belonging to another temperament, or are our strengths limited to our own temperament?" The short answer is that we often do display strengths that are native to another temperament, but as our secondary strengths.

Another common question asks, "Are our strengths a result of our conditioning as children (the parents we had and the culture we were raised in, for example); and were our parents the main influence in determining our strengths" Some believe that, if they were, we could end up with strengths different from our temperament's strengths – possibly the strengths of our parent's temperaments. However, if this were so, knowing the strengths of our temperament will be of no real benefit.

The short answer is that our native strengths are the drives of our given temperament (not the ones we may have developed as our secondary strengths) and can be modified, but not changed, by environmental influences. On the other hand, we may have not used our main strengths and, therefore, they have been minimized. However, each temperament's strengths hold the promise of our greatest fulfillment, and no other will satisfy us like those that are inborn.

Hardwired or Environmentally Conditioned

Let's begin by saying that our strengths (or drives) are hardwired into our human makeup. Temperament is not about our conditioning or our parental influence. It is about our strengths — our hardwired urges — that all of us are given and that we display from birth. We weren't created with a blank slate. Even babies show elements of the temperament they grow up to display.

Environment can modify, but not change, our basic temperament's strengths. What happens to our given strengths if they have been masked by, say, the strengths of our parents? Do they just fall away? Or can they have resurgence and ascend to dominance later in our development? If they are our native strengths, the latter seems likely and logical.

We may admit that the strengths we have that are native to our temperament have not been used, or that we do not even know they belong to our temperament. Not using them or knowing them, however, doesn't change the drives we posses. It simply means they lie latent in us and await our discovery of them. I have found many, when they find their temperament, also discover their strengths for the first time and attest they have found their real selves.

The best conclusion seems to be that we can develop secondary strengths, say from our parents, but our given, native strengths are still there and await their renaissance.

When we read our own strengths as I have listed them under the temperaments in this chapter we may also feel that some of them sound foreign to our nature. They can feel that way because we haven't used them much, or because that particular strength is not a dominant strength among our native strengths. Remember that not all the strengths listed under each temperament are found in every person of that temperament, or in equal amounts, but we will find that most strengths listed under our temperament will be recognizable to us as the drives of our given nature, and they will be verified by us. There is a great deal of variety in each person of the same temperament. No one is able to fool us. We verify our strengths; no one else does.

In thirty years of coaching I have found an impressive degree of accuracy in temperament testing that makes believers out of those I have tested. I have also found cases of false diagnosis, which can happen in any

profession or field of applied knowledge. These, upon accurate diagnosis, have found their strengths to be correctly described and listed.
Why, then, do we say that certain strengths belong to a certain temperament? Because the study of people with these temperaments finds that they commonly report them, and they find greater satisfaction in using them as opposed to using other strengths – a true indication that they belong.

People often don't see themselves fitting into well-defined boxes. They don't. There is, of course, more to a person than temperament. They also develop likes and dislikes from what they feel they should be and what others tell them they should be. These can cloud our self understanding and create fear of identifying our true preferences.

Temperament is simply discovering the similarities that exist among us in our basic drives. We report these as our dominant preferences. However, this discovery will tell us so much about our given strengths and our makeup that we can't afford not to know.

Personally Verified

As we have just said, temperament studies are validated by the persons themselves, not by some predetermined rules. No one will be able to force on you what you don't validate yourself. Temperament is, in a sense, the default mechanism that drives our systems, and under stress, for example, we will naturally revert to the preferences of our temperament. You will know which is your default mechanism, or temperament, when you hear it; and some of your strengths (or drives) you will find you have already noted as "typically you." For you and your child, the identification of strengths will be a profound help to life and to parenting.

Adopting Other Strengths

Let's look at this question of primary and secondary strengths in a little more detail. We are capable of any strength from any temperament, to a degree. If we work at developing a drive that belongs to another temperament we should be able to develop a fair representation of it.

However, two things need to be understood. First, our own temperament's drives will fulfill us at a level the drives of another temperament will not. We can find satisfaction in any achievement, but the ones native to our temperament create a satisfaction and a sense of personal comfort and worth that must be experienced to be understood. I have called strengths that we have developed and that are native to another temperament "secondary strengths." Strengths native to our own temperament I call "primary" or "native" strengths.

Another discovery you will make is that primary strengths – the strengths native to your temperament – will lead you to being the best that you, as a person, can be. You will know this from the success and inner power your primary strengths generate, the way they comfortably fit, and the feeling of being truly you. Secondary strengths will have weaker drives. They will allow you to be successful, but not to the full extent possible as with your native drives.

Focusing on our primary strengths makes good sense, and utilizing all other strengths, as needed, also makes sense. But to reveal what you are made to be, and where you will function at your best and reach your highest potential is the cry and purpose of this book. That goal makes most sense, so focus on your temperament's strengths. This will be the path to helping your children be their best.

Strengths Lead to Potential and Avoid Undesirable Behavior

Developing our children's strengths is the first step in leading them to their potential and in avoiding undesirable behavior. When we exercise our strengths we feel happy, fulfilled and satisfied. This is a key understanding to developing a child's potential. Producing this internal happiness can be a powerful deterrent to unwelcome behavior as well. Prevention is better than cure, so study your child's strengths and encourage their use in positive and healthy ways.

You will find it a pleasant task to watch your children use their strengths as you praise their efforts and show them ways to be more successful. Instead of the conversations between parents always reverting to a report on bad behavior and discussing disciplinary measures, you will find yourselves talking mainly about good behavior and how to grow your children's positive drives. In this *positive parenting pattern* you will be observing their progress, or lack of it, and training them to be who they were meant to be. Knowing their strengths, and observing their fulfillment, you will find confidence and confirmation that your parenting path is the right one. You will not be using a one-size-fits-all method of parenting, but one designed for each child's uniqueness.

When children are engaged in using their strengths constructively, they are not engaged in undesirable behavior. That's an advantage almost too obvious to mention. In the task of encouraging their strengths, you will often be involved in returning your children from negative displays of their temperament to positive, healthy functioning as you develop them for adulthood. How we do this is discussed later. It is the skill of training them to use and develop their strengths according to how they have been made that we will focus on here.

Five Simple Tasks that Will Help Develop Your Child's Strengths Should Fill Your Parental Day.

1. Identify your children's strengths. Use the following list as an aid in identification. It will show you what to look for.
2. Genuinely accept and respect all the positive attempts they make to live in their strengths. Don't ignore their healthy efforts. If you do, they will disconnect from you and puzzle over why they seem not to be able to impress you.
3. Grant them freedom to be themselves, namely, the persons they are created to be, and cease all Pygmalion efforts on your part.
4. Positively reinforce their successes in displaying their strengths. This will assure progress. It's called positive reinforcement. No doubt you have heard of that before.
5. Model your own strengths, not your weaknesses. Be who you are created to be.

About the Following List of Strengths by Temperament

Following is a list describing the main strengths of each temperament as observed by students of temperament covering the period of history from its first mention (Ezekiel, 580 BC) to Keirsey, and others who are still pursuing their studies of Personology today. My own observations can be seen in how I view these strengths and in their selection.

I first list the strength as seen in adults, and then make comments relevant to its appearance in children. However, there is little essential difference between the child and adult versions of these strengths, as you will see.

All strengths are positives; all weaknesses are negatives. These are the native strengths that children will grow up to exhibit, and in which they will find their ultimate fulfillment. Focus on the strengths, not the weaknesses! I'll never grow tired of reminding you of that.

The Temperaments' Orientation to Time

My study in the counseling and coaching room over the years has convinced me that the strengths are primarily oriented to time. Therefore, I will attempt to help you understand this adaptation. We are creatures that inhabit a universe that is governed in the physical realm by laws of physics. We are created to live in this physical environment, so our inner selves must also relate to its demands. Two basic laws of our physical environment deal with time and space. We must live related to time, and are trapped in its conditions. We are also creatures of space, limited to one place at a time, and we cannot escape. We should expect, then, that our inner lives will show a relationship to time and space as well as our outer lives. And I believe they do.

Time and space limit us in virtually all things. Our virtual world (our minds) can escape this realm of time and space in thoughts, dreams and imagination, but we still must live in the world of real time and space. Two of the temperaments relate us to "outer" space (the Ss); and two to "inner" space (the Ns). They also relate us in different ways to time, and empower us to live in our natural time orientation.

Because time is linear and we experience it in passing, we view it in three dimensions: future time, present time, and past time. Three of the temperaments choose one of these dimensions and focus mainly on it. The NF focuses mainly on the future, the SP on the present, and the SJ on the past. The person who focuses mainly on the future lives differently from the person who focuses mainly on the past, and is powered by different drives. Wherever our focus is, there our life is. Whatever we focus on will also intrigue us, excite us, motivate us, and cause us concern. So the way we look at time largely defines the "look" of our temperament.

What about the NT? Their focus is not on the past, present, or future; but on the project or task they are engaged in and they are quite unrelated to the passage of time until they finish the task. Then they wake up, as it were, and say to themselves, "What time (or day) is it?" If we had to choose between past, present, and future for the NT, we would have to go with the future, since they are the far-seeing temperament that plans and strategizes about their interests and concerns.

Each temperament bears the stamp of its focus on time in its strengths. We will attempt to arrange the strengths of each temperament from their strongest relation to time to the least, and discuss that relation as we discuss the strengths of each temperament.

Suggestion:

Copy the sections on your child's (or children's) temperament, and attach them to your refrigerator door for frequent reference until they are written permanently on your mind. You may wish to write only the bold headings of the strengths, and you will have a purse/pocket-sized list.

I have tried to make this section of the book a complete reference to the strengths of each temperament and to act as a handy reference.

Let me introduce you to …

The Native Strengths of the SP Temperament

If you have determined that your child is an SP temperament, run through this list of strengths and highlight the ones you can already see. Of course, some strengths you will be able to see, and some will be hidden from you due to being undiscovered by you or your child, unexercised, or both.

Health is found in living happily in our native strengths. The ones that are unseen by you in your children may be able to be confirmed, or otherwise, by observing your children when you design ways for them to use an unseen strength. Children lock into the moment when they are using their strengths, and you should be able to observe their focus and pleasure. Repeated use and observation will encourage development of the strength, and you will clearly see when your children are fulfilled and happy in the positive use of their strengths.

Remember that not all SP strengths are present in each SP, but most of them are. Likewise, for the other temperaments. Also, some will be more dominant than others. If you scan the other temperaments you will probably see that your little SP has some of those strengths as well. They are present as secondary strengths, as we have already noted. If the child has been using a secondary strength often, it may have become a distinct part of his (or her) behavior. There is nothing wrong with this, but we should still encourage the true SP strengths, since this is where the child's greatest fulfillment is to be found.

An excellent way to know your children and note their progress is to make your own notes on the use of their strengths as you see them develop. Keep a journal on your children. This way you will be able to more quickly spot the weaknesses that will show up from time to time and take appropriate action. Later, this journal can help your children understand themselves, and they can read an interesting history of the development of their strengths.

Now, proceed through each of the strengths and become familiar with them.

Here Is a List of the Main SP Strengths

Orientation to Time: Lives in the Present Moment

Whether child or adult, the SP is related to the present and lives in it with gusto and abandon. If you watch an SP, you will notice how they seem to drain the last drop of excitement and pleasure out of every present moment. If asked to sit still and do nothing, they fidget, fuss, and quickly become bored. They will find a way to inject action and fun into the moment as if they are compelled by some internal force to rescue the moment from waste. For the child, this can result in distracting behavior that can lead to destructive behavior. Their inner drive to find excitement and movement squeezes whatever it can out of the present.

Seldom are SPs chained to the past or excessively concerned about the future. If they live effectively in the present, they feel that the future will take care of itself. To them it is a downer to live in the frustrations of the past. Therefore, they don't plan or prepare much (as does the SJ), nor do they treasure traditions and connections with the past. They want to be "all there" in the present, and, when they are distracted by past or future events, they feel cheated out of a valuable moment of time. The external world is their natural home, and this is where they find so much of their enjoyment.

Living in the present helps the SP find enjoyment anytime, anywhere. A happy child is an easy child to parent. Don't despise this strength. It feeds mental health and avoids unnecessary stress.

Comments on the strength as seen in children

- It will soon be obvious that they do not like to save. Saving for the future is robbing today of its resources. It is living for the future, not the present. To effectively teach them to save, you will need to set your goals low and make a game or competition of the unlikely event. If they don't respond to saving their cents or dollars by exercising self-discipline, teach them via a means they do enjoy.

- Thinking too hard of the future can generate fear. Fear in an SP's life, whether child or adult, is a shameful admission and is to be avoided at all costs. Fear is not fun. Therefore, they do not want to think of the future if it holds the potential for fear. They face fear with impulsive actions and would usually rather take a risk than face the shame of being "chicken." In teenage years this can be dangerous. Teach them to temper their daring with reason and to see reason as sense, not shame.
- They soon show a liking for the advice "Forgetting what lies behind," since what lies behind is where failure and guilt often arise to rob pleasure from the present if they focus on it. Help them enjoy the present, which is where they experience their greatest strengths and test their ability to respond with skill and tactical brilliance.
- You will notice that living in the present seems to magnify the present for them, and they find greater fulfillment in the present as a result. Whatever we focus on we magnify. Remember? If you get them to focus too much on the past or the future, they may become morose, because their self-image suffers.

Brave, Bold, Daring

This is a strength that can be easily observed and seen from the earliest years in their adventures. Ezekiel named them the lions. "As daring as a lion" gives the analogy true meaning. Courage and bravery lead the lion, and the SP, into daring exploits and is a necessary element of character if they are to succeed and excel. If the lion is not daring it does not succeed; it must take risks. So must the SP!

Daring and bravery create a rush of adrenaline, and this can bring great excitement. So the boldness of the lion is related to another strength — excitement. This is what inspires most of its courageous action. Take away the opportunity for the SP to be the bold lion and the SP loses interest in that activity. The SP will not stay long in a group where there is no potential for thrill.

Weakness occurs most often from nonuse of this strength. If they don't use it their self-image lowers.

Comments on the strength as seen in children:

- The brave, daring trait is easily observed. SP children seem to have no fear. Although all children dare without fear to some extent as they test their world, SPs are the real exponents of this strength. They will unnerve the adult, and challenge the adult to match their bravery without thought. They must, if they are going to like themselves. Curbing this daring spirit is a considerable challenge because we want to temper it with wisdom, without taking away the source of the SP's high self-image and self-confidence.
- Some SP children will even act like lions, growling and imitating a lion's courage. It is a high compliment to call them lions. When they use their courage in a good cause, you may want to reward them with a "lion party." Don't invite the real lions. Leave them at the zoo!
- To the little SP, courage and daring is a badge of bravery. So are the results of their daring exploits. When the teenager comes home with a vehicle covered in mud, he doesn't want to wash it. It is the evidence of risk-taking and bravery. He or she can't be expected to remove the evidence of who they are or the badge they earned!
- Where the parents are too protective, damage is done to this strength. The SP's boldness must be allowed to be tested in order to grow. The SJ parents have a real issue with this. They do not want it to grow. They want it to disappear. Press too hard for your SP to give up his daring and war is going to be declared. The goal is to moderate it and temper it with reason – an attainable goal.

Spontaneous, Impulsive

The spontaneous, impulsive ability of the SP is a strength just like sensitivity is a strength for the NF. Both can present you with immediate choices and result in immediate action. Spontaneity enables fast reaction to circumstances and can often bring instant positive (or negative) results. The true SPs will act on impulse. If the results do not turn out positive, they will simply rely on their tactical skills to decipher the next move and take the fight to their opponent, confident in seizing the advantage.

Impulse can be an act of faith that goes into action without the need for thought and mental processing. A weakness is developed when this strength is used wrongly (without reason and wisdom). This kind of impulsive faith defends itself as an act of self-confidence or some other belief. The SP's confidence inspires them to act impulsively without fear and, often, without thought.

Spontaneity can also be very creative. In the fast pace of games or unexpected happenings in life, it proves its worth. The SP is the master of impulsive action.

Comments on the strength as seen in children:

- Both daring and impulsiveness can go hand in hand. Thinking too much about either causes the thrill to subside along with the nerve. Remember that the SP can't bear the thought that they have lost their nerve, so they act and take it from there.
- In children, spontaneity often causes unnecessary accidents, of course. However, to the SP, the accident is a badge of merit — proof of their daring, impulsive spirit. By now, all SJ parents have reached for a sedative and sat down for support! As we have said earlier, not all SPs act with reckless abandon. Some are a muted version, but still gain their self-esteem from their bravery. "Thank God for the muted ones," you SJs say.
- We can think too much at times. The little SP is a reminder that immediate action carries its own reward. Too much thinking can ruin the thrill of adventure and talk you out of the opportunity. An excess of thinking can create fear. Learn your SP child's way of thinking, and encourage bravery and spontaneity in positive exploits where they will do much good.
- Your SP can explore an impulsive nature in many creative fields. For instance, jazz can be a spontaneous musical exercise and an example of spontaneous creativity.

Effective, Tactical, Aggressive

The SP needs to be effective, achieving results in the present moment. They seldom concern themselves with the distant future, unless it really affects a decision in the present. They excel at being able to figure out the best tactic to become effective or efficient in what they are currently engaged in doing. The word tactic comes from a Greek word *taktikos*, which comes from a family of words to do with arrangement and timing. A tactical mind is one that can quickly see what move or arrangement is needed, at what time, and in what manner. The skill shows itself in sports and physical achievements as participants figure out their best moves.

The degree of aggressiveness differs with each SP. Most see aggression not as attacking others, but rather as effectively executing their tactic without hesitation or fear. Nonuse of this strength is a cause of weakness since their self-image suffers.

Comments on the strength as seen in children:

- The young athlete who shows a mental grasp of tactics is likely to be an SP. This is a talent to be trained.
- We all use tactics, but they can be used for damaging purposes (as when a child tactically teases to get revenge). The wrong use of tactics is not to be encouraged and poses the greatest chance of developing a weakness out of this strength. Discourage all hurtful tactics.
- A tactical mind is a special way of thinking, and the more it is used the more it will develop and become an exceptional skill. The child can, and will, use it against the unwitting parent. Beware! If they succeed, expect repeat performances.
- Encourage SP children to use their tactical minds to figure out how to help someone in need, or how to lift the spirit of a sick sibling. Tactics are not only for sport and physical skills. Find opportunities for behaviors that constructively use this strength.

Easily Excited

Here we draw a distinction between the passion of the NF and the excitement of the SP. The excitement of the SP is an emotion raised in the present moment and just as quickly lost in the next. The passion of the NF is excitement that is raised in the present, or even by a dream of the future, and plans to last long into the future. Excitement is born in the senses, while passion is often limited to the mind and the heart.

The SPs are easily excited in the present. They are stirred to perform for the enjoyment of others and for the stimulation of their own senses. Joy is closely related and feeds their spirits. So the SP devours one of the main nutrients for the spirit, thus dispersing such damaging mental conditions as sadness, gloom and depression. Nonuse of this strength is certain to cause gloom.

Comments on the strength as seen in children:

- All children get excited, but the SPs excel in this department. We want to encourage their excitement, but not at the cost of wisdom or care for others. Excitement, on its own, is not a strength. The correct use of it is a strength. If it is used constructively, not hurting others or themselves, their true strength is showing. We are training our children to use their strengths fruitfully in society.
- Excitement does not necessarily feed the soul. Also, what excites one temperament may frighten others. Though important, excitement is not the greatest strength, even though it feeds the SP's spirit.
- Excitement is food for their optimism — a greater strength. Optimism will feed their self worth more than excitement, and will buoy them up in times of trouble. Watch their optimistic attitude more than their excitement monitor, and approve of it.

Want to Make an Impact

SPs do not seek to be significant, but to be noticed. Significance is too abstract a concept. They crave a concrete experience that makes an impact in the world of things and people. SPs make their mark on the lives of others with their competent use of their physical skills and senses. The impact is in the present and, since they live in the present, we find them constantly endeavoring to impress.

SPs seek to impress in performances of all kinds, from excelling in sports to the dramatic and fine arts, to simply being the life of the party.

However, overuse of the need to impress can lead to a pride that predicts a fall. Watch for pride in the SP. The balance is a high self-esteem that stops short of thinking too much of itself.

Comments on the strength as seen in children:

- You won't miss the child who is always trying to impress. They will try to be the center of attraction and the life of the party.
- When they can't make an impact due to rules and regulations or watchful eyes, they misbehave to achieve their goal of constant excitement. They will act up and deliberately disrupt if that's what it takes. "Be noticed" is their motto. For the muted SPs this will take on a more subtle form.
- Give them plenty of opportunity to perform in front of family, friends, and audiences.
- If you want their attention, you will need to entertain or impress them. They are easily distracted. One of the best ways to get them to focus on you is to get them to do most of the talking.

Lighthearted, Playful

This makes SPs very attractive and pleasant to know. Life is not taken too seriously. Parties and adventures may top their list of appealing activities in teenage. Some go to college because of all they have heard about the parties. The academic activity is only secondary to this innate drive to play. They are always "all there" in the present moment, enjoying the excitement and the stimulation.

We have met this lightheartedness lying behind other strengths of the SP, and it serves them well. They should not be taught to be more serious, because that is the opposite of the strength and is not likely to take root. However, the SPs use this strength best when they include wisdom and thoughtfulness, not seriousness. All strengths can be overused. That is when they become weaknesses.

Comments on the strength as seen in children:

- Watch for them to be playmates as opposed to helpmates. Watch how they continue to play and leave the helping to the other children, or to adults. To get them to help, give them something to do that gets attention from others or turn it into a game or contest.
- SPs will be obvious for their ability to make friends. Many friends are the norm, and they call all of them their close friends. All of them are not, however, deep friends, except for the introverted SPs who will have one or two deeper friendships among other nominal friends.
- "Lighthearted" is not equivalent to "empty headed." Their academic achievement can be impressive. Most find their way into tech schools because of their physical dexterity. Some are flighty, but that goes for other temperaments as well.

Ultimate Optimist, Positive, Bullish

The SP stands in contrast to the SJ's inclination to pessimism, unless they are depressed or confined. Optimism characterizes their spirit. The present moment is their world, and the passion of the moment can feed this buoyant spirit. They move with ease from worrisome concerns to enjoyment and fun. But if confined, they can react strongly since freedom and activity is their native urge, and they don't want to give these up.

Depression is unlikely in this atmosphere of positivism. This strength is clearly beneficial and healthy since we operate best when we are positive. Many of life's disappointments and troubles are viewed with a detachment that makes it hard for worry to depress them. Optimism also encourages faith. The SP often confuses optimism with faith. Optimism is an attitude; faith is a belief. Both can appear to be one and the same, but faith is mature optimism that has a precise goal and a firm commitment to that goal.

Faith in themselves is almost a given, endowing them with loads of confidence. SPs can be wonderful encouragers of others, leading others to believe in themselves. The SP's leadership is often assured because of their ability to encourage and maintain an upbeat spirit.

SPs are not usually financial wizards, but if they venture on Wall Street they tend to be strongly bullish. The excitement presented by a risky gamble is more than some of them can resist. A positive view on life is a necessity for all of us, so we can all do well to make this a strong secondary strength if we are of another temperament.

The weaknesses of this strength – over confidence, rash judgment, and failing to see what could be damaging – are all an overuse of the strength. In contrast, if SPs do not use their optimistic attitude, they can become either depressed or troubled.

Comments on the strength as seen in children:

- Attempting the impossible pervades their dreams and their waking life. They do not understand that they might not be able to do things. They boldly try, and when they fail they either move quickly on, or wallow for a moment in the surprise of failure. Impossible, doubt, fail – these are words they do not wish to become familiar with. Encourage this optimism and positivism.
- Faith is a natural challenge to them and calls them to use their strengths. When they fail, simply teach them that it is an opportunity to figure out how to excel.
- Pessimism seems to miss the very purpose of life for them. If you have both an SP and an SJ child, they will balance each other when they are not opposing each other and fighting! There is an upside to the obvious clash of these two temperaments — one needs the other.

Action

SPs usually display physical skills, excelling in sports and any physical skill that requires dexterity. Art, driving large machinery, the use of weaponry, dramatic performances, and the skills of a hands-on trade are all examples of what we might observe in the SP. Anything that keeps them moving can fulfill and excite them. They find it hard to sit still and concentrate on mental activities. It's not that they can't, they are as intellectually bright as any other, but they find activity more to their liking.

Movement keeps boredom at bay. When we live focused on the fleeting moment, a lack of activity in that moment causes optimism to fade. If there is no activity offered by the present moment to keep them positive, we need to find or create some kind of activity (or they will, and it could be destructive). They are constantly on the lookout for what feeds their positive spirits. Action is tied to the constant hunger for a positive attitude.

Nonuse of this strength leads to depression. Overuse leads to trouble with others, at times. The wrong use can cause them to be introduced to law enforcement authorities. Keep them away from things that destroy true pleasure.

Comments on the strength as seen in children:

- Balls and wheels will entertain them forever. They take to sports like a duck to water. Computer games can make them into addicts because it is constant, exciting action.
- The little SP soon shows his or her love of competition. Unlike the NFs who are more comfortable competing against themselves and their own record, the SPs compete against others and enjoy the thrill of victory like no other temperament. The victory stand is the SP's throne. Help them get there often. It will build their confidence. An SP who is excelling in healthy sports is often kept out of trouble.
- Discipline is learned in the rigorous training they willingly commit to so that they can win. Use sports and competitions to teach them discipline and self-control.

A Focus on the Physical, Graceful

Although we have mentioned their physical ability many times, it is worth special focus. Their physical movements are usually graceful and well coordinated. They even walk gracefully. The bodily senses are keenly alive and active in an SP. The feeling of movement and coordination is rewarding in itself to them. For the SP, physical sensations capture life's thrills.

We are physical creatures, and this part of our system floods us with immediate sensations. We can calm or excite our spirits by physical movement. Both the body and the spirit are inseparable in this life, and they influence each other. The SP emphasizes the body while the NF emphasizes the spirit. Both can advantage themselves by using the other temperament's strength more.

SPs seldom move without a purpose. However, the purpose is often to offset boredom or attract attention. Movement stimulates, and they can't live long without it. The nonuse of this strength seems to create more weakness than its overuse. Of course, as for most strengths, the wrong action will create a weakness and possible damage, too! Use the strength as it was designed to be used, to stimulate the physical senses.

Comments on the strength as seen in children:

- You will be able to notice their gracefulness in movement and their obvious love of stylistic action. Drama and theatrical skills are cherished. Dance is favored by many of the SPs.
- They strive for perfection of movement. Notice how they will repeat actions until they are satisfied they have mastered them. Then they will say, "Watch me!" Often after being shown something once they will get it right
- Stationary learning methods bring out the worst or challenge in them the most. This is why they learn physical skills so well. It is learning by movement.
- Major on action in learning. Teach by activity and demonstration, involving them in the demonstration. Make games of the task of learning, and you will find your SP a ready learner. Develop their physical dexterity.

Generous Nature

An easy-come-easy-go attitude contributes to the SP's generosity and kindness. In the confirmed SP, not a moment's thought is wasted on saving things for the rainy day. That only robs the present of its possible resources. Giving things away to someone in need makes real sense to the optimist, who sees more coming anyway. The SP can give more generously of their money and possessions than their time. If the gift of time inhibits the excitement of the moment, they may not be generous. This is not to say they are self-centered. They can be seriously focused on the needs of others. Their protection of their own pleasure is more like the in-flight instruction, "Put the oxygen mask on yourself first, then on your child."

The motive for generosity differs with the temperaments. In the SP, there is a strong desire to bring pleasure. Since they hold their possessions lightly, they give with a liberal spirit. So free are they with what they have, that they earn the name of the "generous temperament." Overuse of this strength is often encountered in them. Nonuse of this strength is seldom found.

Comments on the strength as seen in children:

- The little SP will give his toys away, but with equal freedom, he will acquire another child's toys. Watch out for this behavior. They simply believe that, since they are generous, others should be too. Punishment for feeling this way is certainly not understood. They must be praised for their generosity and helped to understand that not all want to give like they do.
- Also, kindly help them understand that "taking" is not "giving!" Wait till the other child gives freely.
- Don't underestimate either the kindness of their hearts or their creativity in acquiring! Both will surprise you. They are the tactical experts among children and are very clever in finding ways to accomplish their ends.

Dramatic Concrete Language

One final word on the SP's use of language. Being easily excitable they probe language for its exciting phrases. Since they are firmly rooted in the real world with the use of their five physical senses, they use its concrete expressions and generally avoid abstract language or discussions of a theoretical nature. These characteristics can add up to colorful, vivid language and, at times, inappropriate language in the quest for attention.

Comments on the SP's language as seen in children:

- Sometimes too colorful, their language is an expression of their excitement and daring. You will need to monitor their verbal exploits into cursing and the use of obscene phrases. They don't grasp the line between acceptable and unacceptable speech easily because the unacceptable often gets the immediate attention and, in some cases, approval of others. You will need to teach them.
- Novels with expressive and obscene language can attract them. For all temperaments, watch their reading material and monitor their internet wanderings if you want to mold their values.
- They are only too willing to test the limits, particularly of social decorum. "Society should be free," and " liberal self-expression should be the law" is a philosophy that is certainly encouraged by the SP's unguarded love and use of these values.

All temperaments have their challenges because their strengths can be used for wrong and damaging purposes. However, the SP temperament is a pleasure to live with and a joy to parent if you don't try to make them into SJs. All Parents of SPs should read about all the other temperaments' strengths. This way, you will place your own child's temperament in sharper focus.

An SP who is operating these strengths without hurting others will feel fulfilled and happy, and will feel no guilt. Undesirable behavior is then not the immediate problem that it can be with the SP who uses their strengths without consideration for others. There is always a striking difference between a temperament operating in its strengths, and one operating in its weaknesses.

The Native Strengths of the SJ Temperament

If you have determined that your child is an SJ temperament, run through this list of strengths and highlight the ones you can already see in them. Of course, some strengths you will be able to see, and some will be hidden from you due to being undiscovered by you or your child, unexercised, or both.

Health is found in living happily in our native strengths. The ones that are unseen by you in your child may be able to be confirmed, or otherwise, by observing your child when you design ways for them to use an unseen strength. Children lock into the moment when using their strengths, and you may be able to observe their focus and pleasure. Repeated use and observation will encourage develop of the strength, and you will clearly see whether your child is fulfilled and happy in the positive use of the strength.

Remember that not every SJ strength is present in every SJ, but most of them are. Likewise for the other temperaments. Also, some will be more dominant than others. If you scan the other temperaments you will probably see that your SJ has some of those strengths as well. They are present as secondary strengths, as we have already noted. If the child has been using a secondary strength often, it may have become a distinct part of his (or her) behavior. There is nothing wrong with this, but we should still encourage the true SJ strengths, since this is where their greatest fulfillment is found.

An excellent way to know your children and note their progress is to make your own notes on the use of their strengths as you see them develop. Keep a journal on your children. This way you will be able to spot more quickly the weaknesses that will show up from time to time and take appropriate action. Later, this journal can help your children understand themselves, and read an interesting history of the development of their strengths.

Now, proceed through each of the strengths and become familiar with them.

Here Is a List of the Main SJ Strengths

Orientation to Time: Lives in the Past

The past is what guides and fashions the life of SJs. They live their lives "backing" into the future, with their eyes firmly glued on their experiences and those of others. Phrases such as, "You learn from the past;" "Doesn't your experience tell you something," and "You can trust your experiences," support their lifestyle.

All actions are guided by the past, and SJs feel confident only when they are repeating the past. Trusting in change, when it hasn't established itself yet, is risky and, for many SJs, simply foolish. As we will see, many of their strengths are fueled by this relationship to time — the past.

That past holds many lessons to be learned which can be carried with us into the future to make it less problematical. This, the SJ understands and believes with a passion. The danger of this orientation to past time is that they can easily become enmeshed in the past and display reticence to change. They then make little progress as they solidify the rules for their behavior and make even more rules to secure the ones they already had.

Comments on the strength as seen in children:

- You will hear things like: "That's not the way to do it." "We don't do it that way." "Stop changing things."
- As children, the SJ needs to develop a past full of experiences in order to live this way successfully. You can see them developing routines and habits and rummaging through their past for experiences on which they can depend, together with displaying a reluctance to change the established ways. They will defend their actions by reference to what they have done in their past.
- The rigidity of this behavior is especially damaging to the ability to be adaptive and accept new challenges.
- Help them to make little changes just to reduce their fear of change. Facing little changes can make them feel more comfortable with big changes that will come later.

Careful, Cautious, Concerned

This is a strength that you will observe in the SJ's mood. Because of this strength, they are focused more on details. The care and concern also makes them ideal social beings, protecting social traditions and seeking to increase its values. They are not out for fun simply for fun's sake as much as they are for helping and taking care of others. When their duties are done, then they try to relax and have some down-time fun.

Because they are focused on the past, SJs are more afraid of the future and cautious about how they enter it by each moment. Cautiousness causes them to establish rules and regulations to protect what is. What "is" is known; what "is not" is unknown, so the fear of the unknown stimulates their cautiousness.

Caution leads to conservatism, which often does not want to change. This resistance is because the new idea is not worthy, but because it means doing things differently. That, to the SJ, is a challenge. Care, caution, and concern lead also to a somber attitude and a seriousness toward life that makes for a clear distinction from the SPs and their pleasure-loving, in-the-moment mood.

Overuse of this strength is the main cause of weakness. Fear, a critical attitude, and social rejection can all result from overuse.

Comments on the strength as seen in children:

- SJ children are less accident prone than the SP. They look before they leap. Help them to attempt calculated risks to develop a healthy balance between caution and risk. Life cannot be lived without risk. Caution all too easily stimulates fear, and fear cripples.
- Watch for their being helpers. The care in them leads them to want to show that they care. They do so in practical ways, like helping Mom or others. Differentiate between the "loving" actions of the NF and the "helping" actions of the SJ. Love expressed in practical care and concern drives the SJ. Love (for love's own rewards) with an inbuilt passion and sensitivity drives the NF.

- The SJ child's caution is seen in timidity with physical things. If you see frequent fear in your little SJ it is cause for concern. They must be gently encouraged to face their fears and overcome them. In contrast, the SP is not timid unless overwhelmed. You will never make your SJ into an SP, nor do you want to. However, fear in any temperament needs to be addressed and overcome.
- SJs are on the watch for things that may go wrong, hence their belief in Murphy's Law: "if it can go wrong it will go wrong." This negative approach is a weakness that is caused by an overuse of caution and concern. Too much of this strength, and you need to step in and seek to instill a more positive attitude.

Thoughtful, Prepared

The SJ is a planner. If they do not plan on paper, or on their time management system, they plan in their heads. To be prepared, we need to plan. Their minds operate logistically, and step-by-step plans are the favored method.

The SJ will often want to know what is happening next in order to be prepared. They feel more comfortable when they are prepared. Fear of the future is offset in their normal mode of living by planning. Planning is not theorizing or strategizing; it is logical, step-by-step formulas developed by the question, "What do I do next?"

At times, even the extroverted SJs will look like introverts in their somber planning moments. Being prepared is serious business. They know life is risky, and risk is not to be faced without a plan.

Over-preparation breeds a stilted existence, and joy can be lost in carefulness.

Comments on the strength as seen in children:

- Don't hold back information about what is intended and planned for the day or the future. This will only earn you an upset little SJ, and they can vent this annoyance strongly. You will pay for your failure.

- Help them plan positively, not out of fear. They will tend toward pessimism, so optimistic planning helps keep them vibrant.
- SJs will also tend to plan for all the possible negative results, and fail to plan for the positive. "What if this goes wrong," is their first thought and sometimes their last. Teach them to plan for the scenario, "What if this goes well? What next?"

Responsible, Dependable

SJs exhibit a strong sense of responsibility. They long to be known as someone who can be depended upon. Testing the limits all the time does not deliver a reputation of reliability. Therefore, the SJ is less likely than the SP to test the limits. If they do, they do it cautiously or to attract the attention of peers.

In the SJ, you have a temperament that keeps within the bounds, most of the time. Responsibility is a way of behaving prudently in society and keeping within the boundaries. This is true of both the home society and the larger society. It is for the sake of society that they want to be responsible, also for the recognition of being respectable members of that society. When they show no concern for society (home or larger groups), something is wrong with the SJ. Either they don't feel that they belong, or they have been hurt by society and are rebelling against undesirable authority.

SJs love routine and use routine to aid their development of responsible behavior. This is how: Routine creates dependability and, by its regularity, helps a person continue to be dependable.

It is hard to imagine weaknesses that could develop with the overuse of this strength, but nonuse will certainly produce guilt in the SJ.

Comments on the strength as seen in children:

- Observe how this strength emerges in their relationships with their friends and their superiors. "Mom said we had to do it this way," they insist. Following rules is being responsible. Turning homework in as requested is also being responsible.

- When they fall out with their friends, ask why. You may discover that their friends have disregarded the expectations set by their superior, and this has upset the little SJ, or maybe they were laughed at for their concern over following the rules.
- SJs can become judgmental of others when they see others as irresponsible, criticizing them and reporting their lack of "correct" behavior.
- SJs will seek, at times, to impress their parents with their responsibility and reliability. If they are looking for approval they will often do this, trying to extract a comforting word of praise.

Do What Is Right, Law Abiding

Akin to their desire to be responsible and reliable, is their drive to do the right thing. Rules and regulations make sense to all SJs, and established rules are the right thing to follow. Of this they have little doubt. They believe chaos is around the corner if people are not compelled to obey the rules. "Laws are for a purpose," they declare. "If everyone would follow the rules, all would be well." There is no doubting the importance of control factors in social life, but this strength is only one side of the coin for society to run smoothly. The other is the need for free expression in a society – a strength of the SP. Both are strengths, and each must honor the rights and needs of the other.

Nonuse of this strength can cause guilt and develop into self-denunciation and a lower self-image.

Comments on the strength as seen in children:

- Watch for the children who order the others around and make them "do it the proper way." These are your SJs. If you have an SJ child traveling with you in the car, he (or she) will surely point out your indiscretion when you run the traffic light or exceed the speed limit. The traffic department might well consider paying the SJs for their vigilant policing of their parents!
- You will likely be tempted to put these children in charge if you must leave for a moment, because they will attempt to enforce the regulations and will take pride when, upon your return, you thank them for helping

you. However, if there is an SP in the group, the SP will test the control and authority of the SJ. A fight is likely to break out because their drives oppose each other. (The heat of political elections, among adults, is often a display of the opposite drives of law and order on one side and freedom of expression on the other.)

- The SJ displays propriety and responsibility, while the SP displays expediency and successful tactics that can result in the limits being stretched. Think twice before you put the SJ child in charge over SPs, or vice versa.

Strong Need to Belong, Social

The word "society" has come up several times already in the discussion of the SJ. They are the social temperament. Belonging to groups and to society is a paramount drive. SJs can hardly pass up the opportunity to belong to clubs and communities, and their wallets often burst with membership cards. Whatever group they belong to, they monitor with pride and concern.

A society is a group of people, of no particular size, where the actions of all affect the common welfare of the group. The group makes rules for behavior to protect common interests, enforces those rules, seeks to provide for agreed upon needs, and expects each member to act responsibly as assigned duties are performed. All this the SJ does instinctively and purposefully. They accept the social model as the norm for human conduct. Therefore, we expect that they will have a strong drive to belong to such units. The units themselves give the SJ a sense of security. When a social being lacks security, they become nervous, lonely, and fearful. This need sets up the most common weakness – namely, a loss of security – when the urge to socialize is not heeded. The SJ blesses society, of which we are all part, with their careful attention to our needs.

When they feel they don't belong, SJs fall into gloom and despair. Thus, home must be a place where they feel that they belong in order for the SJ to be comfortable. To make them feel rejected is punishment indeed.

Comments on the strength as seen in children:

- At play, SJ children will often make up groups to which they can belong.
- Observe how they divide larger groups into smaller societies so that belonging is more personally satisfying. Then they demand loyalty to their group. Defense of their group can result in serious wars among friends.
- If they don't feel that they belong, it can lead to insecurity. Insecurity leads to either undesirable behavior or to depression if not relieved.
- Unlike the SP who might be pressured into something because of being "chicken," the SJ will be pressured because everyone else is doing it.

Steady, Not Easily Shaken

When a person feels well-grounded in reality and certain that they are right, they show the strength of not being easily shaken. The SJs have their feet solidly planted in reality, and their desires and goals are straightforward, making them (when they feel they are right) the proverbial "rock of Gibraltar" — unmovable.

Society, for its good, needs stability, and the SJs know this. They believe that they are the reason social groups succeed. This firm belief only makes them more entrenched, and they will argue their position with tenacity. "A double minded man is unstable in all he does." This they seldom display.

Because they are the J and not the P (among the Ss), they want to come to closure and move on. Keeping their options open in case more evidence turns up seems like procrastination to them. They accuse the Ps of procrastination readily because they believe it is not productive of immediate results and they want results, now! Actually, they see procrastination as laziness, and even irresponsibility. The SPs and the SJs seem opposites because they live opposing lifestyles.

Comments on the strength as seen in children:

- Your little SJ can be an arguer. They don't argue to win a debate (as the NT does), they argue to hold their ground.
- Their lifestyle will clash strongly with all Ps, and if you have an SJ and a P in your family, war can break out at anytime over issues of timeliness, preparation, and decision-making. It is not the clash of personalities, but of lifestyles — ways of living that do not blend easily. Therefore, don't punish them for their lifestyle "infractions." To do so is to lose respect from a child. You will only consider punishment if you happen to be the opposite lifestyle! Train them to make a place in the family life for an opposing lifestyle to feel welcome. You are teaching respect for others and pointing out the ugliness of judgmentalism. Compliment their lifestyle, but demand they respect others.
- A loss of security, which means a loss of stability in SJ children, will cause them to crater fast. The child becomes worried, nervous, and loses all hope. If this is observed, it must be addressed and rectified, or the little SJ will lose all confidence and desire to do anything.
- Watch how they make an effort, in play and work, to create routines so that they have a stable foundation for their lifestyle to be enjoyed.

Trust Authority

Authority is defended unless it shows itself to be unfair in its decisions, lacking in societal responsibility, or wasteful of resources, etc. The SJ knows that authority is needed for law and order to be enforced, and they will create layers of authority to protect something as minor as a routine. Respect for people in positions of authority follows, and expectations for authority run high.

SJs aspire to be in positions of authority and, when they "arrive," they swell with the pride of status, which is (at times) more valuable to them than the amount of money the position offers. Other SJs measure their success based on money alone. Both possessions and status are equal drives in an SJ.

The overuse of trusting authority leads to acceptance of abuses, and the nonuse leads to personal lawlessness.

Comments on the strength as seen in children:

- SJ children will establish levels of authority in their play. Playmates will be assigned responsibilities, and along with them, the authority to police them.
- They will respect your authority as a parent, unless it violates their expectations of justice (in which case it is a matter of correcting their wrong expectations and beliefs, or changing your practices as the authority).
- Model responsible authority for them. SJs will inspect, supervise, and oversee your decisions and behavior as the authority. Expect it, and be ready to defend or change. You will be judged!

Supervisors, Managers

The SJ's excellent ability to supervise and manage is an outcome of several strengths and drives. The SJs' desire to help, their logistical minds, their sense of being responsible, and their cautiousness and attention to detail, together with their innate honor of authority figures, makes them born supervisors and tenders of the affairs of society. They recognize rank and desire it.

Keirsey labels them well. "ESTJ" means "supervisor and manager," "ISTJ" means "inspector," and "ISFJ" means "protector." All three will be conscientious in their sense of duty to be what they are. This strength (supervision) is the cause of many SP plans to get even. The ESFJ also holds to supervision, but not so rigidly. Society needs supervision, and that belief is not questioned by SJs. It is no surprise that they excel at business enterprises where supervision and the regulation of systems are much needed.

Overuse of this strength creates friction with those they supervise and the belief that SJs may think they are superior.

Comments on the strength as seen in children:

- The ability to organize and supervise others leads to their being perfect babysitters (a skill they seek). It is, for many, the first opportunity for budding supervisors. They will listen to instructions carefully and meticulously, then follow them to the best of their ability to prove their worth.

- Watch them fuss over a younger sibling. Helping Mom with baby brother is a God-sent opportunity. They can proudly show their stuff and be what they are made to be.
- Once they have learned how to do things around the house, they will even try to tell you how to do things! Don't punish the emergence of this strength out of your frustration at being supervised. Walk the line between encouragement and teaching them to be good followers as well as supervisors.
- Differentiate between the ESTJ's supervising of others and the directive advice of the INF child. While the SJ supervises, the INF directs and advises with less interest in following up and enforcing their advice.
- Your SJ may start a roadside lemonade business, a babysitting or lawn mowing enterprise, complete with her (or his) own business card! Other temperaments may be attracted to do this also, but the SJ will show the desire and ability to turn it into a lasting activity.

Stoical

"If bad things can happen they will." This is Murphy's Law that I mentioned under the strength of cautiousness. It was invented by some SJ, for certain. They believe they must always be prepared for the worst, and then they will never be disappointed. This belief develops an attitude that is reminiscent of the ancient Greek philosophy of Stoicism, which asks us to steel ourselves against trouble, and bear it with an iron acceptance and without complaint, since we cannot avoid it.

The mental preparation that this attitude demands, and its conservative interpretation of life, is its strength. However, it is easy to see how this is overused to become a weakness. A negative, pessimistic attitude waits just over the fence, so to speak. You will also notice the SJ's seriousness about life emerging whenever the storm clouds of trouble gather. The SP will show hope and optimism at the onset of trouble, while the SJ will display their strength of seriousness and immediately leap into preparations to handle the worst. If they don't, they fall into worry. "Better to be serious than sorry," they say.

Comments on the strength as seen in children:

- Watch for the depth of disappointment that a let-down creates and you may be looking at a little SJ. Differentiate this disappointment from the hurt, in the NF, that causes anger. Disappointment is one level of letdown. Hurt is deeper and takes longer to get over.
- Watch for the formation of weaknesses that the overuse of stoicism creates. Too much attention to possible troubles or too much preparation for the bad times plunges them into the sadness of pessimism. Their attitude then becomes gloomy and worrisome. It weakens instead of strengthens.
- If your child is constantly morose and sad, consider the possibility that their mind may be full of negative attitudes, all on the dark side of life. They will need to think more optimistically to recover mental health.

Logistical in Work and Play

The logistical mind dominates the mental activity of the SJ and is the brilliance seen in their intelligence. Webster's Dictionary defines *logistics* as the art of calculation. Arithmetic appeals to this logistical mind. Calculating how to get goods or people from one place to another with the attendant issues of placement and timing is a logician's skill. Logistics is the branch of military science dealing with procuring, maintaining, and transporting people, material, and facilities.

Step-by-step planning, doing things in a logical sequence, figuring out how much and how many, and when and where, is the logician's world. They are the masters of this sequential, systems-oriented approach.

Comments on the strength as seen in children:

- In SJ children, you will find this mental skill developing early in their play. They will show a love for order, rules, and a natural ability to organize. The drive will stand out. Encourage it.
- They will systematize their rooms and their homework, and tell you what should be your next step, too. They should be noticed and approved for their logistical skill, or they will neglect it. The more they feel it is helpful and rewarding the more they will use it.

- Of course, this skill complements their drive to supervise and control situations. All of their strengths are a package of drives that support a lifestyle and a preferred way of living.
- Management is enhanced by logistics. Help them handle their finances with a step-by-step system in place. Likewise for other activities. Because they are logistical, help them to manage their time, and start early. You will develop a strong and healthy SJ.

Keeps to the Facts when Communicating, Gives You All the Details

SJs are factual and focus on details. This strength enables their logistical mind. It also keeps them grounded in the real world and contributes to their stability and stabilizing influence over others. If they skip a fact in reporting what they have done, they squirm at it being noticed. They handle the concrete facts of life the best. Details keep their feet on the ground.

SJs know that the devil is in the details, so they are painstaking in noticing and taking the details into account. The problem with this strength is that they can get lost in the details and fail to see the big picture. You can get so focused on the trees that you miss appreciating the forest. The impression that the details of the trees leave is not the same impression as the mass of a forest.

Details and facts also bore the NF who looks at the forest first, and then pays attention to the trees as needed. "Communication should be accurate," says the SJ; and by that they mean "pay attention to all the details."

Overuse creates a weakness and leads to the weakness of getting bogged down in the details.

Comments on the strength as seen in children:

- They tend to tell you what happened to them blow-by-blow, and they don't want to be encouraged to shorten their stories or be interrupted. Be patient with them.

- Details are often remembered without the meanings of the events or their significance. What is happening is that the SJ is remembering the concrete details because they communicate in concrete terms. They also live in the real (concrete) world, and abstract principles and ideas are of secondary interest to them. If they talk about ideas, they want to translate the concepts into concrete facts and happenings. Let them. The NT and NF (who live in a conceptual world) need to translate their ideas into concrete terms to be able to communicate them effectively to the SJ and the SP.
- The significance of an event is not so much how it made them feel, as it is the size of it or the details of its uniqueness. SJs are most impressed by external facts.

Good Samaritans, Helpmates

This helping spirit of the SJ is a combination of many strengths, especially their concern for society, the urge to do their duty, and the desire to be reliable. SJs take "like ducks take to water" in occupations such as nursing, childcare, and helpful workmates of all kinds. Because they want to be recognized as significant contributors to society (be it the home, club, church, community, or nation), they logically see themselves as the helpers of their fellow citizens. Anything that needs to be done should be done. Everyone has a duty to pay back for the privilege of living in a free society, or even for the privilege of living.

When helped by an SJ Good Samaritan, you will feel their care and love in a powerful way. They will attend to details (even sacrificially) and often follow up to see if there is more to do. You can almost always count on an SJ to help. A weakness is developed in their character when they don't use this strength.

Comments on the strength as seen in children:

- Watch the SJ's play and observe the "helpful" quality in action. If someone is hurt, they will fuss over them and do whatever they can.
- In the helpmate, there is a concern for other people's welfare that distinguishes their play.

- Are they helpmates around the home? They should be. It will fulfill them. Expect them to try to help their school teacher, too.
- SJs often show great concern and love for animals, as well.

Non-Dramatic, Concrete Speech

As we have previously noted, SJs are concrete in thought and expression. Unlike the SP whose language is vivid, they tend to a more prosaic way of talking. Exactness in the reporting of details is expected of all people, not just fellow SJs. Often, they will interrupt you and correct you if you have made an error in detail. "It was 6:35, not 6:30, when we left!" They can't let it stand as 6:30 since it was not accurate. If they are caught in saying 6:35 when it was 6:30, they will at times argue that it was 6:35 because their honor as accurate reporters is at stake.

Flowery language is not their norm nor to their liking. Say it like it is, simple and plain! Therefore, some SJs can lack an appreciation of the arts, and prefer science — plain and powerful with its search for accurate facts.

The little SJs will test an NT parent but mesh with the NT, NF and, of course, the SJ. They are solid, if not dramatic, children and often lead in classrooms and family life.

The Native Strengths of the NT Temperament

If you have determined that your child is an NT temperament, run through this list of strengths and highlight the ones you can already see in them. Of course, some strengths you will be able to see, and some will be hidden from you due to being undiscovered by you or your child, unexercised, or both.

Health is in living happily in our native strengths. The ones that are unseen by you in your child may be able to be confirmed, or otherwise, by observing your children when you design ways for them to use an unseen strength. Children lock into the moment when they are using their strengths, and you may be able to observe their focus and pleasure. Repeated use and observation will encourage development of the strength, and you will clearly see if your children are fulfilled and happy in the positive use of the strength.

Remember that not every NT strength is present in all NTs; but most of them are. Likewise for the other temperaments. Also, some will be more dominant than others. If you scan the other temperaments you will probably see that your little NT has some of those strengths as well. They are present as secondary strengths, as we have already noted; and if the child has been using a secondary strength often, it may have become a distinct part of their behavior. There is nothing wrong with this, but we should still encourage the true NT strengths, since this is where their greatest fulfillment is to be found.

An excellent way to know your children and note their progress is to make your own notes on the use of their strengths as you see them develop. Keep a journal on your children. This way you will be able to spot more quickly the weaknesses that will show up from time to time and take appropriate action. Later this journal can help your children understand themselves, and they can read an interesting history of the development of their strengths.

Now, proceed through each of the strengths, and become familiar with them.

Here Is a List of the Main NT Strengths

Orientation to Time: Time Is Relative to the Current Task

Unlike the SP (who lives in the present), the SJ (who lives in the past), or even the NF (who lives in the future), the NT seems to be unrelated to time. The use of their strengths is related to the task more than they are related to time. They absorb themselves in a task, and time is not a concern until the task is over. Then they wake up and ask what time it is.

Like the NF, they are abstract, and time is a concrete reality. How can abstract temperaments be related to time? The NT and the NF solve this issue in two different ways. The NT only relates to time if their project is dependent in any way on time. As scientists, they can indulge themselves in projects that may take decades, since time is of no relative importance unless a deadline looms. When one does approach it disturbs them, because they must share their focus on their project with a focus on a clock. Most of their strengths are related to this view of time.

Strong Will, Determined

With a detachment to reality and time, NTs set their jaws and face life with a determination to find answers and succeed in their search for knowledge. Their road to success leads through the heart of "Determined City." Play is subservient to their goals or projects. Instinctively, they know the power of this single-eyed approach.

Such focus needs a strong will and an unbending determination. They can stay focused on a project for decades. Their cool, calm spirit helps, since determination is most successfully thwarted by emotions. Curiosity also aids a strong will in the NT. They must find out how things work, or why things are the way they are, and whether they can be changed. They seek change, and willpower is the psychological means of bringing change about. Therefore, they seem, to many, to be masters of will power. Their main weakness is a stubborn will that won't change, even when another approach is clearly needed.

Comments on the strength as seen in children:

- Determination breeds a seriousness that is easily observed in the NT child, and sometimes disturbing. Don't confuse it with depression or sadness. Look for the focus and ask, "Is it intense?" If so, it is not likely to be depression. Depression is often associated with a lack of focus.
- Everything must wait for the completion of the project. To drag the NT away from a project when they are not finished is a struggle. If possible, don't. And if not possible, reason with them and bring them back to reality. Like all of us, they must live in the real world and meet its demands at times.
- When their determination demands too much of them too early in life, their determination can lead to depression caused by not being able to achieve their goals or satisfy their curiosity.
- Any depressed state needs joy or pleasure to reverse its decline and, for the NT, joy is often best found in successful projects, or ones that receive lavish praise. Praise your NT for ingenuity and creativity.

Strategic, They Leave Nothing to Chance

Strategy is a way of attempting to leave nothing to chance. The mental functioning of the NT is strategic. Strategy is the science of planning, setting goals, and directing operations. It can also be seen as the artful and scientific means of accomplishing some purpose. Their minds work on schemes, theories, and plans that are designed to accomplish a predetermined goal.

Strategy requires, at times, considerable research, and this is part of the NT's comfortable territory. Strategy is not just planning; it is also the theorizing that underwrites the planning. However, strategy works best in the world of things and ideas, research and discovery, and is often disrupted by the world of people. The NT is not skilled at working with people and within relationships to accomplish a goal. Their relationships are often only marginally successful, because they lack the sensitivity to intuit people's feelings and thoughts and the emotional sensitivity to bond on that level.

The designing of concepts and ideas to form patterns of thought and complex theories excites the NT. They will also spend countless hours designing objects. Seldom are their strategies devoid of some kind of design.

If a weakness develops, it usually is in their failure to understand people, relationships, and the power of emotions. It is an overuse of their analytical strategizing plus their tendency not to adequately observe the human factors involved in their decisions that often leads to this weakness. The NT must learn that rational strategies are not the only tool needed to solve problems in a world dominated by humans and their interests. They need the complex skills of diplomacy and emotional logic to be fully equipped.

Comments on the strength as seen in children:

- Of all the temperaments, this one is the most single minded. NT children focus on designing things and can develop tunnel vision.
- NT children will spend hours with Legos or Lincoln Logs.
- They will tear a toy apart to see how it works, and try to put it back together again, an exercise in knowledge aimed at becoming ingenious.
- They will immerse themselves in books of learning to discover all they can, and use this knowledge in strategizing.
- Time is irrelevant to the NT if they are engaged in the pursuit of a goal, which is most of the time. They will be late to an appointment without conscience. It will become evident that there is no way of getting them to bed without a display of anger from them if they are in the midst of a project. The parents must be ingenious in their persuasive ways.

Intense Curiosity

Curiosity compels the NT to ask why, how, what, and what for — incessantly. If they don't ask it audibly, they are asking it mentally. "When" is of far less importance to someone who is concerned with theoretical abstractions, so they live in their theoretical world, engaged with these four main questions: Why? How? What? What for? In their intense devotion to learning, the acquired knowledge must be examined, and they are lost in its pursuit. Creativity and ingenuity are steps to the same goal.

Everything must be understood and explored to see how it works and how it might be bettered. NTs will probe anything if they detect that it holds promise of a new discovery or a new way of doing things.

Remember the adage "curiosity killed the cat"? The main weakness that can develop from curiosity is its overuse. Overuse can not only kill, but it can destroy one's project, lead to endless investigation with no profitability, and can become an end in itself. Curiosity is a fabulous tool, but, like all other tools, it has a limited use and purpose. This concept the NT will find hard to accept.

Comments on the strength as seen in children:

- They are constantly asking "Why?" An unwillingness to answer adequately can bring on a display of dislike, or even anger, as though you are deliberately standing in the way of their growing knowledge. Take time to explain as though this is a matter of extreme importance. It is.
- Watch them probe things, engaged for hours on end.
- NTs will tend to show other children (as well as adults) their findings and be proud of their discoveries. You must encourage this strength since it supports what the NT is all about, especially since most peers might not.
- Once they have exhausted a toy's potential, or have fully understood its uses, they lose interest quickly and move on to the next. A non-working piece of machinery can be, to them, a precious toy because they can satisfy their curiosity by dismantling it and trying to make other things with its parts.
- Don't be surprised if one of your household appliances becomes their target for discovery!

Questioning, Doubtful

NTs do not trust nor hold the past precious. They wish for the future to be better and to change. The past is of historical interest only, and it is not needed material to guide the future. Their ingenuity and their use of reason is the only needed guide, they feel. This attitude disturbs the SJ terribly. The future is not trusted either, and is in their hands to control and mold to their theoretical fancies. Nothing is sacred to the NT. All must undergo constant scrutiny with the purpose of finding new ways of understanding it, or using it, or of making a better mouse trap.

To find new ways and utilize new concepts, one must possess a natural degree of doubt. "Doubt," for the NT is questioning with a positive purpose, a search for solutions. Skepticism is to take a negative attitude to all you do and think, tearing everything apart except your own cherished beliefs. Doubt is a strength. Skepticism can quickly become a weakness. Skepticism often leads to premature abandonment of an idea or a project. It can develop a harmful tenacity to continue in that skepticism when the exit has long been passed. Weaknesses abound in the overuse and wrong use of this strength.

Comments on the strength as seen in children:

- The NT will not necessarily believe you. You must "prove" your claims and the rationality of your demands. Reason and its "proofs" are almost their god. When they can't prove something, they tend to reject it instead of understanding it. It may be that they simply are not working with all the facts, and their skepticism has short-circuited discovery. In the older NT children, keep them aware of the facts that they are not working with: typically, the facts of the immaterial values and realities of life they all too often overlook or avoid.
- The NT's doubt of you is not personal; it is how they learn. Present reason and evidence to them. You may have to go on a learning spree of your own to be able to do this, but this will also help gain their respect.
- They do not regard you as an authority, and, if by chance they do, they will still question all you say, since no one is an absolute authority. Their own reason is the only authority they care to follow. Again, help them see that this is, in itself, quite an illogical approach. From where does their reason gain such authority? Who said that there are not many facts in this universe that are beyond reason's ability to discover?

- If they take on a negative, critical mental attitude, it can lead to the common occurrence among them of an obnoxious pride.

Independent, Self-Reliant — "It Is Up to Me"

Independence, in an NT, is a strong drive. If things go wrong, they believe that they must find a way to fix it, often refusing help. They will struggle excessively in the belief that they must do it alone, or because accepting help is failure. Only with independent effort can they feel proud of their accomplishments. There lies the core of the issue of NT's independence: I must do it myself or I have proved to myself that I am lacking in ingenuity and mental acuity. We want people to be independent and self-reliant; but we are social beings, dependent on each other to be able to live in our complex world. We depend on others for our food, water, shelter, and a thousand things. Total independence is not an achievable goal since male depends on female, and vice versa, to begin with! Teach them the limits of independence.

Their self-image drops dramatically when they fail to be self-reliant. For the NT, having to depend on anyone else, including parents, is failure of a devastating nature. These are seldom the ones that stay at home and rely on the support of parents, unless it is the INTP who has lost direction and is circling without a strong motivation. This condition is otherwise known as "an NT living in his or her weaknesses."

Independence can feed self-approval to the point of pride. Pride is defined as thinking more of one's self than the facts justify. The facts justify that I am a dependent being as well as one who must exercise an appropriate amount of independence. The weakness of pride is simply an overuse of this self-reliant attitude in the NT, or in anyone.

Comments on the strength as seen in children:

- The adult who does not appreciate the NT's achievements is not included in their center of interest.
- You will see the NT choose friends who show appreciation and awe for what they do. Their self-image is dependent on this feedback.

- Encourage this trait since you don't want a child who is still dependent entering adulthood. Don't over-encourage it, or you will create a standard too high for a healthy self-esteem to achieve. Your NT will then fail too often in his (or her) own estimation.
- Help them develop a sense of needing others and you develop their social skills too.

Calm, Cool, Collected

The NTs have been accused of having "ice in their veins." However, calmness can be a very necessary strength because a calm spirit often handles the pressures of life best. They can face extreme criticism and pressure without flinching and without panic. Most of us would wish for more of this natural, NT ability.

Passion and excitement are kept inside and, since both of these border on emotion, they must be kept in control. The NT appears to have no emotions until you try to inhibit their freedom to explore or make them conform when they don't think it makes sense. Then you find they do have emotions after all. The cool, calm exterior is a control on emotional engagement to further enable a purely rational process of the mind.

If they are ruffled, you can be sure they are living in their weaknesses, and this strength is simply not being used. Teach them to use it. NTs are also the ones with a strong will power who can be told "Use your strength" or, "Be calm now, and think clearly;" and they can usually do this, if they want to.

Comments on the strength as seen in children:

- Watch for this cool, calm exterior in your child. If it is connected with curiosity and ingenuity, you have an NT operating healthily.
- Watch their lack of need to have emotional warmth, such as touching, and don't force them to be "cuddlers." They detest the emotional display.
- The cool approach supports their mental development. Encourage it. If, as a mother, you pine for more emotional connection with your little

NT, you are best advised to set your goal low for the benefit of both of you.

- Even when they are excited, NTs are cool and calm, which can make a parent feel they are never really happy. They are, if they are achieving.
- If you are an NF parent, don't try to make them into your image. They will look upon you as weak and pathetic. Their drive will prevail, and you will fail.

Logical, Reasonable, Must Make Sense, Analytical

Again, almost everything in this temperament supports the common goal of ingenious discovery. Logic, analysis, reason, and the drive to do only what makes sense creates an atmosphere of discovery. This temperament is not in sole possession of logic, but they are distinct in that their logic is usually devoid of emotional disturbance, as though emotions have no place in intelligence (which is, of course, not true). Emotions discover and verify things just as logic does.

If it makes sense, is reasonable, or is approved by them as logical, NTs can be easily persuaded to do it. They will normally just do it. Reason and logic are their ultimate standards of judgment. When logic is used alone in the field of human relationships, much can be missed and misinterpreted. Thus overuse of this strength is a prime mistake of the NT.

Comments on the strength as seen in children:

- What surfaces earliest is their staunch opposition to do anything that doesn't make sense to them.
- Watch the effectiveness of reason to change behavior. It works best with this temperament, and starts early in life as a useful force in parental control measures.
- Please study the NT method of discipline (under "Parenting Styles") for an understanding of how they will do what makes sense to them and how you can use this strength to aid your discipline issues with the NT.
- They are little nonconformists, struggling to make sense of their world. Don't over-correct their dependency to rely on what makes sense. Respect the strength, but guide it.

Ingenious, There Must Be another Way

The NT is the intuitive mind with the compulsion to find better ways of doing things and create a better world. Their intuition is governed by reason more than by feelings. Therefore, their ingenuity is confined more to the cerebral than the intuitive insight and discovery of the NF. NTs can take longer to come to their ingenious discoveries than the NF. The lightening speed of intuition in the world of emotions and feelings can bring immediate results for the NF. (The NF tends to see things faster where emotion is involved.) Ingenuity via reason takes time and careful thought. The NT majors on this analytical approach, while the NF, using both reason and emotion (but majoring on insights) often sees in a flash of inspiration.

Ingenuity is a combination of strengths that center the NTs' powers in the analytical, or logical, mind. NTs generate and organize ideas and concepts in their minds in resourceful, insightful, and clever ways. This we refer to as being ingenious.

Comments on the strength as seen in children:

- Look under the strength "Strategic" for comments that are also applicable here.
- Ingenuity will evidence itself in an incessant urge to build things and find new ways to do things. NTs will conceive of different ways to use their eating utensils, writing instruments, and just about anything.
- Building toys (such as Legos) are favored, and they may show an early desire to play games of strategy like chess.

Efficient, Effective, Achieve

The self-image of NTs depends on their achieving! Without results, they feel they have proven to themselves that their drives are devoid of effectiveness. That hurts! To achieve, they set goals and create expectations. They are then driven in their desire to reach them and even exceed them. Everything about their temperament is designed to succeed in discovery and ingenuity. When expectations are not met and must be dismissed, the NT suffers the pain of defeat.

In their drive to efficiently achieve their goals, the NT usually does not equal the logistical skills of the SJ who plans the efficient movement of goods and people. Efficiency of thought and strategy is more the skill of the NT, not logistics. It is not easy to observe the difference.

Comments on the strength as seen in children:

- Depression sets in and they lose interest in all things pleasurable when they are not achieving their own independent goals. Parent them in a way that will help them achieve. Assist in achievement, but don't do it for them. It must be their achievement.
- Watch for a loss of industrious curiosity. It is a flag of dismal things to come. Dampened curiosity is a real low for an NT child.
- Promote personal achievement, and you will help them grow all of their many related strengths. Make sure you pay as much attention to their ingenious Lincoln Log constructions as you do to the sports successes of your other children. Even spend time sitting watching them build and explore the possibilities of their physical world.

Abstract in Speech

If you are an SP or SJ there will be a communication barrier with the NT. You will find them difficult to follow at times. Abstract conversation does not feature in concrete facts and details, but rather uses the language of concepts, ideas, and theoretical abstractions. You will find yourself saying "Tell me plainly" or "Put that in real details."

NTs think like they talk. Therefore, a concrete, real life example may be difficult for them at times, since it causes them to think of the various abstract possibilities that can distract them from the reality of the real life example. Making sure you understand what they are trying to say is the way to solve most communication problems between Ss and Ns.

Comments

The NTs, though rare, will open up a new world for both parent and child, and their strengths will be enriching to life. Like any other temperament, their weaknesses are not helpful. However, they can be the calm element in a family that holds it together as long as the family sees the NT's strengths positively. An NT can bring great joy and pride to understanding parents.

The Native Strengths of the NF Temperament

If you have determined that your child is an NF temperament, run through this list of strengths and highlight the ones you can already see in them. Of course, some strengths you will be able to see, and some will be hidden from you due to being undiscovered by you or your child, unexercised, or both.

Health is found in living happily in our native strengths. The ones that are unseen by you in your children may be able to be confirmed, or otherwise, by observing your children when you design ways for them to use an unseen strength. Children lock into the moment when they are using their strengths, and you may be able to observe their focus and pleasure. Repeated use and observation will encouragement development of the strength, and you will clearly see whether your child is fulfilled and happy in the positive use of the strength.

Remember that not every NF strength is present in each NF, but most of them are. Likewise for the other temperaments. Also, some will be more dominant than others. If you scan the other temperaments you will probably see that your little NF has some of those strengths as well. They are present as secondary strengths, as we have already noted; and if the child has been using a secondary strength often, it may have become a distinct part of his or her behavior. There is nothing wrong with this, but we should still encourage the true NF strengths since this is where their greatest fulfillment is found.

An excellent way to know your children and note their progress is to make your own notes on the use of their strengths as you see them develop. Keep a journal on your children. This way you will be able to spot more quickly the weaknesses that will show up from time to time, and take appropriate action. Later, this journal can help your children understand themselves, and read an interesting history of the development of their strengths.

Now, proceed through each of the strengths and become familiar with them.

Here Is a List of the Main NF Strengths

Strengths related to time

Orientation to Time — Lives In the Future

Are you saying to yourself that it is impossible to live in the future? I agree, if you are talking about living with the five physical senses in the future. But NFs live in their minds more than they live in the physical world. As they walk through the real world they are living in the imaginations and realities that they create in their minds. You can live in the future in your mind! The NF has fashioned this "living in the future" to (among other things) refresh their spirits by creating and enjoying idealistic dreams.

Their relation to the future is also a searching for its possibilities. The future is full of possibilities. Some are predictable, and others are not. Most of their strengths are related to a pleasurable, idealistic search for meaning and fulfillment, held and hidden in the possibilities of the future, and experienced by them for a second time in the realities of the present moment and, for a third time, in their memory. Whereas the SP squeezes every ounce of pleasure out of the present moment, the NF gets the most pleasure out of the future, and wrings out the rest of their refreshing pleasure from the present and the past.

Everyone can try to enjoy everything three times: in expectation, in the actual experience, and in memory, like they do. However, the SJs are not so skilled when facing the future. The NTs are too busy to bother (and some consider it too fanciful), while the SPs don't really want to look too hard at the future or the past. That leaves the NFs as the experienced experts of future enjoyment and possibility programming.

The NF stands facing the future, searching and evaluating its opportunities, and walking passionately into its possibilities. This can create an optimistic attitude if the possibilities look bright. However, depression ensues if the possibilities are not impressive enough to generate the pleasure of passion.

Like the SP (whose optimism is hard to dampen), the NF can display some Epicurean pleasure. However, the NF's pleasure must be meaningful, or it is empty and too shallow to be indulged. It is relatively easy for the NF to be caught up in tomorrow's hopes and promises, living the imaginative pleasure of them today.

It will be interesting to discover how many of the drives that propel the life of an NF are related to this future time orientation. In the terminology of Disneyland, they live in "Tomorrow Land."

Comments on the strength as seen in children:

- Children are creatures of hope. However, that hope can be snuffed out early in life and cause them to suffer from a malfunctioning system. Hope is an essential lubricant for the mind. Although essential for all, hope is a major part of the NF's orientation to life. Therefore, it is something to watch for in your NF. "Is hope healthy in my NF?" you ask yourself. If not, depression is lurking.
- Dreams are an integral part of life for the NF. Their dream life keeps them gazing longingly into the future. Don't disparage their dreams by day or by night.
- This interest in the future encourages the NF's use of imagination. Imagination is so vital to the mental functioning and the progress we make in our world that it is to be especially treasured in the NF and the NT. Listen to their dreams and their hopes, and show great interest.
- Faith is easier for NFs if they are allowed to dream, and if their self-images are healthy. Encourage their faith and trust in things unseen and their faith in themselves whenever it falters. Encourage their dreams.
- Watch for and be happy with periods of daydreaming, since these activities are refreshing to the spirit of NFs and build their imaginations. If the child is an INF, these periods are recharging times for when their batteries are flat.

Idealists, Possibility Seekers

No temperament is so affected by ideals as the NF. They see almost every possibility with the optimism of the idealist. They create visions of the ideal, strive for the ideal, imagine the ideal, and live in the ideal creations of their minds. This is why, when the ideal image they have created and set on their pedestal of hope falls, they are so desperately devastated and shocked. They have already lived it in their minds and walked its golden streets in their imagination; so, to see their vivid versions that were displayed in living color in their virtual worlds smashed is like losing reality. It was real to them!

NFs are the masters of trusting relationships, and everyone they trust or love is created as an ideal. When these idealized people disappoint, the image falls off the pedestal, and great is the fall thereof. Idealists can be called the optimists of the "not yet." As long as they see the future in this hopeful mold they are happy and above despair.

Often the word *idealist* is seen as overestimation, exaggeration, rashness, and miscalculation. And sometimes it is. However, there is a more sober, needed meaning to the NF's idealistic dreams. To see the future through the eyes of hope, and to hope for the ideal conclusion to something is better than to look dismally and negatively, doubting the good and magnifying the bad. So it is that there is health and happiness reserved for the hopeful optimist. The NF idealism is a form of optimism.

Is it too much to say that this is a strength the world needs to see? The world would do well to enjoy the idealistic dream while it lasts. Isn't it better than looking at the equally unpredictable pessimist's projections of the future? A considerable number of the NF's dreams are actualized: more than we remember, for we count our disappointments religiously while we tend to forget our realized dreams and hopes. Trouble registers in not-to-be-forgotten colors; realized dreams pass and we move on to the next. Idealists are often the visionaries and leaders. Gandhi is a powerful reminder. Gandhi was an NF.

The most common negative reflection of this strength is its nonuse. Without it, weakness in the NF character is rife.

Comments on the strength as seen in children:

- Little NFs see their ideals fall so often that they can quickly learn to destroy them in order to avoid embarrassment and hurt. This is a personal disaster. The world needs their idealism. And they need it also, to live healthy, happy lives. Much of the NF's fulfillment and pleasure comes from their ideals and the dreams that create them. When their ideals are dashed, take steps to comfort and encourage the NF to dream and hope again. Never join in the destruction of their ideals. A parent of an NF must see this as a prime area of NF child management.
- Likewise, when a girlfriend or boyfriend dashes expectations and dreams, help and comfort the child's wounded heart and refresh it with much love.
- Listen with patience to their ideals and plans for the future.
- Read fantasy and make-believe to them. Join in their dream-world and don't ever pour cold water on their fantasyland.
- Always commend imagination that creates the ideal. Imagination is the next strength that we will consider.

Imaginative

Imagination belongs to everyone, of course. But some have sharpened its use, and none more so than the NT and NF, because they live primarily in their inner world: their minds. It is here that imagination flourishes and grows. Unlike experience that exists only in the real world, imagination exists and thrives in the virtual world. Imagination leads to all kinds of discoveries. In the NF, the imagination is fueled by the emotions as well as reason and is most potent. The NF is the master of imagination.

Imagination goes beyond reason to probe the possibilities, and often discovers what reason cannot. It drives passion and makes the future much more exciting. I cannot imagine what it would be like to live without imagination lighting up the path into the future.

The main weakness related to this strength is its nonuse. It can be overused and wrongly used; but its nonuse cripples the world of possibilities.

Comments on the strength as seen in children:

- Children's imaginations are pure. Try not to adulterate them.
- Watch for NF children to imagine their toys to be monsters, real people, or anything, actually, is possible. Anything!
- An NF's room can be littered with imaginary realities that are very meaningful to the child. Tidy it up with the child's permission and direction!
- Real life is often seen by those with little imagination as superior to flights of fantasy. Sad thought!
- The combination of intuition, imagination, and sensitivity is the potent recipe for genius that occurs only very occasionally, of course.
- Imagination in a child can be so enhanced as to cause them to imagine reality even when the reality did not occur. They have often been accused of lying when they truly thought that what they were saying was real, and that it was what actually happened. Some temperaments find this unbelievable. It is, for those temperaments. Be careful to judge justly and if needed help guide the NF to reality.

Passionate, Enthusiastic

If NFs are anything they are passionate. Now, of course, you may not see the passion very easily at times, and that confuses some. Surely passion can be seen, you may argue. Especially in the introverted NFs, passion is being experienced at a high level of intensity within them, but not shared. Therefore, it is not seen. Often, all you will see is the intensity in their demeanor and nothing more.

Passion comes from the Greek word *pathos*, which means suffering. Passion is a form of suffering. It revs up the senses, and the inner intensity it causes can be stressful, even ultimately damaging to the system. The NF's passion can express itself in anger or love, in hurt or happiness. Anything can become a passion. And its command of their system means it is essential that some form of control over it must be learned in order to avoid the malfunctioning of the human system.

Passion is not an unmixed blessing. Choices about our passions and wisdom in their execution are mandatory or they do harm. The wrong use of passion is its greatest weakness, although overuse often leads to the wrong use.

Comments on the strength as seen in children:

- Watch for the sudden explosion of emotions, which to the SJ will seem like an over-sensitivity of the senses. Passion is known to explode and implode. Watch for both.
- Your children will be parented well if you teach them self-control of their emotions. To help them, urge them to use their strengths constructively. That is the number one way to promote self-control. Don't focus on their destructive use of passions. Focus on what you want — the constructive use of passion. Focus on "do," not "don't."
- Their emotions are just under the skin (if that deep) and can erupt in pleasure or distress at any second. You already know this if you parent an NF!
- Parents can become over-reactive or, in fear of these emotions, do nothing about them. Rather, this is the opportunity to inject reason, love, and appreciation into a child's life and help promote self-control.
- Passion is the NF child's energy and motivation, so don't destroy it. Direct it.
- Watch for over-sensitivity and over-passionate expressions, and you will be ready for the over-passionate actions that follow quickly.
- The NF's speech will also betray them. The use of exaggerations declares their passion.
- The NF's passion will often lead them to hurt others or themselves. Be mindful of this.

Trusting

The tendency to trust others increases the NF's ability to influence and motivate people, but when thoughtlessly applied it becomes a weakness. The weakness appears as misplaced trust and an unwillingness to disconnect when trust has been violated. Some will tend to trust everyone. NFs feel that trust brings out the best in people. The strength relates to their desire to please, as well as their search for pleasant, harmonious relationships. Trust is the basis of all relationships, of course. Without it, no love can be authentic or relationship stable.

In relationships, NFs trust readily and will often not disconnect (even if abused) because they feel there still are possibilities for change and the ideal may return. Understanding themselves and their temperament's strengths (a step often neglected in counseling) — especially this excessive urge to trust — will help them best handle an overuse of this strength.

Trust is also related to possibilities and, since the NF finds possibilities in everyone, God can be easily trusted too. However, if they believe they have been jilted or unjustly treated by the Divine One, trust can turn to bitter resentment and outright opposition.

Comments on the strength as seen in children:

- Teach the NF to manage this strength carefully. If they do not learn to trust others several of their other strengths are also crippled. Keep the trusting attitude in place, but controlled. Help them evaluate more carefully where strangers are involved. Teach them to develop, as secondary strengths, the SJ's caution and a little of the NT's doubt — just a little! Skepticism and doubt do not fit well on the shoulders of an NF, unless they are deeply hurt.
- Watch the way NFs quickly include others in their circle. Even the introverts (who are, by nature, territorial) will include others readily before they wilt from too much people contact and seek solitude.
- The SJ can be cautious of others; the SP, welcoming, but selective; and the NT, at times, anti social. The NF child will stand out in the arena of relationships as the trusting one.
- Be very cautious of their choices in relationships, as they can easily commit and give away full trust based on only a warm feeling. NF children do this readily, and so do many adults.

Personal Growth, Seekers of Meaning and Significance

The goal of the INFJ is to lead people to realize their highest potential, and the INFP desires to heal the wounds and bring wholeness (which, to them, is a fullness of life). Both the ENFJ (who teaches and exhorts with the same goal in mind) and the ENFP (who champions a cause) are focused on people's personal growth, as well as their own. When they fail to achieve this goal in everyone they know, they feel like failures and question their abilities to influence and cause vibrant growth. Life only has meaning when we live near our potential, NFs believe. It is then, and only then, that we become significant to others and to our world. Weaknesses develop when they don't use this strength. They wander aimlessly through life, and that can mean trouble.

Comments on the strength as seen in children:

- The ability to assist others in personal growth is in the developmental stage while young, and you may see only glimpses of it.
- Meaning and significance can be observed in the way they react to friends and events. Only the meaningful will likely be repeated.

Strengths Related to Sensitivity

In the NF, there is a very noticeable second pole around which the strengths can be grouped. After twenty-five years or so of observation, time is the first one and, to me, sensitivity is the second.

The first cousins of sensitivity are intuition, emotion, empathy, caring, kindheartedness, people skills, reality and authenticity; romanticism, introspection, and perfectionism.

Sensitive

Sensitivity is a finely tuned response to stimuli, both outside of us and inside of us. The word comes from the Latin word-family for "sense" or "senses." Sense impressions are received physically (through the five senses) and spiritually (through inner mechanisms, one of which is intuition). Imagination, thoughts, and emotions can emit sensations too, just as truly as touch, taste, and smell. When we say the NF displays the strength of sensitivity, we mean they are sensitive to all external sensory input, and particularly to the inner senses.

Therefore, unseen, inner experiences can suddenly affect them and engage their complete attention. This feeling, for the NF, can be very forceful, and can overpower them at times. Many have described the NF as being over-sensitive. So watch for them to be sensitive to even the slightest thing. Just to make it difficult, they will often show no signs of being affected by outside or inside stimuli because they internalize all they sense and feel. And they often don't feel the need to let you know what is going on inside of them. This makes knowing them almost impossible. "Now you see it, now you don't" is what you will have to get used to with the NF.

Sensitivity alerts us to danger and opportunities. Both are good. Therefore, we should not see this strength of the NF as unnecessary or harmful just because we consider their sensitivity to be over-reactive. Only the nonuse, overuse or wrong use of a strength is damaging. However, because it is seen as the cause of their emotional volatility, people (including the NF) want to eradicate it. What a mistake!

NFs need to be very sensitive for their intuition to function well and for their creativity, love, empathy, and people skills to flourish. Artists (of which there are quite a few NFs) rely on it to create their masterpieces. Many more create masterly relationships from the same strength.

Managing their responses to sensitivity helps NFs master its powers and reduce its damage, particularly if they over-internalize things.

Comments on the strength as seen in children:

- You may observe above-normal sensitivity to physical pain in your NF child.
- NFs are often very easily upset by the slightest thing. This is their sensitivity in action.
- Not only what is said can upset them, but what is not said, because their expectations are suddenly denied or somehow changed. This can be a real inner hurt to the NF.
- Atmosphere affects their behavior and mood. The NF can be at home and happy in one room, and simply changing rooms can depress their spirit rapidly and create aberrant behavior.
- Watch for a combination of intuition and sensitivity to cause a heightened perception. Extra sensory perception (ESP) can become

apparent in your child. It is not necessarily damaging though others fear it can be.

- Since NFs live, most of the time, in their minds they can be very responsive intellectually, quickly grasping the big picture and becoming bored with a detailed description. Sensitivity, imagination, and intuition can result in this kind of intelligence.
- The sensitivity can also be seen in aesthetic appreciation. They may not want to wrench away from a sunset or other attraction because their inner receptacles are being flooded with pleasant sensibilities. Some "place" may hold a pronounced value to them.
- Such things as physical closeness are also deeply rewarding and quickly activate their emotions, creating deep satisfaction. Hug them often and triple it if you are a T!
- Don't make derogatory remarks about their sensitivity. When it poses a problem, help them manage the emotions it causes. They have to learn this self-control for adult life, and the earlier, the better.

Intuitive

Intuition is the knowing of something without the use of the five physical senses or the power of reason alone. Intuition finds its full expression in the NF. This intuitive knowledge can cause them to be able to look at someone and perceive their thoughts, feelings, and attitudes – but not at will.

It can be "creepy," especially to the S who questions, "How do we know things that our five physical senses can't tell us?" Obviously, some other dimension is involved. We can deny this, but if we do, we must have a reasonable explanation for the experiences of intuition and extra sensory perception. The person who lives across the country and yet knows, by intuition alone, that his father has just died is an example of raw intuition. Coincidence does not explain it, unless we give to coincidence the same powers we have given to intuition. But then all we have done is change the name. There is a Christian explanation that involves the human spirit and God's Spirit. Since this is not the place to discuss intuition's rationale or spiritual basis, we will simply accept its reality in our human experience.

NFs are especially given to visions, dreams, and extra sensory experiences. If we call these things (or only some aspect of them) "intuition," we will be acknowledging its reality even if we know little about it.

Intuition is commonly experienced as knowing what another person is thinking or feeling, or that something is wrong with someone when no indication of it has been observed. Counselors and coaches who have a high degree of intuition frequently intuit their client's inner condition. Intuition and empathy often work together.

Temperament assessments that are built on the Myers Briggs and Keirsey models accept that intuition is a way of gathering information from the world around us distinct from the use of the five physical senses. This appears as either an "S" or an "N" in the temperament profiles.

Intuition can easily be misinterpreted, misunderstood, or even inaccurately recognized. Regardless, it is still a reality and a force in our experiences.

Comments on the strength as seen in children:

- Children can be frightened by intuitive feelings. Little children often see creatures in their room, or tell us amazing things about which we know they had no knowledge. Premonitions occur in children as well as adults (perhaps even more clearly than they do in adults).
- What the parent is thinking might suddenly be reflected in the child's behavior or speech. This seeming knowledge of another's thoughts or feelings can indicate the presence of a strong intuition.
- They will often have just the right thing to say or do, showing intuitive (not observational) knowledge of what the other person needs.
- This perception seems to be clearest in childhood because there is little in the way of personal doubts to intrude and cloud their reception.
- Intuitive knowledge is often amazingly and frighteningly accurate.

Emotional

The emotional content of love and hate is undisputed. The NF is capable of extremes in both directions. Anger them, and they may release a verbal broadside of gigantic proportions or keep an equally forceful reaction inside themselves. Love them, and you can be the recipient of overwhelming expressions of love. Hurt them, and the opposite will visit you.

The control of this strength is hard for the NF to accomplish. Their EQ (emotional quotient) depends on the control of their powerful emotions, so it is worth much effort to teach them self-control before they reach teenage. If you don't, it will be a trying time for both parents and teenager to learn emotional intelligence in those turbulent years and beyond.

Emotions are such a complex drive that it is impossible to do justice to their importance within the scope of this book. All of us find them difficult to manage when they are stirred. They can interrupt the briefest of encounters and change a relationship in seconds. However, we would live a sterile life without them. When the negative powers of our emotions are in full flight, we often wish we did. Parents sometimes pay more attention to developing a child's IQ, when EQ will have more to do with success or failure in life. To create a mature and successful adult, give most of your time to teaching your child emotional control and the positive use of emotions. Parents should read Daniel Goleman's *Emotional Intelligence.*

Weaknesses are many from the overuse of this strength, which is most common; but don't forget those created by the nonuse and the wrong use of emotion.

Comments on the strength as seen in children:

- Teach them to accept delay of gratification. This is, perhaps, the simplest and most effective way of training them to control their emotions. A simple game of waiting 15 minutes before they eat their treat in order to get a second treat is a good way to start. Teach them, also, to wait for things and be patient with other people. This teaches self-control of emotions, too. Reward their successes.
- Teaching children consideration for others is another simple way to help them use their emotions constructively. Positive reinforcement of

this evidence of emotional control, encourages repeat performances. Remember, the more we use a strength, the stronger it gets.

- Teach and encourage the expression of healthy emotions, such as love, gentleness, kindness, etc.
- Discourage negative emotions (emotions used to hurt themselves or others). Perhaps I should emphasize that not all anger is negative. Negative emotions are defined as above!

Empathetic

The ability to feel another's pain and empathize is an NF's native strength. The other temperaments can sympathize, but it takes real effort and a special quality of the human spirit to empathize. Empathy is produced by intuitive qualities and an alert sensitivity, together with sensitive emotions. Empathizers project their personality into the personality of another so that they may understand them and their feelings better. This is not so much a deliberate effort as it is giftedness.

Here is a further explanation of empathy for those who want to understand it better. The English word comes from the Greek word *empatheia*, which conveys the idea of passion, affection, and concern. It suggests that our emotions are involved in positive concern for another person. Sympathy could be defined that way too, but empathy takes sympathy a step further. It is one personality entering the other personality and fully understanding, usually with the purpose of sharing the burden of their feelings and concerns so that they can be helped. The ability to sense the feelings of others, know what is felt or thought, and share their pain is what is meant by the strength we call empathy. Sometimes it will be just a knowing; sometimes a feeling; often both, and always with concern. Intuition is not the same as empathy and is a knowledge that does not necessarily result in concern.

Some NFs are so empathetic that they find it hard to function when experiencing the pain that others feel. Sharing the pain of another, even to the point of becoming sick or depressed is not uncommon.

Most of us would agree that empathy is a wonderful gift and does much good in any society, particularly the small society of a home. It is hard for

NFs not to be empathetic, so they usually develop a weakness from this strength by overuse, causing them to overload and stress over other people's concerns.

Comments on the strength as seen in children:

- Notice if your child weeps easily with others, or shows exceptional concern for the suffering of others. Warmly commend their empathy; but don't actively encourage it, since children can hurt unduly from the pains of others and it can be a burden too great for them to bear. Adulthood can bring a greater understanding and wisdom to know one's empathetic limits and learn to disconnect where needed.
- Help them modify their pain by showing them how to help the person they feel for in practical ways and by reasoning away the excessive case of de-motivating pain that cripples their emotions. Get help if your child is being negatively affected by empathetic feelings.
- Show sympathy and understanding for their empathetic experience and they will share more with you, allowing you more opportunity to help.

Humanitarian

Humanitarianism surely is expected in a temperament that majors on empathy, concern for others, love, kindness, and emotions. A humanitarian is one who promotes the welfare of our human race — put simply, one who helps humanity by seeking to eliminate pain and suffering.

Some NFs extend this humanitarian concern to all living creatures. If they inadvertently squash a bug they become upset and feel guilty. Others are selective and they show concern for all living creatures except, say, snakes or spiders.

Comments on this strength in children:

- This humanitarian trait is to be encouraged alongside of their kindheartedness.

- Whereas you may notice the SJ child being the helpmate of people who have fallen on hard times, the NF sees the condition as another call to help humanity as well as the individual and show concern to all.
- The world needs more of this strength displayed with wisdom and understanding. Compliment your child!

Seekers of Harmony, Haters of Discord

Since the NF is all about relationships, any lack of harmony registers on their radar. So strong is this love of unity that, when disturbed, it can actually incapacitate them. Discord is hated with a passion. Of course, they must take care that their own passion doesn't draw them into escalating the discord.

Harmony calms the NF, and they become productive. It is the sign of health in relationships. Harmony is not the same as agreement. Harmony can exist when disagreement is accepted and respected.

Comments on this strength in children:

- When upset because of disharmony in a relationship, you may see either anger or withdrawal. Withdrawal should not be seen as an indication that they are not really upset. Instead, it may be a sign they don't know how to deal with it or they are on the verge of deep anger.
- Emotional upset often stems from a lack of harmony. Before you react to their outburst or withdrawal, determine whether disharmony is at the root of their actions.
- The solution to your child's upset lies in addressing and lovingly restoring harmony, if that is possible. If the source of disharmony is you, it is in your interests, as well as theirs, to make every effort to restore harmony. Remember, NFs are all about relationships and can't function well if a close relationship has been disturbed.

Kindhearted

With all this sensitivity and emotional concern for others, kindness seems an essential medication in an NF's first aid relationship kit. It is. The SP and the SJ are also very kindhearted. Differentiate between the SJ's kindness (displayed as helpfulness), the SP's kind generosity, and the NF's touching attempts at creating a world of love.

Kindness has been with us from the beginning. Plato believed the idea of the good (*agathos*) is all embracing — the highest most dominant idea or thought for us as humans. He equated this goodness with kindness. Kindness, then, is a great thought and most noble when it is translated into an action. Aristotle, also, in his *Ethics* defines kindness as the goal of all action! The Greeks believed that in order to be kind, we need to free ourselves from material ties. The NF is the spiritual temperament who can easily embrace this ancient and still valid idea of kindness.

The Greeks had several words for kindness, including *chrestos*. Just like all the ancient understandings of this strength, *chrestos* links goodness with kindness. A "kind" wine was a good wine. Kindness was seen as having a friendly nature and a mildness about one that shunned roughness. The NF, living in his or her strength, exemplifies this!

Perhaps of interest is that *chrestos* was, on occasion in ancient literature, mistakenly used for *Christos*, the Greek word for Christ. He was, in effect, being named "Kind," instead of Christ. It is a happy mistake, as the core of his teaching is love that is practically expressed in kindness and a love that would eventually give birth to hospitals, mercy missions, and the spread of kindness in our world. Kindness is love incarnate. Kindness has been emphasized, by all leaders who view goodness, as important to social welfare. It expresses love practically and effectively. That is what the NF who is living in this strength is doing — expressing and showing love. They long for a world where everyone is kind. Kindness is strengthened by caring, humanitarian concerns, empathy, and other strengths of the NF temperament.

The most common weakness that relates to this strength is the nonuse of it when NFs have withdrawn due to anger. Sometimes that anger is due to a kindness being shunned or thrown away, which huts the NF deeply.

Comments on the strength as seen in children:

- Note how long it has been since your NF did some kind deed for you, or touched your heart with their genuine love. Was it not so long ago? You should see it often in a healthy NF. All temperaments will do this; but the NF is the master of empathetic kindness.
- You will see a kindness in your NF, particularly when they detect some sadness in you, or need for comfort and help. Accept it.
- If they withdraw from you (they can and will), you will know that they somehow were hurt by something you did or did not do. They are waiting, and inwardly hurting, while hoping that either they or you will find a way to mend the wounds and restore the all too needed harmony. Once it is restored, kindness is the order of the day again.
- Of course, encourage this strength.

People Skills

Diplomacy is the ability to bring opposing parties together and to work with people in difficult circumstances to respectfully merge opposite agendas. It does not, in my opinion, describe the intellect of an NF. Keirsey thinks it does and, of course, I respect his reasons. He calls the NF the "diplomatic intelligence." This is true. But I think the NF's intelligence is more than simply diplomatic in its functioning and has other dominant functions as well. Diplomacy describes the NF's ability to use both emotion and rationality to find solutions to complex problems.

NFs purposefully use diplomacy to bring people together or to maintain relationships. They are the masters of people skills and will often sacrifice personally just to maintain morale in the workplace. The urge for creating harmony among people is what drives them to intervene and attempt reconciliation with their people skills. At this, they are very skilled.

People skills lead them into occupations where people management and the powers of persuasion are paramount. As sales people, they show a strong desire to please the customer and sell only what they believe will be for the customer's good. To sell the customer something they do not need leaves them feeling guilty.

The nonuse of this strength is seen most often when they are angry or disturbed.

Comments on the strength as seen in children:

- Watch how the NFs attempt to bring people together and bring resolution to sticky relationship problems among their friends. If you see them trying to negotiate a peace between their playmates, you can smile and later compliment them warmly. They are being what they are.
- Encourage this skill because if they can't bring people together they suffer from the disharmony and can even become sick as a result.
- "Little counselors" will quickly attempt diplomatic activity with their parents if they detect trouble in their parents' relationship. They will give advice and often will not let the matter drop until both parties accept a resolution. They can be tenacious!
- Leave them in charge of their peers and you can be assured of an all out attempt to barter a diplomatic peace.
- Don't, in a derogatory manner, call them "people pleasers." They may then attempt to show a stern rough manner just to prove themselves acceptable to you.
- Furthermore, understand their desire to please is not only due to self-esteem but to their desire to show kindness and build harmony.

Real and Authentic, Ethical

Being false or less than authentic eats away at the NF, as it does with all the temperaments, and causes real guilt. But this feeling seems more prevalent and persistent in an NF. Being a real, genuine, ethical, person is so important to them that they will often sacrifice their goals and comfort just to be seen as authentic. The NF is the ethical temperament that feels a strong urge to follow its own ethical standards.

Ethical inconsistency in their virtual worlds, where they live most of the time, amounts to war with themselves. They can be slow to see that their anger, at times, is a loss of personal integrity because they are not being true to their desire to love. The NFs are very sensitive to any disturbance inside themselves. Every failure or lack of integrity is internalized and, unfortunately, in most is mulled over and becomes their focus. Their self-esteem suffers.

For them, inner purity is the only way to live in peace. They are the judges of their inner purity, too; and they can judge harshly, often establishing exaggerated guilt. This strength can turn quickly into the weakness of self-condemnation, even causing self punishment.

Comments on the strength as seen in children:

- Watch carefully because NF children can often be very angry at themselves and you may think they are angry with you or someone else, instead.
- Standards of personal authenticity can be placed very high, and failure to reach them is then certain and, at times, results in depression.
- Extreme and unwarranted guilt can eat away at them, so the closer your bond, the more likely you will be told of their inner struggles. You then can help with teaching, comfort, and understanding.
- Since the above conditions are internal and cannot be seen, watch for depression and sadness. They will flag you that something is amiss.

Romantic

Two days ago at a seminar, an NF who was known to everyone there described himself as "incurably romantic," and the chuckles of agreement collapsed the whole group into understanding laughter. Everyone knew this romantic had correctly identified himself. Read the list of NF strengths again (the bold headings) and I think you will see many strengths that contribute to this one, including idealist, passionate, sensitive and emotional.

For the NF, romance extends beyond people and relationships. The atmosphere of a favored restaurant can be romantic. A sunset can bring out their romantic feelings, and nearly always does. All temperaments can wax romantic, but the NF is accompanied by romantic feelings to the extent that they are characterized by them.

Romantic surroundings initiate feelings of love, and an NF is deeply stirred by its power. Weaknesses enter when they don't welcome their romantic feelings, and life then becomes prosaic and stale. NFs don't believe that they can ever overuse this strength.

Comments on this strength as seen in children:

- NF children readily warm and become attentive to romantic environments. Their inner intensity increases and their sensitivities come alive in romantic settings. An NF child will cherish the flowers brought to their mother or a candlelight dinner as much as the recipient.
- Make their special days (birthdays are an example) romantic with candles, colors, and decorations that suggest the feelings they cherish most. This is positively stimulating to them.
- Be ready to calm the emotions of an NF who is disappointed or hurt by romantic rejections.
- Try to share their romantic moments, even if the same moments are not stimulating to you. This effort will enhance their experience and further bond them to you as they appreciate your effort.

Introspective

"Introspection" means internalizing things and NFs tend to internalize everything. They compare themselves to others constantly. . They consult how they feel about themselves, mercilessly inspecting their performance in the light of others.

Introspection is meant to be self-examination for the purpose of understanding where we need to improve. Positive introspection builds self-image, but negative, harsh or misplaced introspection destroys it. Weaknesses develop easily in an NF when they wrongly use their introspection to inflict condemnation on themselves. Negative self-talk fuels the damage. So remember that introspection helps find shortcomings so that we can clean house and create a positive confidence, not a self-condemning attitude that destroys mental health. A positive conscience and feeling about yourself is the goal of introspection.

I haven't found an NF who doesn't introject everything. I have found many who either overuse or wrongly use this strength.

Comments on the strength as seen in children:

- The NF will suffer guilt for their wrongdoing, sometimes to the extent that it cripples their lives. The SP would never let it cripple his (or her) life. An NF child who is suffering from too much inner self-condemnation can become depressed and will need help.
- Self-depredation is common in the inner life of an NF, and it is usually because they see themselves as less than worthy, even most of the time.
- Watch for a possible fall into depression by children who are suffering from self-judgment. Help them establish positive self-talk.
- Tell them over and over how wonderfully they are made and how they warm your heart. This is the first-aid they need daily for their self-inflicted, inner wounds.
- Of all the temperaments, be very careful in the use of guilt to change behavior. The NFs already tend toward guilt and the use of guilt by the parent, without a way for reconciliation or a positive way out, will amplify guilt in the NF.

Perfectionists — Must Do and Be Right

It is not too great a leap from high self-demands to the desire to be perfect. Every perfectionist is a perfectionist in some, not all, of the things that they do. Perfectionism is a strength when it comes to motivating us to high achievement. It is a curse when it is over done or wrongly applied as self-judgment.

Again, we face a strength that needs careful application and pruning. We are limited beings, as is evidenced by our need to go to bed every night for the rebuilding of our bodies' strength. Therefore, we cannot be perfect in the absolute sense. A perfectionism that condemns us more than it stretches us will de-motivate us and keep us from achieving its intended goal — namely, calling us to better things.

The weaknesses that the overuse and wrong use of this strength can create are only too clear. Watch for the NF's perennial habit of setting high standards and (whether they are reached or not) raising the bar constantly until they cannot clear it, then sinking in self-condemnation and defeat. Introspection and perfectionism combine in the NF to create a dangerous climate for the building and maintenance of self-esteem.

Comments on the strength as seen in children:

- Keenly notice the frustration that comes to children when they are unable to meet their own high demands in, say, test results or their self-determined standards of behavior. Perfectionism is its own prophecy of failure.
- Perfectionism de-motivates, even freezes actions, whereas appropriate high standards and an ability to accept failure lead to healthy development. Modify the strength and help define it positively in your children's minds. Teach them that their perfectionist tendencies call them to higher achievement, but these tendencies must never condemn them for not reaching their goals.
- Teach the child to set realistic goals, or a lofty goal divided into small steps.
- Teach the child that failure is an opportunity, not a cause for despair. Failures are good. All we need to do is learn the lesson they teach. "You failed? Good! Now you have a chance to learn what will take you to the next level!"

Abstract in Speech

NFs prefer to speak abstractly. They talk about concepts, ideas, and possibilities: what if, what should be, what could be, and what might be. They often don't finish their abstract statements as their minds race on to the next thought and they've imagined they've already explained it! The SJ parent can't follow such fast-paced, abstract thinking without anchoring to some detail. "Details!" says the NF, "We'll deal with them later. Let's get the big picture in place first."

If you are an NT, communication with an NF should be no problem. All Ss will feel that NFs are in the clouds much of the time and not grounded in the real world. They mean "not grounded in the details." Don't worry.

Just ask for the NF to say it again, slowly, and with some details if they can do that. Then you will understand them.

The NF's vocabulary will enrich yours (if you are an S) since they are the masters of the superlative, graphic, poetic expression, and they talk in metaphor and simile. Plain Jane language is not their best performance. Encourage their metaphoric style (unless they are writing a scholarly paper), since this is their best contribution.

Comments

The NF's strengths can bless your home. But they need much care and coaching to let the NFs be all that they can be! Yes, let's admit it, the NFs need much more care than other temperaments due to their complexity and unpredictability.

Their low self-image (due mostly to damaging self-talk) will need your attention, too, if they are to attain a healthy self-image. The sky is truly the limit for their possibilities. However, reaching the highest is no easy task. Prepare them as best you can, since their goals are always flying somewhere in the hazy blue yonder.

Beliefs, Dreams, Skills, and More

> *Seek not to understand that you may believe, but believe that you may understand.*
> *~ St. Augustine*

Chapter Fourteen ♦

Creating Positive Beliefs and Changing Undesirable Beliefs – How to Do It!

We now focus on the task of creating positive beliefs in our children, because positive beliefs help our children build their strengths even faster and with greater consistency. Positive beliefs fuel our preferences. Negative beliefs fuel our weaknesses, but by nonuse, overuse or wrong use of our strengths. Therefore, the importance of this chapter should be clear.

What Qualifies as a Positive Belief?

Positive beliefs include any belief that does not damage ourselves or others. They build relationships and do not destroy them. They center on constructive beliefs about our world, others, and ourselves. Damaging beliefs lead inevitably to damaging behavior. Positive beliefs build, lift, and encourage, pointing our way to success, fulfillment and the reaching of our highest potential.

Lift that Self-Image

Josh was a gifted child who could use his people skills and astonish his parents with his love and kindness. He was also mentally bright and when he focused, he solved problems and learned at a remarkable speed. He did not, however, believe that he was really any good. Although his social and intellectual gifts were clearly there, he felt socially inept and intellectually less than average, and he often moaned that he was no good. His belief about himself was holding him back.

Josh is typical of those whose self-beliefs need lifting. Beliefs either empower or defuse the exercise of our gifts. What he needed was a concentrated effort to understand who he was and how good he was. It is always hard to change a child's (or, for that matter, an adult's) self-image. Slowly, Josh learned to think of himself as a unique and wonderful person, every bit as good as anyone else. The use of his giftedness immediately increased. Beliefs raise our ceilings or lower them, and we never really out-perform them. Josh was taught by example and precept to focus on his positive thinking patterns, not his negative condemnations, and he built a strong foundation for his talents.

Parenting a child with a high self-image is a lot easier than parenting a child with a low self-image. It is to your advantage, and your children's, to lift their self-images by building positive beliefs.

This is no surprise. I want to introduce you to ways you can instill positive beliefs and discourage, or change, negative beliefs in yourself and your children.

Belief Drives the Human System

Your children do what they do because of what they believe. Belief drives the human system. We never do anything unless we <u>believe</u> we should do it. Therefore, both helpful behavior and unhelpful behavior stem from belief.

Our first task will be to create in our children positive, helpful beliefs that will result in positive actions (not to focus obsessively on changing the negative ones). We will also bear in mind that undesirable behavior stems from undesirable beliefs and, when those beliefs are damaging to others or ourselves, they should be changed. Our children need to learn how to change undesirable beliefs, how to create desirable ones, and which comes first. Parents will need to spearhead this educational experience and instill its principles to aid children to maturity.

Creating or changing beliefs is not usually a quick fix. Beliefs often take time to instill or replace. However, once new ones are created they are a long-term fix to undesirable behavior if they are accepted and absorbed into a person's life.

Do I Teach Beliefs or Behavior?

We know that desirable beliefs lead to desirable actions, and undesirable beliefs inevitably lead to undesirable actions. However, we tend to focus on teaching the right actions, rather than the right beliefs. Perhaps that is because approximately 86 percent of the population is focused on the outer world of action, what we call the "real" world. This 86 percent are the SPs and the SJs. If a person is lost in their inner world ("inner space cadets," we sometimes call them), we perceive them as not being well grounded in reality. These are the NTs and NFs. The inner world is where beliefs are formed, and the outer world is where actions are performed. As a parent, what should you focus on? Here is a guide:

- Address behavior for the short term and beliefs for the long term. If you need an immediate change in behavior, attempt to change the behavior by distracting the child and helping the child focus on something other than what is causing the unacceptable behavior. This approach will make an immediate change in the behavior.
- Make it your top goal to create repeated desirable behavior. To achieve this, teach and create desirable beliefs and ferret out undesirable beliefs. If you do, you will become a "super" parent. **The super parent is focused on strengths and beliefs.** Remember, beliefs create patterns for the long term.
- Parents usually look for paths to immediate peace. The stress of parenting drives them to this. However, if all you do in your parenting is put out fires, you will never plan for the development of "firebreaks" and other preventive measures. Parent constantly for the long term, and you will parent your child more successfully and reduce your stress in the process.

Model Beliefs

If we want to teach our children desirable beliefs, we must first honestly examine our own beliefs. Are our own beliefs modeling what we are trying to teach our children? Some children have contradicting beliefs because their parents do. They say one thing and act another. Children are quick to pick up on such inconsistency because they are absorbing all they can from their environment, and contradiction is easily noticed when we are trying to absorb new material.

Contradiction leads to confusion. Confusion leads to undesirable behavior. We are the lesson, as well as the giver of lessons. If I had to choose between verbal instruction and modeling with the life, I would choose modeling as the most effective method for training a child. Remember, we can't teach what we are not modeling.

Changing the Mental Landscape

(The plasticity of the brain and how to use it to help create desirable beliefs and to correct undesirable behavior)

Understanding how our brain works and how our mind affects our brain is very helpful in creating desirable beliefs and behavior and in getting rid of unwanted patterns of thought that plague us. Children can get emotionally "stuck" and hold the hurt or the upset in their consciousness for a long time, limiting the growth of their self-control and damaging their relationships. When they do they not only practice an undesirable pattern of behavior, but they develop undesirable beliefs.

They blame others for their condition, or even their behavior. This kind of thinking soon consolidates into beliefs that negatively affect the entire life. They begin to think and believe:

> "Why don't people love me and do more things for me?"
>
> "If only others would be kinder to me, I would be better."
>
> "Everyone is horrible. I can't help what I am doing."

"So and so is the fault and is to blame, not me, because if only he had done such and such, I would not have acted the way I did."

Science has previously maintained adamantly that the brain is pliable and malleable in childhood, but fixed and unchangeable in adulthood, which means, of course, there is little we can do to change an adult pattern of thinking and acting. We now know this is false! The brain remains plastic, even in adulthood. It redesigns its "landscape" constantly as we think new thoughts. So, no matter what the age of the child, the brain's plasticity presents our best opportunity for change.

However, it is true that the adult brain does not make major changes as readily as the young brain. Nonetheless, it is still very malleable, as the following facts will reveal. Here is an understanding of how children, teenagers, and adults change their brains by changing their minds (cognitive behavior). Here, also, are some methods to use with children and teenagers, in particular.

How We Change

- The brain changes constantly with our changing thoughts. The past does not determine the future, unless we welcome its memories into the present moment and continue to entertain those memories in our minds. Hence, it is important to install new thoughts first, if we want to eliminate damaging thoughts.
- The present moment is a tiny slither of time that is gone as fast as a thought is gone. If we want to change our future, we must change our thoughts **in the present moment,** and hold onto that new pattern of thinking. The new pattern will change the brain's functioning, its landscape, and structure for its next conscious moment.
- The present moment determines the immediate future of our feelings and our behavior. When caught up in a tantrum, the child is dragging the hurt or disappointment from the past and holding it in the present by repeatedly rehearsing it. We often say people are "carrying the baggage of their past" into their immediate future by rehearsing its pain. This baggage is what we want to be able to help people leave in the past.

With this knowledge we can see why distracting the child (or adult) works. New thoughts enter the mind when it is distracted and change the "landscape," thus changing the immediate future. The stuck emotions that are creating the tantrum, or the hate, are then "unlocked." Here are two ways we can cause an effective distraction in a young child.

1. Distract children's thoughts by changing the environment. For example, take them to a different room, go outside, take them for a ride, or direct their attention to something they readily respond to. We have all seen how fast a tantrum can disappear if the child's friend arrives at the door.
2. Distract them by all kinds of enticements. Of course, there should be a limit to the use of this method.

Helping Older Children to Change Their Thoughts

If the child is old enough, we can change the mental landscape with reason. Using reason, try to get the child to see that he (or she) is on a fruitless journey that will be damaging to himself, and no one else. For the NT and NF temperaments, this has a better chance of working and of working earlier in life, but it works for all. After all, this is the method that the child must self-employ in adulthood to be able to achieve emotional control. The rational mind can and does influence the emotional mind. This is a basic principle in the way we influence others and ourselves. Use it. You don't need complicated methods if you are not using this one. You probably will never need them if you use reason consistently.

But please, focus on the positive correction, not the negative. If you are all the time correcting instead of building, criticizing instead of teaching, reason will not work well because emotion will be aroused and clouds the landscape of reason.

Reasons for Change Can Center On:

- The uselessness of the child's present course, since it will not get the child what the child wants. For example, anger does not get cooperation, and revenge does not build relationships.

- The hurt they are bringing to themselves. All negative responses hurt us more than they hurt others. Ask them, "Why are you hurting yourself? Does that make sense?"
- The damage they are doing to their relationships with others and to others.
- The unreasonableness of making no sense. This is a reason the NT child should understand. NTs do not want to do what makes no sense. It makes no sense to hurt ourselves in the process of trying to feel better. None of the temperaments want to be known for making no sense, so use it for all.

If you are the object of their anger, there is little use saying, "You are hurting mommy!" They intend to hurt the object of their anger, and will be glad to hear that they are succeeding.

With younger children in particular we can simply ignore undesirable behavior, forcing them to figure out whether their present course of action is achieving anything. Children will learn to do what is in their own best interests. Getting nowhere with their present behavior is not in their best interests.

With some children, they will deliberately hurt themselves as long as they feel that, in the process, they are hurting you. If you suspect this is what they are doing, then ignoring them and showing that they are not infuriating you can be the best course of action. Even a young child will figure out after a while that this is a loser's game.

If the child makes a display in front of others just say, "Sorry for the disturbance, but we are learning an important lesson today," and ignore the child's attempts at controlling the situation by embarrassing you. Smile, and let people think what they will. Most will respect you for your wisdom and self-control.

Using the knowledge of the brain's plasticity to help train your children to change the "landscape" of their brains is the way to produce lasting results and prepare them for adulthood by giving them the capability to self-govern their lives.

Steps for Changing or Creating New Beliefs

The above methods will not only help change the immediate landscape of the brain, but also the beliefs of the child. When something doesn't work the mind is willing to open and consider other options.

To create a new belief we often must start by changing the landscape, as I have described above. We first change the focus by any of the above methods, making the child think differently. Next, we teach new beliefs, because the mind does not want to get rid of what it already has in place and, as a result, create a vacuum. The new belief then fills the mind and eradicates the negative belief.

Four Steps

I have laid out the process in steps (though, in reality, you may be doing more than one at a time). They start with discovering what the damaging belief is. Memorize the steps so that you do them automatically during your parenting tasks. This change process should become a way of life for you as a parent.

1. **Discover.** First discover the belief behind an undesirable action that you have noticed.
    a. To discover it you can take the direct approach. Ask the child, "What do you really believe or think when you do such and such? Why do you believe it, and what for?" The child is then aware of what you are doing, and older children will learn that their beliefs are somehow important and are related to their actions, and this can also be used as a tool to coach them to self regulate.
    b. Next, question the response you get from the child. Ask yourself whether the reply seems true and if it is an adequate cause for the child's actions. In other words, evaluate your child's answers. Your child may not be telling you the truth and may not want to or may not understand his own belief. Therefore, this step is important in the information gathering stage. If the child's answer leaves you skeptical, then rather than

pressing the child for what you feel is an honest answer, go on to the next step.

c. If you are puzzled, confused, or can't get an adequate answer, ask your spouse or an expert coach what he (or she) thinks might be the belief behind the actions. Someone familiar with temperament can use it as a guide to behavior and evaluate the child's answer from that point of view. The accuracy of this approach is amazing. You can do this, too, by reviewing the strengths in your child's temperament (as discussed in this book). You will often find the real reasons and beliefs behind the actions because temperament uncovers their preferences, and their preferences can reveal their beliefs. Of course, experience also helps. Thoroughly understanding a temperament's preferences also aides when the child doesn't know the real reason themselves. When you simply bug children for answers, they know you don't believe what they have said, and harm can be done to your relationship and to the child. The child may also react and embark on a campaign to hide his (or her) motivations from you even more.

2. **Calm the emotions.** We can't teach positive beliefs in a negative emotional environment.

    a. It is not helpful to work in the heat of negative emotions. Your mind is clouded, and so is theirs. More importantly, when emotions run high, the emotions and the disconnectedness they induce become the center of attention. The original issue is lost in personal accusations and hurt feelings. Keep emotions out of it as much as you can, and keep to the discussion of the behavior at issue.

    b. Don't make accusations before you have heard your child out and are sure you have discovered the truth. Emotions flare at accusations. Your children feel they have a right to be heard. After they have defended themselves, the truth can be stated if needed. Personally, I view accusations as negative. Keep everything as positive as possible and respect them as persons, even if you must reject their behavior. Too often, parents paint a picture of an evil person, rather than an unacceptable and damaging behavior.

c. Speak calmly and softly. Remember the magic of volume. Raising the volume raises the emotions. Lowering the volume lowers the emotions!

d. When the emotions have calmed, question some more. You may not have received a truthful or realistic answer. Discovering their real beliefs does not have to be a rushed task. Ask for a sufficient cause for their actions. Tell them they have good minds and can tell you. Why did they do it? What were they thinking? Tell them you want to help them sort out what it is that makes them act this way and suggest ways more to their liking. If you can calm the emotions and develop a cooperative discussion, you are well on your way to discovering the real truth.

e. The whole process should become an exercise in teaching your children self-awareness of their beliefs and the way they affect and result in their actions.

3. **Instill another belief.**

   a. Show them the damage their belief is going to do, or is doing, to themselves and others.

   b. Show them that there is always damage to themselves, and eventually to others, when they believe something that is not constructive and positive.

   c. Explain and defend a new reasonable and positive belief — a way of looking at things that benefits them the most. A positive belief, as opposed to a negative belief, also makes their system function as it was designed to function. Use reason to show the effect a positive belief will have on their emotions.

4. **Help them refocus their lives around the new belief.**

   a. A change in lifestyle may be needed. Don't leave it to them to figure out the changes needed to make their new belief a new habit. This is a most important step because it is required to put the belief permanently in place.

b. Beliefs result in action. If they don't, they are not really beliefs, just ideas that are given temporary approval.

Brain Lock

If the above does not work, the child is in "brain lock." Brain lock can be caused by any of the following, and you must address the cause of brain lock first, before trying to effect change since they apparently can't get past it. Seek to remove these roadblocks.

Fear.

- Fear of repercussions from others or simply the fear of peer reaction.
- Fear of failure, or even of success.

Worry.

- Worry is a fear, and sometimes we feel it as a vague undefined feeling in the pit of our stomachs.
- The source of worry can be something that happened in the past (the likely source for an SJ), or something that may happen (or not happen) in the future (a likely source for the sensitive NF). If the SP and the NT worry, try searching for a fear of failure. Look for the fear of not being perfect in the NF.

A simple lack of understanding about the issue in question can also lead to brain lock. When we don't understand, our minds often feel lost in a fog.

A familiar way of thinking that has hardened into a habitual way of thinking is a common cause of mental freeze up. The mind is closed.

Desire to please others, or any other temperamental tendency that children can't seem to let go of and are over-using, can cause them to be locked into a negative mental pattern.

How to Break Brain Lock

- Replace their negative belief with a positive one. Help your children discover a belief that will not harm them or others, and one that will positively increase their pleasure. A positive belief will always have a positive pay back.
- Refocus their lives on their new positive belief. This is so often the really important part. If we adopt a new belief, we must refocus our lives around it, or the replacement will not last long. Show your children how they can refocus their lives around a better, more rewarding belief.
- Repeat refocusing and the development of new habits to strengthen the new belief.

Here are the steps "in a nutshell":

1. Discover the belief behind the action.
2. Calm the emotions.
3. Instill another belief.
4. Help them refocus their lives around the new belief.

If this does not change the behavior…

1. Suspect brain lock in their beliefs caused by such things as fear, worry, or a lack of understanding.
2. Break the brain lock by addressing the fear, or whatever the problem is, and reasoning it away. Then…
    a. Again replace the negative belief with a positive belief.
    b. Help them refocus their lives on the new positive belief.
    c. Help them repeatedly refocus on the new belief. This strengthens the belief.
3. If still not effective, repeat the above.

If you feel overwhelmed at attempting this task of creating positive beliefs, follow the "in a nutshell" steps as simply and methodically as possible, dealing with one step at a time. You will find it will come to you easier than you think.

The knowledge of your child's temperament, and your own, is the best help you can get to simplify parenting and lead you to the help you and they need.

When Emotion Precludes Reason

Stan was a normal boy of 11, sitting in the van with his sister and mother. They had stopped to pick up some grocery items and, on leaving, his mother spotted a neighbor's child who looked as though she needed a ride. The neighbor's child was 11 too, and Stan secretly wished for a relationship. He had made no approaches because he was nervous and couldn't find the words he needed.

Stan's mother invited the girl to accept a ride. As the girl approached the van, Stan jumped up and accidently kicked his younger sister's leg as he stepped over her to exit the van with the purpose of letting the girl get in first. (He wanted to get in next so that he would have to sit next to her.) He was simply being a clumsy opportunist who hurt his sister inadvertently.

His sister complained, and cried loudly, causing the mother (who did not know what exactly had happened behind her) to yell at Stan and berate him for hurting his sister. The scene was set for embarrassment, anger, feelings of being judged unfairly, and disappointment. Tempers flared between Stan and his mother. Stan was humiliated in front of the neighborhood girl and his mother was steaming with her own case of embarrassment. An "Are you okay?" addressed to the younger sister and a promise to find out all about it later was all that was wise at that stage.

His mother later reported the incident, still not thinking that she needed first to find out what happened before she acted in anger, and still not realizing that she had made the incident worse by her own heated actions. We are human and can't see clearly when our emotions are still high.
Parents are also sometimes nursing hurts of their own and can react to their children in just this manner. However, the parent is the parent. Much damage was done and a lot of trust had to be rebuilt. So follow the steps above. And please, find out what really happened before you make accusations. Keep the heat of engagements down low, for your own advantage at least. Speak to an offender when you have the best opportunity to effect real changes in their behavior. And be calm, just, and fair in your training.

This chapter and its suggestions can sharpen our skills as parents and lessen the guilt a parent often feels.

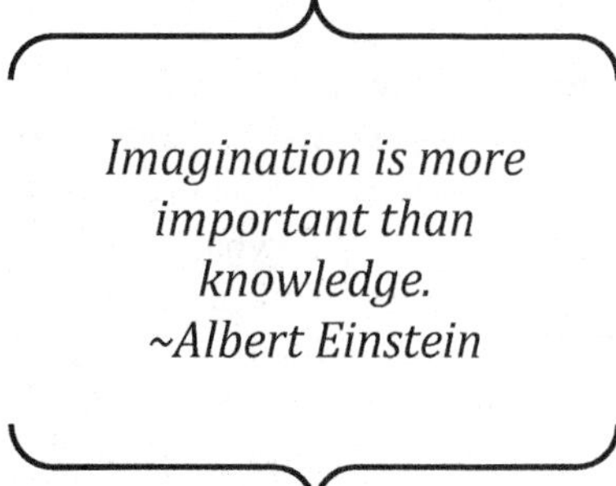

Chapter Fifteen ♦

Building Your Child's Dreams Walking Together Into the Future

"We live in death without a dream."

Without hope, children perish (adults, too), and hope is what a dream is all about. There are three essentials for a life to have value and meaning. They are faith, hope, and love. The three really are essentials! Without all three, your children will not develop into their full potential. They will live a death.

The lack of faith, hope and love, of course, will result in undesirable behavior – a disaster for them and a disappointing and frustrating parenting experience for you. Dreams (the magical creation of a vibrant hope) will nurture love and challenge faith. All should then be well. What humans hope for and love, they dream about, and faith will be called on to bring it to pass. Focus on creating this healthy process in their lives. Dreams never happen without focus.

Take hope out, and the castle of life crumbles. Children must believe in something, and if their hopes are dashed, they will fill the emptiness with a faith built on a hope from some foreign soil. That foreign hope may be inspired by their peer's passions and can be anything at all. Unfortunately, it can often be what you know is damaging to them.

Lesson? Watch their hopes as well as their beliefs. Belief, hope, and love are all interconnected. What they love will lead to what they hope for. What they believe in will bring reality to their hopes. Likewise, their dreams will point to their hopes and their growing beliefs. If a dream is the culmination of what children love, believe in, and hope for, understanding dreams is a necessary step for parents who want to parent their children to be the best that they can be.

We will find the relationship of their dreams to their temperament and their strengths. We will also remark on the effect dreams will have on their potential — limiting it or stretching it.

Shattered Dreams

Children are all too often the victims of shattered dreams. Unfortunately, they are shattered at times by parents who call their imaginings stupid, or simply "unrealistic." Imagination, a tool for the creation of dreams, is fragile. Its edge can easily be blunted. The "wild" imagination of the NF child is often seen as dangerous or, by some, even as a sickness that must be discouraged. Children report imaginary friends and toys that take on another reality (such as a monster or a princess). They report happenings that at times do not square with the facts, only with their inner realities.

The truth is that imagination is more important to success than reason or the cool, calm nature of logic. It leaps the barriers that logic, by nature, must encounter. And it boldly and creatively ventures into the unknown. Once shattered, imagination lies dormant, waiting for something or someone to awaken it. If that happens later in life, the imagination is stunted from lack of growth during early years. The result is that the adult struggles to perform at half power. The potential of imagination is, unfortunately, largely lost in childhood because it is not encouraged and respected, and too many children grow up to be could-have-beens.

The number of stories that I have been told by adults whose parents endeavored to stamp out their fantasy and imagination when they were children, is astounding. They must rank in the hundreds, and that is only <u>my</u> experience. I ponder some of my actions as a parent, and think I probably caused damage in unguarded moments too.

A human being is a treasure trove of possibilities and unknown potential. Who knows what a human can be? Parent, you are raising one of these precious wonders. We certainly are created in an image far above all other creatures, if results are the standard of comparison. I guess the nearest creature to us in intelligence and potential is one of the apes. And the distance between the musical creations of Beethoven and the non-existent compositions of the ape cannot be over-exaggerated. The difference between the ingenious, complex systems and technology that make up a 757 aircraft, compared to the primitive tool usage of the ape, is also too great to be meaningfully stated. We are made in an image that calls us to yet undiscovered heights.

The potential we can unleash when we parent one of these little lives should motivate us to our very best. You, my reader, are one, no doubt, who is so motivated.

Dreams and Strengths

Dreams are extraordinarily motivational. They are realized when we use our strengths and our imagination. It is not likely that they will be always framed within the expectations of society, of our close friends, or even family. Our dreams may take us beyond the expectations of the limited reality of others because our strengths have unlimited potential, which seldom we reach.

Dream as big as your strengths and imagination will allow you to dream. Your view of your strengths may limit the realization of your dreams. If and when it does, enlarge your strengths! Train, exercise, and develop them. Think more of their potential and stretch them further in real life by constant and challenging use.

Model the building of your own strengths for your children. Let them take the ride with you as you speed to your dreams. This, more than anything, will teach and motivate them. A parent without a dream to showcase to their children is a parent without a fully developed hope and faith.

If your dream is anchored to your strengths it is not "pie in the sky" – no matter how big it is. Your strengths are your map to success; so are your child's strengths. Become a dreamer of astonishing things. But before you do, be willing to pay the price of the development of your strengths and the cost of their demands.

If you are (or your child is) an SP and, perhaps, dream of extraordinary physical achievements in sports, don't dream unless you are willing to endure hours of sweat and pain in practice.

If you are (or your child is) an SJ and dream of a business that goes public and commands leadership in the marketplace, you will need to commit to hours of hard toil in developing its systems and its product or service to the point of standout excellence. Your life must be disciplined and balanced. And you must find the niche that will distinguish you and utilize your greatest strengths.

If you are (or your child is) an NF, you must serve people with a superiority that makes you indispensable as a teacher, writer, coach, counselor, advisor, healer, or champion of causes par excellence.

If you are (or your child is) an NT, you must apply yourself in the field of your choice with ingenious thinking and tireless tenacity to discover newness and uniqueness at all cost.

You must lead and be an example to your child. You can lead them no further than you have gone yourself. At that point, they are on their own and must find their own path. So I urge you to pay attention to your own life, or you will not be able to lead them far, and (unknown to you) if they are fired with a dream, they will have discounted your leadership. Parents build the dream of the child more by modeling the path than by verbal instruction, of course, and they light the way to success or failure for their own progeny. It is a foundational mistake to pay too little attention to the goals of your own life, if you would parent superbly.

In a nutshell:

- Develop your own strengths, and let your children see and feel you stretch and struggle to achieve your goals
- Discover their strengths. Go first to their strengths by temperament and discover what they hunger after.
- Coach them in the development of these strengths.
- Model the passion of rising to your potential.

How Do We Discover Our Children's Dreams?

- By sharing our own. Talk often about your dreams with your children.
- Share with them how your dreams are taking shape. Your journey of hope is the best tool you have to teach your child what it is to hope and what the journey looks like.
- Ask them about their dreams. "What do you dream to be?" "What do you want?" But don't always ask only about what. Ask how they intend to reach their dreams. Enter into a partnership with them, encouraging their dreams and suggesting things they can do and ways they can reach their goals more efficiently. In the early years it is all about encouragement.
- The more we, as parents, talk of dreams and hopes, the more our children will open up and feel it is a natural thing to dream and a normal thing to share their dreams with those they trust.
- Place your hope in them, and they will hope. Children who feel trusted, accepted, and admired will be very willing to share their dreams.

The main problem you will have is with the introverts (approximately 25 percent of the population). Of the introverts, the ISTJ (who is the most unlikely to communicate about their inner life) can make it very difficult. Persist. Both the INFJ and the INFP can also be difficult to draw out, because they fear excessively about being thought odd or being laughed at, and they are ultra reserved about what is in their inner world. Make it a normal activity in your family to share and talk about your dreams, encouraging all to reach them. They likely will open up very slowly, so start as young as you can, and be patient.

Caution: Please don't label a belief or dream as "undesirable" because it is not what you had hoped your child would be or do. Let them be what they are created to be. Attempt to change the dream or the belief only if it is damaging to your child or to others.

Here are the steps in a nutshell:

1. Discover your child's dreams.
2. Share your dreams.
3. Approve of their dreams (unless they are damaging).
4. Encourage the fulfillment of their dreams.
5. Develop their dreaming potential by becoming engaged.

Chapter Sixteen ♦

I do not want the peace
that passeth
understanding, I want
the understanding which
bringeth peace.
~ Helen Keller

Essential Parenting Skills Don't Go Home Without Them

All temperaments can fall into their weaknesses, and do. Oh, how we wish we wouldn't. Whenever we don't use our strengths, overuse them, or use them in a destructive manner toward others or ourselves, we develop our own unique weaknesses. Unique, because our temperaments, stamped with their own mix and degrees of strengths, gives our weaknesses their own fingerprinted reality, their own individual twist. Have you noticed that those who know us often identify us by our weaknesses as well as our strengths? Since we are not perfect, these weaknesses creep into our parenting, of course. Our goal is not to avoid weaknesses, but to maximize the positive contribution of our strengths in our parenting model, which will minimize or eliminate the weakness.

Hence we need to practice the positives that will eliminate the negatives. Write this on your mind: **Practice the positives to eliminate the negatives**. Here are some of the major positives that will eliminate the negatives in our parenting.

Focusing on the Positive in Parenting Eliminates Negative Obsessions

When we become concerned and emotionally involved with our child's behavior, any temperament is likely to focus on the problem instead of the solution. Disaster! This means we magnify the problem in our minds, and, at the same time, we are diverted from placing our focus on seeking solutions. It's like taking two steps back, not one: a double retreat. The success of our parenting will depend more on our positive solutions than our negative musings. Sadly, these musings are often accompanied by a display of frustration in angry bursts of devaluing language directed at the worthlessness of our child.

Whenever we fall into such frustrated behavior, the smart child knows he or she has snatched control of the situation and has possibly even secured control of the family – at least for a while. Our child's attempt at control is then likely to be repeated.

Focusing on the positive reaction to frustrating displays of temper by our children keeps our hand on the controls of our own emotions, and of the family. Someone must be calm and steer with a steady hand, or the home reverses its direction and slides into chaos. Tell yourself you must remain in control, and that means remaining calm and steady, thoughtful and patient. It can be done if we practice calm responses to meltdowns. I said, "Practice!" It won't all come instantly. Reward yourself for progress on the way. Why not? Parenting is a learning curve. You are not supposed to have all the answers. Take it in simple steps.

- First, reward yourself for identifying the potential game-losing issues: the moments when you need to keep a firm hand on the controls, but are likely to lose it. Most parents omit this step and wonder why they can't parent calmly. Don't miss this practice that sharpens identification skills. You can only improve insofar as you identify and become aware. Replaying the day's ups and downs, while identifying the curve balls and rehearsing the right responses, is mind changing. Mind changing is life changing!
- Reward yourself for every calm, rational response you make. I know you have a tendency to beat up on yourself when you fail, right? That

draws the mind's attention to this damaging behavior and because the mind does not know the difference between a negative and a positive, it responds by saying, "So this is what you want me to do. I get it. I'll not let you down next time!" Why punish yourself? It makes little to no sense, and it is damaging. Draw your attention to your right responses, and pay no attention to the failures except to learn from them. Focusing on failures is what losers excel at doing.

- Reward yourself for every time you "save" and turn a potential meltdown into a moment of education for your child. Are you complaining that if you do all this rewarding you'll be rewarding yourself all the time!? You couldn't do better to bring about real changes. Go for it!

When we "lose it," and react to our children in anger or heated loud words (which for our personal comfort we rename "frustration"), we reinforce our child's bad behavior by displaying our own. This is called regress, not progress! However, don't be depressed at your failure to keep calm. Step up into the belief that you will do better next time, and not down into self-recrimination. Every time we fail we have a choice to step up or down. To avoid falling again into your weaknesses, focus on doing a good job of the steps above.

United You Win; Divided You Lose

There is power in a united front — in parental unity. A child is seldom skilled enough to control both parents when they stand together. With intuitive insight, children know that to divide is the way to conquer, and whenever they can drive a wedge between the parents, they have a good chance of conquering. Dividing the parents on any issue is, in itself, a victory for the child. Keep a united front and you not only secure success, but also discourage the child from attempting to fight you simply for his (or her) own advantage. Children are smart. They only persist doing what they perceive has a chance of success.

How do you maintain a united front? First, maintain your own relationship and invest in its care. If there is disharmony between you as parents, don't let the sun go down without restoring harmony, forgiving each other, and showing love and respect for each other.

Joe and Erica were beyond solutions, or so they thought. The stress of children, who were way out of control and (in their belief) uncontrollable, had taken its toll. The tenderness that once made togetherness so rewarding was now a thing of the past. Mentally they thought of each other as incompatible and even enemies at times.

Nights, like the days, were times of separation. When they woke, they got up without a warm word of greeting or welcome to the new day, and their home had become two world's that touched only when they bumped into each other, and then it was with irritation. Sometimes it was revenge that motivated their disagreements over what the children could or could not do. They needled each other and used parenting differences to drive home emotional pain. "Why can't you at least agree with me for once!" they yelled at each other. The children had taken control of the home (if you could still call it that). We talked.

"Can you see that you have abdicated control to your children?" I asked. Two people who loved each other and wanted to build a family together, now think of each other as aliens in the same house. You have lost love because you have allowed your beliefs about each other to be changed by stress, anger, and bitterness; there is only one way back. You must put your relationship first. Nurture it with weekly dates, lots of thoughtful comments, and little acts of kindness which will soon revive your strangled love. Go all out! Find some money somewhere in your budget, and spend it on a lovers' weekend retreat. But before you do any of this, forgive each other.

Forgiveness, I reminded them, was for themselves, not for the other person. Not forgiving is a sure way to hurt yourself and reinvigorate the hurt every time you recall it. For your own sake, forgive the other. It's the only way to begin again with a fresh, clean page. Then, after you have done this, let's talk about getting the control of the home in your hands again and parenting your children with success.

It sounded like humiliation to Joe and also like sweeping his hurt under the carpet, but, as I reminded them, to forgive is divine. Hurt changes its chemistry when bathed in forgiveness, in little acts of kindness, in loving caring thoughts, and sweet renewals of past memories. They reluctantly tried and, to their surprise, found that they liked trying! The power of love was about to heal their relationship and open the door to parenting success. The children were about to see the model of a great relationship and reconciliation.

Parents who are having trouble with their own relationship seldom can have a united front. This is essential to parenting success since, without consultation and mutually accepted methods and limits, your child will wrench the control from you. Increased undesirable behavior inevitably follows. So, add to renewing your relationship, times to discuss and unify your approaches – councils of war (as some call them), strategies for the enforcement of a few rules and for the handling of negotiations over all the negotiable issues of the home.

One more factor is essential. Communicate with the children about how all issues will be handled. Explain that, for the few nonnegotiable rules the family has, everyone keeps to the rules. For negotiable issues, either all issues are to be referred to one parent or, where needed, consultation between the parents will take place before a decision is rendered. Maybe you can decide to simplify the matter by simply informing them that both parents are going to back each other up! If you actually disagree as to what should be done, let one lead and talk about it later. Fine-tune your future decisions as needed. Have frequent evaluations of how your unified front is working.

I am suggesting these two steps for a unified front. First, make sure your relationship gives your children the clear message that you can't be divided since love reigns between you. And second, devise a clearly communicated strategy for how all issues are to be handled. Remain open to changing all decisions that need to be changed if, and as, situations dictate. Always communicate all changes effectively.

The Competitive Nature of Volume

Volume is magic! The parent's volume of speech should be the standard for discussion, debate, and any resolution of differences and discipline in the home, and it must be LOW. Never let the child control or dictate your volume level! When you are frustrated, this is what automatically happens — their level of volume dictates yours. They yell at you, and you return the same emotional volume in order to obtain control, believing that your volume, as the authority, will outdo theirs. Not so; the higher the volume, the greater the loss of control – not the opposite. So, set a volume you can live with. Also consider this, your children will outdo the volume you set. They want to be the authority, and volume is an instinctive way (to them) of asserting control.

Low volume also means low emotions. Low volume means, "I have control of this situation and I don't need to get emotional or loud to convey my control." It's like saying to the child, "You are not getting to me with your high volume, since I am in control of this situation, not you. I have no need to get loud or upset." Emotional levels rise and fall with volume. If you lower your voice, they will soon lower theirs until it rests at a level just above yours. The wonderful thing is that as they lower their volume, their emotional heat lowers too. The exchange becomes more of a discussion than a yelling match. Lowering the emotion also focuses the attention on the issue, rather than the emotions that surround the issue. You always win when you lower the emotional level.

If you are wise you will set the volume low, real low. I mean soft and emotionless. All your discussions with your children should be held at a predetermined, low volume. Don't let them rattle you. And if they do, return quickly to your practiced low volume to gain control again. If you don't predetermine the volume, the emotion of the occasion will determine it and you, not they, have lost!

Why must you win? You must teach, and winning control is the only way to do it effectively. Creating an atmosphere in which calm, rational discussion can take place is your goal.

"Why can't I stay out late?" their son yelled. "You're not old enough to be out that late!" John, a frustrated SJ father, yelled back. From there, it quickly deteriorated into the usual, "I hate you!" with some graphic expletives. What was this? A home? It sounded like an enemy camp. John and his son were not getting along, obviously. The mother, who was an NF, was cringing in horror in the kitchen. She wanted to explode at John. He was treating their son, Mike, in a horrible manner, degrading his personality and making him angry, she thought.

John had a distinctively different opinion. As he put it, "My son is going to respect me, or I am going to die in the effort to make him." I asked him why his son was going to respect him. He saw it this way, it was his responsibility to make his son respect him.

And why should he be respected? John was Mike's father, and children had to honor their parents. Didn't the "Good Book" say, "Honor your father and your mother?" John was, of course, misquoting the "Good Book" (as he put it). The "Good Book" was addressing children with the dictum, "honor your father and mother," not giving the parent the right to demand it. Respect is not a right we possess, but something we earn. Parents must earn the respect of their children – constantly.

You see, to John, parenting was all about the parent when, in fact, it is all about the child. He was yelling at Mike because he was trying to gain the upper hand, trying to enforce his authority and power. In a clouded kind of way, John was feeling defeated by his son and feared where all this would lead. He sensed his wife's concern also, and wanted to demand that she support him and join in the fray.

It was his wife, Anne, who came to me asking if anything could be done. She was also afraid that she was wrong, since she felt her own reluctance to enter in the conflict. Was she just running away from conflict? Should she be supporting her husband and fighting Mike too? Was her husband right about demanding honor and respect from their son? She really didn't know.

This had been going on for some time. The volume was out of control. I asked them to do one thing to start with. Since the volume was contributing to the wild behavior that Mike had become used to, they needed to drop the volume to a very low, soft, caring kind of level, and simply observe Mike's surprise and momentary loss of knowing what to do. "Keep it up. Always speak softly and slowly, and let your concern and love shine through," I added. "Don't expect overnight miracles, since Mike will test this astounding change of events." Anne welcomed the quiet loving manner, and they would, in the process, draw closer together. Mike, who was a volatile NF, would be affected and, soon, they would see a different Mike.

They did, and it didn't take long. This twelve year old was responding quickly, as all NFs do, to love and respect. And John and Anne were discovering that volume did indeed control emotional levels. Positive parenting is low-volume parenting. By the way, in case you wanted to know: ***You get respect by giving it!***

Quick Neuroscience Lesson

Mirror neurons speed learning and they don't know the difference between good and bad results. Since our mirror neurons (located in our brains) mimic all they detect, we can learn a lot from their job description. "Read the data and mimic it." That's their short, but important, job description.

Mirror neurons do not detect what is acceptable input to the brain as opposed to what is not acceptable. They are neutral in their replicating of the data they receive. As parents we often model the wrong behavior for our children, even inadvertently. The mirror neurons mimic the data and undesirable behavior on the part of the child follows. At least we should expect that these mirror neurons are going to do their job. Parents living in their strengths usually have a positive effect on their children for this same neurological reason. Mirror neurons are at work replicating what they detect.

Mirror Neurons at Work

Children are being impacted by outside stimuli constantly. Many of the stimuli are routed to our mirror neurons for replication. The mirror neurons help us discover, for example, how to walk. Their purpose is, among others, to aid the complex task of learning simple actions. These neurons gather information of how to act by copying people, such as when children observe their parent's behavior. If we think of how these neurons operate we can understand their importance. Here are the salient points:

- All stimuli are received by the young child's brain without question because it is, in a word, stimulation. Children learn from whatever stimuli they receive.
- If confused signals are received, all are processed and erratic behavior usually results until they have sorted out the confusion.
- During these periods of confusing signals, children learn how to use their strengths and operate their temperamental preferences. Unfortunately, sometimes that means learning to overuse, not use, or wrongly use their strengths. Weaknesses follow.

Parenting is enhanced and made easier if the parent models the right behavior. Focus on the positive behavior you want your children to model and you will make their mirror neurons work for you.

Reward Trumps Punishment

The goal of discipline is to teach, not punish. Keep the teaching and training of your child as your focus, even when you must hand out some form of punishment. Punishment is a last resort. Except for the SJ child, it motivates least. When a child misbehaves, our goal is to change the negative behavior to positive actions. Fear is the only motivational factor punishment effectively uses, and then not always. It can make the SP child decide this is the time to show no fear. The direction of their motivation is to be brave, not to change, to defeat their opponents, and not to cower. For the NF child it can be deeply hurtful by focusing the child on the broken relationship, not the change of behavior. Of course, it is not without its uses. Sometimes it is the only remaining tool and can have a deterrent effect, despite the efforts of some to prove to the contrary. Effective or not, focus on the more powerful, preventive option and reward good behavior. Keep the reward appropriate. Rewards can range all the way from praise and attention to a gift of some sort, or a treat.

Act Only When Calm

First, don't punish a frustrated child. If they are frustrated they do not deserve to be punished. What they need is an end to their frustration. Guide them to it. Frustration often occurs when the parents don't understand the child and the child senses it. Not only is the child confused about what to do, but equally confused over why their parents can't help them. The guidance is usually not forthcoming because the parents are confused, too. Strangely, this can result in escalating anger, because both feel the other is not being helpful or cooperative – even stubborn and rebellious. Frustration is a common cause of anger in parents and children.

Now, here comes the part that is easy to say. Act only when calm, and avoid punishing what angers you. If I am going to say it, I need to at least offer help to make it easier. Understanding the temperaments, yours and your child's, will make this much easier. I offer these steps.

Steps to Help You Remain Calm

- Review and understand your own temperament. Think through how you typically react and what pushes your buttons. Understanding why you behave the way you do is mind opening and your side of the interaction will come into focus. Why you are feeling this way is now half answered because you are refreshing your mind on your tendencies and preferences. You are taking advantage of the wise advice to "know yourself."
- This refreshed understanding of your makeup will also bring an awareness of the reasons and emotions that lay behind your actions, even before you act. It will prepare you for the next similar encounter as well.
- No solution to our problems can be effected, if we are not aware of what is happening. Practice asking yourself, "What is the state of my mind at this moment?" Practice this awareness anytime, all the time, and you will be amazed at the keenness you develop. Ask yourself, "Is my mind negative or positive? On the verge of losing control or in control?" I know. If you are frustrated, it is seldom positive and controlled! That's my point! Becoming aware, in a timely manner, of the negative climate of your mind alerts you to the cause of much of your actions. Self-knowledge is empowering, not just wise.
- Becoming aware of a negative mental climate helps you find calm and hold onto it before you lose it. Therefore, to maintain control of your mental climate, call for a time-out for you to consider the issue, and go somewhere where you are unaffected by what is happening. When alone, breathe deeply and think. Ask yourself, "What is my child's temperament?" As you refresh your mind, you will find a way to reach the child, and this is the key to parenting by understanding and skill. You will be talking to them from where <u>they</u> are in <u>their</u> minds. You will be honoring their temperament.
- Now that you have the knowledge (from understanding their temperament) of why they are acting and feeling the way they are, it is much easier to remain calm. You can now take the roll of the mentor, rather than combatant, the teacher, rather than the disciplinarian.

Try this and practice it. I think you will not be disappointed, and you will like the new role, along with your lowered stress level.

Understand the Source of Anger

Don't punish outbursts that are typical displays of your child's temperament either. For example: an NF's anger at being hurt; an SJ's anger at a loss of security; an SP's anger at authority; or an NT's anger at a loss of achievement. Instead, help them work through to a decision and a behavior that will enable them to relate effectively within their temperament to others, including you. When you can do this you are a super parent.

"Super Parent Theresa" was mystified as to why her daughter, Bridget, was stubbornly disobedient and spoke to her in bitter anger most of the time. Theresa had asked her daughter to clean up her room, but to her annoyance, found the room trashed instead of tidy. Her surge of anger was instant. (This is your signal that you are about to lose it emotionally, and can either gain or lose control of the situation. Take a time out, breathe deeply, and think! Recover your calm, controlling, manner.) *"How dare she defy me like this," she thought. Instead of handing out an immediate punishment in anger, Theresa followed the above steps. She withdrew to think clearly. Her daughter, she thought, always kept her room neat and tidy. This was so unlike her to trash her room.*

Theresa remembered that her daughter was an SJ temperament whose greatest threat to living in her strengths was insecurity. Could she be feeling insecure? The answer was near at hand. Bridget had just come home with a poor report card, and she had been reprimanded by her teacher who she looked up to and felt connected to. It was, admittedly, four weeks since the divorce. Could this (and the teacher's scolding) have climaxed in a fit of rage and rebellion against her mother? Perhaps, even the whole world? This fit could be the expression of an insecure, frightened little girl.

Theresa called Bridget to her and, assuming this was the cause, began to comfort her and go over these events, suggesting they could be quite upsetting and destabilizing. The dam broke and amid big tears, the mother discovered her daughter's fears and heard "I'm sorry, Mother." An SJ parent had rediscovered her SJ child and become the comforting mentor and understanding parent Bridget so needed. Super parenting!

Fulfill Your Child with the Gift of Yourself

A fulfilled child behaves well. Gifts don't fulfill. Using our strengths fulfills us. Therefore, center the gift of your love around the time and effort you spend building up your child's strengths, not on giving them material gifts.

All the time we spend in building their strengths in which they find true fulfillment is an investment in good behavior. Expect good behavior if you have spent the time encouraging it, or take your medicine if you have not!

Love that is lavished on children or even spouses by giving material things is not satisfying to the human spirit, only to the sense of emotional and sensual gratification that all of us know too well. We must get in touch with our real source of fulfillment if we are to find true happiness. We must constantly introduce our children to their inner sources of pleasure and satisfaction, and lead them away from materialistic happiness. Love that gives itself as a gift is priceless.

Placating a child with material gifts is not parenting with positive powers. It's parenting with money. Real love is felt in the way parents give themselves to their children. In parental discussions, explore how much time you have spent building your child's strengths and dispensing practical help and encouragement.

Support, Don't Control. Over-Protection Creates Weakness

It's hard not to overprotect your children. You want to keep them safe from harm, and relieve them from struggle and stress. But if you do, you rob them of needed mental and emotional exercise and perpetuate their immaturity. Muscles grow with exercise. Will-power grows with use. Emotions are controlled by facing difficulties and having to learn self-control. "Control freaks" raise weak children. The road to letting go of your controlling attitude is tough and painful, but absolutely necessary. The wise parent has to watch and suffer along with the child, letting the child find his (or her) way, and fight his own battles. Too much parental sensitivity to the child's needs can be really damaging.

Wise parents strike a balance between rescuing their children from trouble and letting the children struggle and grow. Because of parental intervention children seldom solve their problems independently. Therefore, the problem-solving pathways in the child's brain are infrequently used and underdeveloped. In extreme cases, increased harmful activity can reach a point where the synapses (important spaces in the nerves), in effect, fuse and lock in place, creating a deeply negative, entrenched habit of dependence on others. The child faces a gigantic task if, and when, he wants to change these connections. Good parenting does not control, but enables independent action. Synapses that are not used very often destabilize and fall away. "Don't use it and you will lose it" is the simple pattern for pruning undesirable synapses and connections. In other words, use determines whether a connection will be maintained or dropped. Have them use the powers they have – the positive ones they will need to depend on so often in life – to overcome their struggles. Here are some points to guide you.

- Children must learn to achieve on their own, or they don't achieve.
- Independence is what the child must develop, not dependence.
- Children need to feel you are cooperating, not controlling.
- Controlling behavior will drive the child away from you.
- Challenge them. Coax them. Show them. Guide them. But don't control them (except in the case of physical danger).
- Controlling, along with a number of other inadvisable parental actions, provokes a child to anger. "Don't provoke [them] to anger" is sound and ancient advice because, when you provoke them to anger, you increase the electrical currents and the production of neurotransmitters in their brains that enlarge the mental and emotional highways — the very ones that you have been trying to get your child to change! The more traffic on a highway, the more effectively it stimulates its target and hard-wires the connection.
- The <u>child</u> must win. Not much good is done when the parent succeeds <u>for</u> the child.

Super parents don't over-parent or over-protect their children.

These essential, positive parenting skills should help guide you through the maze of challenges you face, and, combined with knowledge of yours and your child's temperaments, they will make you a **Super Parent**.

Chapter Seventeen ♦

To seek help is to seek wisdom.

When Will You Need Help?

Seek help when any of these conditions or signs appear.

1. **When your child shows signs of depression.**
    - Depression can be noticed in children who seem to have lost pleasure in things that normally excite or interest them.
    - They may also seek solitude when, for them, it is not normal, or for introverts, you may notice that they stay secluded for longer periods of time than you normally expect of your introverted child.
    - Signs of constant irritability may also flag you.
    - A constantly sad countenance, with no adequate reason for it may be a clue.

2. **When you simply don't know how to handle them.** Don't use them as guinea pigs for your trial and error experiments.

3. **When they seem out of control emotionally** and your efforts have proved to be ineffective.

4. **When you find yourself reacting to your child out of frustration or anger,** have a desire to inflict harm, or anything less than a controlled spirit. Get help for yourself.

- When out of control, the parent can cause much harm.
- Children mirror your anger, and they learn what you are displaying.
- They can be hurt by your emotional outbursts and think they are to blame.
- The emotional heat can escalate to dangerous levels.
- When out of control, the parent's stress only increases, and the dangers of over-reaction with it.
- Your child will withdraw from you for self-protection and you will lose the intimacy of relationship you desire.
- The self-image of your child may suffer.

5. **When you have mixed temperaments in your family that seem beyond your ability to understand or support.**

6. **When you need help in developing their spiritual life.**

7. **When differences are perpetually causing conflict among siblings.**

Parents are in the process of becoming experts but are not there yet. None of us are. Don't hesitate to invest in your children and their care by further educating yourself, gaining understanding, and learning helpful tools. It is better to pay for expert help for either you or them than to buy them another toy!

Conclusion

The journey you have taken with me into the inner secrets and preferences of our lives has, hopefully, not only helped you meet yourself anew (or even for the first time), but helped you understand your child in the deeper world of how we function and choose to live on the inside.

Some of the secrets of how we get rid of our weaknesses and develop our strengths could well have revolutionized your struggle and created a home where peace, understanding, respect, and fulfillment will now live and bloom.

Our website will point you to seminars and other ways of finding answers to your questions, as well as continuing education to advance your knowledge and skills. Go to www.raywlincoln.com.

Appendices

Appendix I

Parenting the Temperaments with Love and Confidence

The Fast Track

For those who want a fast track to parenting with understanding and skill, here it is.

The best way is to read the book through first, and then make sure you follow the steps in "The Fast Track." I know, some of you read the last pages of the book first! So, for you, and for those who want to make a speedy start, I suggest you read the Fast Track and start applying its steps. As you can, go back and read the sections in the book that will give you a complete and in-depth understanding of what parenting with understanding and skill is all about. Here's your map:

1. Start by answering the **Temperament Keys** for both you and your children, which begin on pages 39 and 52.

2. Determine the two-letter temperaments for you and your children, pages 47 and 67.

3. Read the appropriate descriptions of temperament for both you and your children, which begin on pages 81 (children) and 145 (parents).

4. Read the appropriate temperament for both you and your children in "Strengths and Weaknesses," beginning on page 229.

5. Read "Essential Parenting Skills," beginning on page 325.

By now you should be able to make some changes in your home by parenting with love and understanding. However, continue, because the next step is also necessary if you are to complete the task and graduate as a **Super Parent**.

6. Once you've been able to establish some change, it's essential to go back and complete the rest of the book in order to understand and apply the principles of parenting with love and understanding.

Appendix II

The Four Faces of Humanity – Religious Roots of Temperament

(Ezekiel to Irenaeus and the Greeks)

Most scholars begin their survey of temperament with Hippocrates (circa 460-377 BC) with good reason. He identified similarities among people, weaved a theory of cause and effect around his discovery and was the first to talk about the similarities in some detail. However, the first suggestion of temperament in literature appears in approximately 580 BC in the book of Ezekiel. When recording his visions, Ezekiel was probably living in Babylon (modern day Iraq) or maybe residing in Persia (modern day Iran).

Judeo/Christian Literature

As Stephen Montgomery has pointed out in his editorial note to David Keirsey's *Please Understand Me II*, there appear in Judeo/Christian literature some "tantalizing hints" of the four temperaments. The case for this observation having some credibility is set out in Montgomery's comments, and I will attempt to flesh the case out here for interested readers.

The same term for a living being or living creature used in Genesis 2:7 (where it says, "The Lord God formed the man from the dust of the ground and breathed into his nostrils the breath of life and the man became a living being") is used in Ezekiel 1:5. There, Ezekiel records what he saw in a vision with these words, "...and in the fire was what looked like four living creatures (same Hebrew term as in Genesis 2:7)." He then proceeds to begin, in verse 6, to describe them as having four faces: "the face of a man... the face of a lion... the face of an ox... the face of an eagle." This is the first intriguing reference to living creatures as fourfold.

If you read all of Ezekiel's vision you will find yourself suddenly plunged into the strangeness of apocalyptic language, a form of literature no longer used. In those days apocalyptic language was a legitimate and accepted way of communicating unseen realities. It is, in its nature, highly symbolic and unusual.

The living creature in Genesis 2:7 is a human. Did Ezekiel have humans in mind, too? Interpretations vary. Some say Ezekiel meant angelic beings; some say humans, and some say both. At least we can't exclude the idea that humans may have "four faces." Add to this the fact that the four names used here — man, lion, ox and eagle — are accurate suggestive names for the four temperaments observed by Hippocrates 200 years later, and the intrigue is under way. Here is the parallel, including the letters I have used throughout the book.

The choleric of Hippocrates is the sensitive, caring creature Ezekiel refers to as man (NF); the sanguine is truly a lion — brave, bold and adventurous (SP); the melancholic is the reliable, hard working ox that is all about duty and reliability (SJ); the phlegmatic is the independent, far-seeing eagle (NT). Could there be a connection between what was observed by Hippocrates and seen in a vision by Ezekiel?

The story does not end here with what might be seen as simply fascinating, imaginary coincidence. In Revelation, John repeats the faces of humanity that Ezekiel saw, but in a different order, "... like a lion... like an ox... a face like a man... like a flying eagle," Revelation 4:7. Again, the interpretation varies. Some see these creatures in John's apocalyptic vision (the whole vision occupies chapters 4-7 of Revelation) as referring to some kind of angelic being, some see it as a reference to humans, and some both.

The descriptions of the four horsemen in chapter 6 also draw a parallel with the descriptions of temperament that should not go unnoticed. They are the first indication in literature of the damage that can be done when the four faces of humanity use their strengths wrongly to destroy and wreck damage on humanity itself. Our news reports are filled daily with examples of this wrong use of our temperaments.

The first horseman rides on a white horse, holds a bow and is bent on conquest by the use of force — the choleric (NF). When poisoned with power and tasting the significance of violent victory, the NF can lose their sensitive caring for others, their love and empathy, and in hurt and anger can fight for glory using their passion in an evil selfish cause. Montgomery reminds us that the Choleric (NF) is like Apollo, the archer god. Truly, the spiritual NF has gone wrong.

The second horseman rides a fiery red horse and carries a large sword — the sanguine (SP). Men slay each other, showing their skill in the use of weapons. The craftiness and courage of the lion is evident. It is a temperament that relishes its competitive physical skills and succeeds in creating widespread fear. In Revelation, it looks like the SP gone wild without ethical restraint.

The third horseman rides a black horse and holds a pair of scales — the melancholic (SJ). The SJ is the logistical master of commerce. A quart of wheat costs a day's wages and the luxuries (oil and wine) are withheld. Famine and hardship must be endured when the SJ mismanages the resources for personal gain and creates worldwide famine. This is the SJ temperament consumed with greed.

The fourth horseman rides a pale horse, and death and Hades follow close behind him — phlegmatic (NT). The NT temperament uses its ingenious abilities to turn nature and its resources against humanity. Weaponry, biological warfare in the form of plague, and the harnessed powers of nature threaten the world. Again, we see a temperament demonstrating its powers for wrong purposes — the mad scientist in unrestrained passion.

Yet all of these faces of humanity are meant to bless us, not curse us. This possible interpretation is interesting and breathes the reality of life as we experience it. We see that what was intended to bless becomes the weaponry of curse in the vision. Humans can and do self-destruct and destroy each other when they lose all ethical boundaries.

It is hard to determine the symbolism with dogmatic clarity, of course, and that may not have been intended. Nevertheless, the descriptions of the four faces seem to have established themselves in this visionary literature as having a recognizable meaning.

Christian Tradition

That recognizable meaning surfaces again in the writings of Irenaeus, Bishop of Lyons, who in his defense of Christianity against the Gnostics makes a strange reference to the four Gospels — Matthew, Mark, Luke and John — as being quadriform. He explains that they share the same faces as living creatures to which he also refers as quadriform. His point is that the four Gospels were written by the four different faces of humanity, the four faces spoken of by Ezekiel and John. If this is so, we would expect that the four writers, Matthew, Mark, Luke and John would bear some obvious similarity to the four faces. They do.

Matthew is the laboring ox, Mark the bold adventurous lion (medieval art preserves the lion as the symbol of Mark), Luke the eagle, and John the man. The striking parallel is made even clearer when we compare the styles within the Gospels to the four temperaments as Hippocrates observed them and also as we now understand them after much scientific research.

The Four Temperaments in the Four Gospels

Matthew's Gospel

The Gospel of Matthew fits the SJ temperament perfectly. Matthew was busily occupied in the world of a scribe and book keeper as he oversaw the collection of taxes — an SJs world if ever there was one. Leaving this occupation, he became a follower of Jesus and the resultant book that Matthew wrote of Jesus' teaching and life breathes the concerns of an SJ.

The Book of Matthew is detailed and concerned with matters of law and rightness. The issues that plague an SJ like worry (Matthew 6:25-34), concerns over being able to forgive those who wrong us (Matthew 18:21-35), and the issue of faith versus the SJs dogma of "anything that can go wrong will go wrong" fill its pages. Matthew focuses on the moralistic side of Jesus' teachings (Chapters 5-7) and presents Him as the ultimate teacher. SJs often gravitate to teaching as a career with the same concerns. It is a concrete presentation of Jesus' life and an explanation of the future, also fully concrete in its language.

The case for Matthew being a view of Jesus through the eyes of an SJ is abundantly clear.

Mark's Gospel

We know that Mark was writing for Peter who shows evidence in his letters as being unskilled as a writer. Both Peter and Mark show clear evidence of being SPs. Peter, for example, was impulsive, brave and daring (he took on the temple guard single handed), and a person of action to which he returned immediately when opportunity arose.

Mark's Gospel is the Gospel of action. The deeds of Jesus are in focus, and a brave exciting Jesus is presented to us. It is fast paced and full of vivid descriptions of events and characters — truly an SP's "action view" of Jesus. Few long speeches are found in its pages.

Both Matthew and Mark write of the same incident (Matthew 21:21; Mark 11:22-25) and note the expanded, more pointed, action-packed phrasing of Mark. Mark, for the SPs! Jesus is the lion in its pages and Peter is the admirer of such a worthy quality.

Of interest is the fact that Jesus chose an SP to lead the church when, in contrast, the church today is predominantly SJ. Was it the bold Peter who would not run scared of risk that was the reason for Jesus' appointment?

Luke's Gospel

The first few verses of the Gospel of Luke make clear that we are in the hands of an NT. Luke details his attempts at assembling the facts and, please, only the facts. He declares his concern for accuracy and he gives evidence of the scholar he proved himself to be. Luke is the non-passionate observer and chronicler. The style is classical and scholarly with a matching use of the Greek language. Luke shows himself as the quintessential NT. Note the bare facts, presented as unbiased and poignant in the account of Christ's birth (Luke 2: 1-7). We could say

Luke's Gospel is factual to a fault. The absence of emotion in his writings is also a mark of the NT.

Luke's second book, "The Acts of the Apostles," has been hailed for its historical accuracy. He was by profession a Doctor of Medicine and was undoubtedly familiar with Hippocrates. Many Doctors of Medicine are NTs and they exhibit the cool, calm presence of an NT. The Gospel of Luke appeals to the reasoning NT.

John's Gospel

What can I say about John's Gospel and its imaging of the NF? I can't say enough. John is undoubtedly the NF and was even reported to be quite emotionally reactive. After all, he was nicknamed a "son of thunder."

The introverted NF (John is an NF) is known as the deep thinker, obsessed with the big issues of life, and often becomes the philosopher. Read John 1:1-14 for a true philosophical approach to the introduction of Jesus as well as evidence of John being an NF who contemplates the big questions.

Witness also his intrigue with the miracles of Christ (try John 2:1-11) and their mysterious nature. His book is full of symbolism. In fact, The Gospel of John is framed around the signs that John claims prove who Jesus really is. The language is often symbolic and mystical: "I am the bread of life," he reports Jesus as saying, along with other claims such as "I am the resurrection and the life." John is the spiritual temperament and his gospel reflects that spirituality. His love of long dissertations and interest in meanings mark his writing. Significance, soulful experiences, and metaphorical phraseology fill the pages of John's Gospel and pound home its emotions while the philosophic musings of Jesus frame its message. All these factors are evidence of the NF mind and heart.

The intuition that lies behind John's portrayal of Jesus and the scholarly interest in his ideas and concepts also betray the abstract mind of an NF. His later book, Revelation, is a certain give-away of his imaginative, intuitive, abstract, studious, and poetic nature. Want to show Jesus to an NF? Take them to John was Irenaeus' point.

When compared with what we know about the temperaments today the evidence is compelling that the Gospels are quadriform as Irenaeus maintained, and they reveal Jesus through the eyes of the four temperaments. Could this be deliberately designed to reach the four faces of humanity? Irenaeus' tradition thought so.

Biblical Characters

Perhaps the most useful tool for understanding the personalities of the characters of the Bible is the use of temperament. The details of the biblical characters are often brief, but mostly they are informative enough to know the person's temperament. Once that is known, the narrative can be understood with accuracy and meaning that otherwise escape the interpreter. People act according to their temperaments. The Bible characters are no exception. When we interpret the Bible stories and events according to temperament they come alive and touch people with a sense of realism otherwise not discovered.

Here are just a few of the Bible characters' types and temperaments.

Paul, INFJ (NF)
Peter, ESFP (SP)
John, INFP or J (NF)
Elijah, INFJ (NF)
Moses, ISTJ (SJ)
Thomas, (NT)
Matthew, (SJ)
Luke, INTP (NT)
Mary (NF)
Martha (SJ)

Read the descriptions of these temperaments in this book and then read the writings by or about these characters, and you will be amazed at the insight it will give you.

The Religious Roots of the Greeks

Keirsey, in his first book *Please Understand Me*, sees the temperaments as accurately described in the nature and descriptions of four gods of Greek mythology. This perhaps can be imagined as the religious roots of the Greeks for the four temperaments that Hippocrates observed, so I mention it here. Whether Hippocrates based his descriptions on Greek mythology we will probably never know, but the correlation is interesting.

Keirsey portrays the parallel like this: Myth has it that Apollo (NF) gave humans a sense of the spirit; Dionysus (SP) displays a sense of joy; Prometheus (NT) is the giver of ingenuity and science; and Epimetheus (SJ) is the god of duty and responsibility.

The people who worship Apollo, the god of spirit, do not worship Prometheus, the god of science. And those who worship Dionysus, the god of joy, don't worship Epimetheus, the god of duty. This is how Keirsey explains the divergence in the Greek's religious roots. This comment certainly points out clearly the great gulf in the attitudes people hold toward each other, found so often in the four temperaments.

The SPs loathe the cautiousness of the SJs, while the SJs despise the flippancy of the SPs. The NFs shudder at the earthiness of the SJs and cringe at the lack of emotions in the NTs. The NTs despise the emotions of the NFs and stand in dismay at the shallowness of the SPs. The disapproval of each other's urges is well documented every day in our reactions and thoughts toward each other.

Put another way, the divine and all that is symbolic capture the NF; the use of tools captures the SP, while the sense of obedience and loyalty captures the SJ, and the desire for power over nature and its forces captures the NT. Although Keirsey doesn't explicitly state the fact, it appears that this idea of difference seems to pervade his understanding of the parallels to Greek mythology and the religious roots of the Greeks.

Taking these parallels a step further than Keirsey did, we can see that this divergence leads to no good. (Keirsey does not suggest it does.) Only if and when we learn to respect each other and see the good in each other can we, in Jesus' words, love each other as he has loved us. The home, the workplace, the world in all its corners needs an infusion of such love.

Selected Bibliography

This is by no means a complete listing of all the books and sources I have consulted in the making of this book. My hope is to provide you with interesting and studious sources for your pursuit of the understanding of human nature and makeup. They are presented in what may be the most helpful order for further reading.

Keirsey, David and Bates, Marilyn. *Please Understand Me: Character and Temperament Types.* Prometheus Nemesis Book Company, 1978.

Keirsey, David. *Please Understand Me II: Temperament, Character, Intelligence.* Prometheus Nemesis Books, 1998.

--------- *Portraits of Temperament,* Prometheus Nemesis Books, 1987.

Montgomery, Stephen. *People Patterns: A Modern Guide to the Temperaments.* Archer Publications, 2002.

--------- *The Pygmalion Project: Love and Coercion Among the Types. Volume One, The Artisan.* Prometheus Nemesis Books, 1989.

--------- *The Pygmalion Project: Love and Coercion Among the Types. Volume Two, The Guardian.* Prometheus Nemesis Books, 1990.

--------- *The Pygmalion Project: Love and Coercion Among the Types. Volume Three, The Idealist.* Prometheus Nemesis Books, 1993.

Harkey, Nancy and Jourgensen, Teri. *Raising Cuddlebugs and Bravehearts, Volumes 1 and 2.* Authorhouse, 2004.

--------- *Parenting by Temperament,* (Publisher unknown) 2009

Jeffries, William, C. *True to Type.* Hampton Roads Publishing Company, Inc. 1991.

Briggs Myers, Isabel with Myers, Peter B. *Gifts Differing: Understanding Personality Type.* Davies-Black Publishing, 1995.

Kroeger, Otto and Thuesen, Janet M. *Type Talk.* A Dell Trade Paperback, 1988.

Hirsh, Sandra and Kummerow, Jean. *Life Types.* Warner Books, 1989.

Kagan, Jerome. *Galen's Prophecy: Temperament in Human Nature.* Westview Press, 1998.

Briggs Myers, Isabel and McCaulley, Mary H. *A Guide to the Development and Use of the Myers-Briggs Type Indicator.* Consulting Psychologists Press, 1985.

Campbell, Joseph, Editor. *The Portable Jung.* A Penguin Book, 1971.

Von Franz, Marie-Louise and Hillman, James. *Lectures on Jung's Typology.* Spring Publications, 2006.

Hall, Calvin S. and Nordby, Vernon J. *A Primer of Jungian Psychology.* A Meridian Book, 1999.

Keirsey, David. *Abuse It — Lose It: Logical Consequences for Teaching Self-Control to Mischievous Children.* Prometheus Nemesis Books.

Eliot, Lise. *What's Going On In There? How the Brain and Mind Develop in the First Five Years of Life.* (Interesting notes on temperament and child growth.) A Bantam Trade Paperback. 1999.

Friel, John C. and Linda D. *The Seven Worst Things Good Parents Do.* Fall River, 1999.

Go to our website, www.raywlincoln.com, for additional helpful resources by Ray W. Lincoln.

Relevant to *I May Frustrate You, But I'm a Keeper! (Parenting the Temperaments with Love and Confidence)*:

Lincoln, Ray W. *The Four Temperaments: A Study for Parents.*

--------- *The Path to Positive Internal Power: How to Build Self-Esteem in Children and Adults.*

About the Author

Ray W. Lincoln

It was not by accident that Ray Lincoln became the international speaker and coach that he is today, and acquired the ability to guide so many to a happier, healthier, more fulfilled life. Ray has studied extensively in the fields of Theology, Philosophy, Temperament Psychology, and Personology.

Ray's is a professional life coach and an expert in human nature. His 40 plus years of experience in speaking, teaching, and pastoral counseling began in New Zealand and have carried him to Australia and the United States. He speaks with energy and enthusiasm before large and small audiences. His expertise has been used as a lecturer and professor, teacher and keynote speaker, seminar presenter, counselor and coach. He teaches and leads in staff trainings, university student retreats and parents' educational classes, as well as other seminars and training events. He also trains and mentors teachers and other professionals and executives — all with the goal of understanding our own temperaments and those of others.

Dr. Lincoln's next book, *Would the Real Me Please Stand Up! – Discovering Myself and Unleashing My Strengths (***InnerKinetics***™)*, will join the list of books that he has authored.

Ray lives with his wife, Mary Jo, in Littleton, Colorado where they enjoy hiking, snowshoeing, fly-fishing, and all the beauty the Rocky Mountains offer. Both are highly involved in their work (which they feel is the most important and most fulfilling work of their entire career lives), both filling the roles for which they were designed, as they travel to speak to groups, and to present seminars and workshops throughout the US.

If the message of this book has inspired and enthused your parenting and you'd like to share this book with others, here are some ideas we call:

The **Passionate Parent** Project

You may have already begun telling others as you experienced success from the understanding and skills you have acquired here. So, if you are passionate about loving your children and your new understanding and appreciation for their uniqueness, here are some ways you can help other parents, grandparents, teachers and anyone who cares about children. Who knows, you might help to change the world!

1. Give the book to friends (especially new parents) as a gift. They need a magnificent glimpse into the way they and their children are made.
2. If you have a website or blog, consider commenting about the book and how it has helped in your parenting – and maybe in your own life.
3. Write a book review for your local paper, favorite magazine, newsletter or a website you frequent. Ask your favorite radio show or podcast host to invite Ray as a guest. (Journalists and media representatives often give attention to the requests from their watchers, readers and listeners.)
4. If you own a shop or business, consider putting a display of the books on your counter to resell to customers. The books are available at a discounted rate for resale. For individuals, we offer a volume discount pricing for 6 books or more. Please contact us for details.
5. Buy several books and provide them to battered women's shelters, prisons, rehabilitation homes, and such where people may need help connecting with their children – or themselves.
6. Talk about the book in your e-mails, groups, clubs, forums you frequent, and other places where you engage in conversation, whether in person or on the internet. Share how the book has helped you and others; and offer people the link to the Ray W. Lincoln web site.
7. If you know of people (authors, speakers, etc.) who have websites, blogs or newsletters ask them if they would review a copy and make some comments about it to their audience, fans and subscribers.

We welcome your comments and success stories. You can send them to info@raywlincoln.com. Happy parenting!

www.imakeeperkid.com

Our website is a great place to order additional copies of ***I'm a Keeper!*** We also have additional FREE resources there to help you with your parenting.

Before you go to www.imakeeperkid.com, however, go to :

www.raywlincoln.com

At this website you can:

- ✓ Sign up for our FREE monthly newsletter, which entitles you to:
    - Receive 15% off all purchases at www.imakeeperkid.com and www.raywlincoln.com.
    - Receive a FREE .pdf download of Ray's article, ***Leveraging the Power of Your Mind.***
- ✓ Find more helpful resources and information about our services.

OUR SERVICES INCLUDE

Professional Life Coaching

Educational Seminars and Training

Keynote Addresses

Educational Materials

Free Monthly Newsletter

CPSIA information can be obtained
at www.ICGtesting.com
Printed in the USA
FSOW04n0823260116
16062FS